First
Certificate

Language Practice

Michael Vince

HEINEMANN

Heinemann English Language Teaching
A division of Heinemann Publishers (Oxford) Ltd
Halley Court, Jordan Hill, Oxford OX2 8EJ

OXFORD MADRID ATHENS PARIS
FLORENCE PRAGUE SÃO PAULO CHICAGO
MELBOURNE AUCKLAND SINGAPORE
TOKYO IBADAN GABORONE JOHANNESBURG
PORTSMOUTH (NH)

ISBN 0 435 28165 8 – without key
ISBN 0 435 28164 X – with key

ACKNOWLEDGEMENTS

The author would like to thank everyone who has made comments on this book,
and in particular the editors, Sue Jones and Xanthe Sturt Taylor.

The publishers would like to thank Dave Millican.

Illustrations by:
Rowan Barnes-Murphy p.7, 8, 33, 34, 67
Ian Kellas p.76, 77, 108, 123, 134, 137, 153
Gillian Martin p.45, 97, 112, 114, 181, 184, 201
David Parkins p.14, 81, 82, 89, 129, 145
Peter Richardson p.2, 104, 122, 174
Bill Stott p.74, 79, 128, 136, 149, 151

Cover design by Warren Kerley, Pentacor
Designed by Mike Brain

Typeset by Tradespools Ltd, Frome, Somerset
Printed and bound in Great Britain by The Bath Press, Avon, England

95 96 97 98 10 9 8 7 6 5 4

Contents

Vocabulary

Formation rules   225

Word list   227

Grammar index   236

Introduction

This book is designed to revise and consolidate grammar points at the level of First Certificate. It also provides practice in key lexical areas.

There are regular progress tests which include forms of testing commonly used in First Certificate examinations.

It can be used as a self-study reference grammar and practice book, or as supplementary material in classes preparing for examinations.

If used for classwork, activities can be done individually or co-operatively in pairs or small groups. The grammatical information provided can be used for reference when needed, or worked through systematically.

The grammar section includes recognition and concept-checking activities, as well as production activities.

Each vocabulary section includes focus on phrasal verbs, prepositions and particles, and collocations.

Unit 1 Past time

Explanations

Narrative

1   Main events
    The Past Simple is used to describe finished events in the past.
    *Susan **went** into the station and **bought** a ticket.*

2   Background description
    The Past Continuous is used to describe actions still in progress, and is used for background description.
    *There were a lot of people waiting in the station. Some **were sleeping** on the benches, and others **were walking** up and down. Susan **was looking for** Graham, so she didn't sit down.*

3   Past before past
    The Past Perfect is used to describe a past event which took place before another past event.
    *By the time the train arrived, Susan **had managed** to push her way to the front of the crowd.*
    It is not always necessary if a time expression makes the order of events clear.
    ***Before** the train arrived, Susan **managed** to push her way to the front of the crowd.*

4   Interrupted Past Continuous
    We often contrast an action still in progress with a sudden event which interrupts it.
    *While Susan **was trying** to get onto the platform, a man **grabbed** her handbag.*

5   Participle clauses
    Participle clauses are introduced by the time expressions *before*, *after* and *while*. They have the same subject as the following clause.
    *After **struggling** with him, Susan **pulled** the bag from his hands.*

Habits in the past

1   Past Simple
    The Past Simple is used to describe past habits or states. A time expression is usually necessary.
    *I always **got up** at six in those days.*   (Habit)
    *I **lived** in Austria for several years.*   (State)

2   *Used to*
    Used to is used to describe past habits, usually in contrast with the present. A time expression is not necessary.
    *I **used to get up** at six, but now I get up at eight.*
    Used to can also describe past states.

1

*I **used to own** a horse.* (I owned a horse once.)
Note these forms of *used to*:
  *I **didn't use to** like beer.*
  ***Did you use to** swim every day?*

3 *Would*
   Would is used to describe a person's typical activities in the past.
   It can only be used to describe repeated actions, and is mainly used
   in writing, and in personal reminiscences.
     *Every evening was the same. Jack **would turn on** the radio, light
     his pipe, and fall asleep.*

4 Past Continuous
   The Past Continuous can be used to describe a repeated action in the
   past, often an annoying habit. A frequency adverb is necessary.
     *When Peter was younger, he **was always getting** into trouble.*

Politeness and
uncertainty

The Past Continuous with the verb *wonder* has a polite meaning.
  *I **was wondering** if you could help me.*
With the verb *think* the Past Continuous suggests uncertainty.
  *I **was thinking** of having a party next week.*

Activities

1
Choose a suitable
caption for each
picture.

a) When he left, Peter forgot that he had put his passport and wallet in his
    other jacket.
b) After phoning the airport, Peter packed his suitcase.
c) Peter put his passport and wallet in his jacket pocket.
d) Before leaving, Peter phoned the airport to check his flight.
e) While Peter was packing his suitcase, he realised that he hadn't checked his flight.
f) While Peter was packing his suitcase, the phone rang.

2

Choose the most suitable tense. The first one is done for you.

a) I suddenly remembered that I forgot/had forgotten my keys.
b) While Diana watched/was watching her favourite television programme, there was a power-cut.
c) Tom used to live/would live in the house at the end of the street.
d) Who was driving/drove the car at the time of the accident?
e) By the time Sheila got back, Chris went/had gone.
f) David ate/had eaten Japanese food before, so he knew what to order.
g) I did/was doing some shopping yesterday, when I saw that Dutch friend of yours.
h) I used to like/was liking sweets much more than I do now.
i) What exactly were you doing/did you do when I came into your office yesterday?
j) Laura missed the party because no-one was telling/had told her about it.
k) Tanya would/used to be a doctor.

3

Put each verb in brackets into a suitable tense. All sentences refer to past time. Only use the Past Perfect where this is absolutely necessary.

a) While I (try) *was trying* to get my car started, a passing car (stop) .... and the driver (offer) .... to help me.
b) The police (pay) .... no attention to Clare's complaint because she (phone) .... them so many times before.
c) Mary (not wear) .... her glasses at the time, so she (not notice) .... what kind of car the man (drive) ....
d) Nick (lie) .... down on the grass for a while, next to some tourists who (feed) .... the ducks. *had hɑt*
e) Tony (admit) .... that he (hit) .... the other car, but said that he (not damage) .... it.
f) Sorry, I (not listen) .... to you. I (think) .... about something else.
g) Helen (feel) .... very tired, and while she (finish) .... her studying, she (fall) .... asleep.
h) The police (get) .... to Clare's house as fast as they could, but the burglars (disappear) .... *had disappeared*
i) I (phone) .... you last night but you (not answer) .... What (you do) .... ?
j) We (not go) .... out yesterday because it (rain) ....

4

Decide whether the tense underlined is suitable or not.

a) While I had a bath, someone knocked on the door. *unsuitable*
b) Sally didn't go to a boxing match before. ....
c) Harry tried to repair the car, but he didn't really know what he was doing. ....
d) What did you wear to the Ponsonbys' party? ....
e) Were you eating spaghetti every day when you lived in Italy? ....
f) I didn't know you had bought a new car. ....
g) They all wanted to believe her, but suspected she was lying. ....
h) As Peggy walked home, she tried to remember what happened. ....
i) 'What a terrible day!' thought Lucy. Everything had gone wrong! ....
j) Although it rained a lot, I was enjoying my holiday last year. ....

5

Put each verb in brackets into a suitable past tense.

When Professor Mallory, the famous archaeologist, (1) *invited* (invite) me to take part in his expedition to find the Lost City of the Himalayas, I (2) .... (not hesitate) to accept his invitation. Mallory (3) .... (discover) an ancient map showing the position of the city, although no European (4) .... (ever go) to the area before. In fact, most of Mallory's colleagues in Oxford either (5) .... (believe) that the city (6) .... (never exist) or (7) .... (feel) that it (8) .... (vanish) long ago and simply (9) .... (become) a legend. According to the Professor, the builders of the city (10) .... (hide) it among the mountains in order to protect its immense riches. He (11) .... (believe) that the descendants of these ancient people (12) ....(still keep) themselves apart from the rest of mankind for the very same reasons. So when we (13) .... (set off) on a cool May morning towards the distant mountains, each of us (14) .... (look forward) to exciting discoveries. For a week or more we (15) .... (climb) higher and higher, following the map, which Mallory (16) .... (study) from time to time. Then one afternoon, while we (17) .... (rest) at the top of a valley, we (18) .... (notice) that a rider on a horse (19) .... (wave) at us from the other side of the valley. A rider whose clothes (20) .... (shine) like gold!

6

Rewrite each sentence, beginning as shown, using a participle clause.

a) Norman collected the parcel. Then he realised it was the wrong one.
After *collecting the parcel, Norman realised it was the wrong one*.

b) Sue left the house. But first she checked that she had her keys.
Before ....

c) Mark was parking his car when he noticed the wing-mirror was broken.
While..

d) Julia cleaned the house. Then she fell asleep on the sofa.
After..

e) Brian bought a new television. First he checked all the prices.
Before ....

f) Alan was skiing in Switzerland. He met his old friend, Ken.
While..

g) Kate took two aspirins, and then she felt a lot better.
After..

h) Sheila went out for the evening, but first she washed her hair.
Before ....

i) Michael was taking a bath when he heard someone at the door.
While..

j) First Trudy read the book. Then she decided that she didn't like it.
After..

7

Complete this table of irregular past tenses and their verb stems.

STEM	PAST TENSE	STEM	PAST TENSE	STEM	PAST TENSE
beat	....	feel	....	shoot	....
bend	....	fly	....	sink	....
.....	bit	.....	froze	.....	sprang
.....	bled	.....	held	.....	stole
blow	....	hurt	....	stick	....
build	....	lay	....	swing	....
.....	caught	.....	meant	.....	tore
.....	chose	.....	paid	.....	trod
cost	....	rise	....	wear	....
draw	....	send	....	win	....
.....	drove	.....	shook	.....	wound
.....	fell	.....	shone	.....	wrote

KEY POINTS

1   The Past Simple describes events in the past, such as the main events in a narrative. It can also describe habits and routines in the past.

2   The Past Continuous is used for:
a) Background description.
b) Actions in progress, often contrasted with a sudden event.
The Past Continuous cannot be used to describe past routines and habits.

3   Participle clauses can introduce a clause giving the main event.
The subjects of both clauses must be the same.

4   The Past Perfect describes a past event which took place before another past event. If *before* or *after* is used, the Past Perfect is optional.
The Past Perfect is not used to show that an event happened a long time ago in the past.

5   *Used to* only refers to past time, and has no present form.

6   *Would* can be used to describe habitual actions in the past, usually in writing, but not when they are contrasted with the present. Compare:
   *Jim **would always make** his mother a cup of tea after lunch.*
   *Jim **used to drink** tea, but now he prefers coffee.*
Would cannot be used to describe states:
   *Sally **used to be** a dancer.*

SEE ALSO

Unit 5
Progress test
Unit 2
Present Perfect
Units 7 and 8
Unreal past tenses
Unit 14
Time expressions

Unit 2 Present Perfect

Explanations

Recent events

Present Perfect Simple

The Present Perfect Simple is used to describe recent events without a definite time. The idea of time or place in the speaker's mind makes the event recent. A time expression may emphasise recentness.

I've left my shopping bag behind.

I've just broken my watch.

We can also describe events that have not happened.

I haven't found her phone number yet.

The event may be connected with the present, because the result of the event is present. No definite time is given for the event.

I've broken my arm, as you can see.

Indefinite events

1 Present Perfect Simple

No definite time is given for the event.

I've been to France three times.

2 Compared with Past Simple

Events described using the Past Simple have definite times.

I went to France last year.

The tense used can depend on the time expression.

This is the first time I have eaten Japanese food.

3 Definite places

If we think of a definite place for an event, this may suggest a definite time.

I left my shopping bag on the train.

Extended or repeated events

1 Present Perfect Simple

With verbs that describe states, the Present Perfect Simple describes a state which lasts up to the present.

I've lived in this house for five years.

2 Present Perfect Continuous

The Present Perfect Continuous can also describe a state which lasts up to the present moment.

I've been living in this house for five years.

There is little difference of meaning between Simple and Continuous in this case, or with *How long* questions. The verbs *sit, lie, wait, stay* prefer the Present Perfect Continuous.

How long have you been waiting?

6

3 Present Perfect Simple

The Present Perfect Simple can describe a habitual action in a period of time up to the present moment.

I've never worn a tie to work, and I refuse to start now!

For, since, ago See Unit 14 for contrasts between these time expressions.

Contrasts between simple and continuous

1 Not completed

Use of the Present Perfect Continuous can suggest that an action is not completed, or has recently finished.

We've been walking for hours! Let's have a rest.
I've been digging the garden. That's why I'm so dirty!

2 Completed

Use of the Present Perfect Simple can show that an action is complete. Giving the number of actions suggests completion.

I've written ten pages of my homework assignment!

Activities

1

Choose a suitable caption for each picture.

a)

①Did you enjoy the match?
2) Have you enjoyed the match?

b)

1) What have you been doing?
2) What have you done?

c)

1) He was married six times.
2) He has been married six times.

d)

1) How long have you been here?
2) How long are you here for?

e)

f)

1) I've been waiting for two hours.
2) I waited for two hours.

1) Where did Wendy go?
2) Where has Wendy been?

2

Choose the most suitable tense.

a) Did you see/Have you seen my bag anywhere? I can't find it.
b) Larry is writing/has been writing/has written his novel for the last two years without getting further than Chapter One.
c) From the minute he got up this morning Gary asked/has asked/has been asking silly questions!
d) Have you given/Did you give Helen my message when you have seen/saw her?
e) Sorry, could you say that again? I didn't listen/haven't listened haven't been listening to you.
f) The police think that they found/have found your missing wallet, so call this number.
g) I don't think we'll go swimming after all because the weather changed/has changed/has been changing.
h) How was your holiday in Italy? Did you visit/Have you visited lots of interesting places?
i) Did you two meet/Have you two met before? Eric, this is Amanda.
j) Did you meet/Have you met anyone interesting at the reception?

3

Put each verb in brackets into a suitable tense.

a) I'm sorry about not coming last week. I (have) *had* a cold and so I (stay) .... at home.
b) Wait a minute. I (have) .... an idea. Let's go and see Roger. We last (see) .... him a long time ago.
c) It's nice to be back here in London. This is the second time I (come) .... here.
d) I'm phoning about your advertisement for a bicycle for sale, which I (see) .... in the local paper. (you sell) .... it?
Or is it still available?
e) This place is in a terrible mess! What on earth (you do) ....?
f) And now for an item of local news. Hampshire police (find) .... the dangerous snake which (go) .... missing earlier in the week.
g) This tooth (kill) .... me lately! So I (make) .... an appointment with the dentist for Tuesday.

h) I can't give you the report I (promise) .... for today because
I (not finish) ....
i) Harry (not look) .... well since he (go) .... on a diet.
j) It says in the paper that they (discover) .... oil in Wales. They (look for) .... it for ages.

4
Choose the most suitable time expression.

a) I haven't seen Gerry (for)/since a long time. How is he?
b) It's ages ago/since I last went to a football match.
c) I've written to Deborah last week/recently.
d) What have you been doing today/yesterday?
e) Have you eaten Italian food before/already?
f) I've been living here in/since the end of last year.
g) Actually I had dinner with Sue last night/lately.
h) I've been trying to get in touch with David for ages/for the last time.
i) Terry hasn't been to Edinburgh since/when we went there together.
j) I can't remember how long/when I've had this watch.

5
Rewrite each sentence, beginning as shown, so that the meaning stays the same.

a) Steve started learning the violin a month ago.
Steve has *been learning the violin for a month.*
b) I haven't been to an Indian restaurant for ages.
It's ages..
c) When she heard the results, Mary began to feel more confident.
Since hearing the results..
d) The last time Nancy came here was in 1986.
Nancy hasn't..
e) This is my first visit to Japan.
This is the first time..
f) How long have Helen and Robert been married?
When...
g) Jack bought those trousers last month, and has been wearing them ever since.
Jack has...
h) It's a long time since our last conversation.
We ....
i) Thanks, but I had something to eat earlier.
Thanks, but I've...
j) This is my first game of water-polo.
I..

6
Put each verb in brackets into either the Present Perfect Simple or Present Perfect Continuous.

a) Someone (eat) *has eaten* all the cakes. I'll have to buy some more.
b) What (you buy) .... your sister for her birthday?
c) My throat is really sore. I (sing) .... all evening.
d) Brenda (learn) .... Russian, but she finds it difficult.
e) How many people (you invite) .... to your party?
f) Those two cats (sit) .... on that branch for the last hour.
g) It (rain) .... all day! Why can't it stop!

9

h) Diana (wear) .... twelve different dresses in the past
    week!
i) I (do) .... everything you asked. What should I do now?
j) Graham and Pauline (try) .... to find a house for ages,
    but they can't find one they can afford.

7

Put each verb in brackets into either the Past Simple, Present Perfect Simple, or Present Perfect Continuous.

It was announced in London this morning that the British Oil Corporation (1) .... (discover) oil under the sea near the Welsh coast. The company, which (2) .... (drill) for oil in the area since 1990, (3) .... (find) small amounts of oil near Swansea last month, and since then (4) .... (discover) larger amounts under the sea-bed nearby. Last year the government (5) .... (lend) over £50,000,000 to BOC, and (6) .... (give) permission for the company to build an oil refinery and other facilities in South Wales. The reaction of local people to today's news (7) .... (be) mixed so far. Local MPs (8) .... (already welcome) the news, pointing out that the oil industry will bring badly needed jobs to the area. But local residents are worried about the danger of pollution. 'Nobody (9) .... (ask) us yet what we want,' said Ann Griffiths, leader of the Keep Out The Oil Campaign. 'Look what (10) .... (happen) when they (11) .... (find) oil in Scotland in the 1960s. The oil companies (12) .... (get) rich, not the local people. BOC (13) .... (not tell) us the truth about what this is going to mean for our people.' A BOC spokesman later (14) .... (refuse) to comment. Meanwhile local campaigners (15) .... (ask) the government to hold an inquiry.

8

Complete this table of irregular past participles and their verb stems.

STEM	PARTICIPLE	STEM	PARTICIPLE	STEM	PARTICIPLE
beat	....	feel	....	shoot	....
bend	....	fly	....	sink	....
bite	....	freeze	....	spring	....
bleed	....	hold	....	steal	....
blow	....	hurt	....	stick	....
build	....	lay	....	swing	....
catch	....	mean	....	tear	....
choose	....	pay	....	tread	....
cost	....	rise	....	wear	....
draw	....	send	....	win	....
drive	....	shake	....	wind	....
fall	....	shine	....	write	....

KEY POINTS

1   The Present Perfect Simple describes indefinite events. These events take place in a period of time leading up to the present moment, or the result of the event is still present. No definite time is given.
    The choice between the Present Perfect Simple and the Past Simple can depend on how the speaker thinks. Compare:
    A: *'What's the matter?'*   *'I've had an accident.'*
    B: *'What's the matter?'*   *'I had an accident.'*

In the second example, the speaker thinks of the event as finished rather than still connected with the present.

2   Events described with the Present Perfect Simple may be recent, or not.

3   The Present Perfect Continuous emphasises the length of time of an action. It suggests that the action is unfinished, or recently finished.
The Present Perfect Continuous is not used where the completion of an action is emphasised. Compare:
   I've been reading. (Completion is not emphasised)
   I've read this book. (Completion is emphasised)

4   *For* refers to a finished or unfinished period of time.
   *He's been sitting there **for ages.***
   *I waited **for three hours.***
Since refers to the point at which an unfinished period of time began.
   *He's been sitting there **since two o'clock.***
Ago refers to the time of a finished event.
   *Jill arrived **a week ago.***

SEE ALSO
Unit 1
Past time
Unit 5
Progress test
Unit 14
Time expressions

Unit 3 Future time

Explanations

Prediction

1 *Will*

Will is used to make predictions. It is often preceded by *I think* or by opinion words like *perhaps*. A time expression is also necessary.

> *I think **it'll rain** tomorrow. Perhaps **she'll be** late.*

In speech, both *will* and *shall* are contracted to *'ll*. Use of *shall* after *I* and *we* is more common in formal speech.

See also Units 21 and 22 for functional uses of *will* and *shall*.

2 *Going to*

If a predicted event is very near, and especially in impersonal statements, *going to* is also commonly used for predictions.

Will can also be used in these examples, with no change of meaning.

> *You're **going to fall**!* (See Present cause)
> *Liverpool **are going to win** the Cup.*

3 Present cause

We often make a prediction because we can see the cause of the event.

> *Look out! There's a bus coming! **It's going to hit** us!*
> *I can see **you're going to have** a baby. When is it due?*

4 Future Continuous

The Future Continuous is used to describe a situation in the future at a particular time.

> *This time next week **we'll be eating** lunch on the plane!*

It is also used to predict a future state or habit at a particular time in the future.

> *In ten years time I expect **I'll be living** in London. And **I'll** probably **be cycling** to work.*

5 Future Perfect

The Future Perfect looks back from a point in the future and refers to indefinite time up to that point.

> *By the time we get there, the film **will have started**.*

This means that at the future time when we get there, we can say:

> *The film has started.*

Future time clauses

1 After time expressions *when*, *until* and *as soon as* a present tense form is used, although this refers to future time.

> *I'll wait for you here **until you get** back.*

2 The Present Perfect can be used to emphasise the completion of an event.

> *I'll wait here until **you have finished**.*

12

Intention	*Going to* *Going* to is used to describe a present intention. **I'm going to fix** the television tomorrow.

Plans and facts

1 Present Continuous
   The Present Continuous is used to describe plans and arrangements which are definite. Such arrangements may be written in a diary.
   *Sorry, I can't help you, **I'm leaving** in the morning.*

2 Present Simple
   The Present Simple is used to describe future events which we cannot control. They may be facts, such as events in a timetable, or a law.
   *The plane for Paris **leaves** at 9.45.*

Activities

1

Choose the most suitable tense.

a) Why ⟨are you going to buy⟩/will you buy a new mountain bike?
b) Don't phone between 8.00 and 9.00. I'll study/I'll be studying then.
c) Look out! That tree will fall/is going to fall!
d) Let me know as soon as Louise will get/gets here.
e) Great news! Jean and Chris will come/are coming to stay with us.
f) According to this timetable, the bus is going to arrive/arrives at 6.00.
g) I have a feeling that something strange is going to happen/happening in a minute.
h) The doctor says I will have/am going to have a baby!
i) Can you call me at 7.00, because I'll leave/I'm leaving tomorrow.
j) If you arrive late at the sale, the best things will go/will have gone.

2

Put each verb in brackets into the most appropriate future time form. More than one answer may be possible.

a) I can't see you on Thursday afternoon. I (visit) *am visiting* our Birmingham branch.
b) George (not be) .... back until six. Can I take a message?
c) What (you buy) .... with the money you won in the lottery?
d) I don't think you (have) .... any problems at the airport.
e) (you take) .... your dog with you to Scotland?
f) Can you answer the phone for me? I (lie down) .... for a while.
g) All the hotels are full. Where (we spend) ....the night?
h) You'd better not come in July. My mother (stay) .... with me then.
i) What time (your plane leave) .... ?
j) Leave the car here. Maybe the police (not notice) .... it.

3

Put each verb in brackets into a suitable future time form. More than one answer may be possible.

a) By the time we reach home, the rain (stop) *will have stopped*.
b) This time next week I (lie) .... on the beach in Spain.
c) In ten years' time I (work) .... for a different company.
d) If we don't get there by six, Jack (leave) ....
e) In July they (be married) .... for twenty years.
f) In the year 2500 a lot of people (live) .... on the moon.
g) When you get to the station, I (wait) .... for you outside.
h) Don't worry! The plane (land) .... in a moment.
i) By the time you come home, I (finish) .... the decorating.
j) Come round between eight and nine. We (watch) .... the match on television then.

4

Put each verb in brackets into a suitable tense.

Have you ever wondered what exactly (1) *you will be doing* (you do) in ten years' time? Well, according to computer expert Tom Vincent, computers (2) .... (soon be able) to make accurate predictions about the future. Professor Vincent, from Cambridge University, (3) .... (hold) a press conference next week to describe the computer which he calls 'Computafuture'. 'This computer can tell us what life (4).................. (be) like, based on data describing past events,' explains Professor Vincent. For example, Computafuture can predict how many people (5) .... (live) in a particular area, or whether there (6) .... (be) a lot of rain during a particular period. Professor Vincent also believes that by the year 2050, computers (7) .... (replace) teachers, and (8) .... (also do) most of the jobs now being done by the police. 'Computers are becoming more intelligent all the time,' says Professor Vincent. 'Soon they (9) .... (direct) traffic and (10) .... (teach) our children. And telling us about the future.'

5

Put each verb in brackets into a suitable tense. All sentences refer to future time.

a) When I (see) *see* you tomorrow, I (tell) .... you my news.
b) As soon as we (get) ....there, we (phone) .... for a taxi.
c) I (go) .... to the library before I (do) .... the shopping.
d) We (wait) .... here until the rain (stop) ....
e) I (get) .... some money from the bank when it (open) ....
f) After you (take) .... the medicine, you (feel) .... better.
g) You have to stay until you (finish) .... your work.
h) I (let) .... you know the minute I (hear) .... the results.
i) Before we (paint) .... the wall, we (have) .... a cup of tea.
j) We (climb) .... over the wall as soon as it (get) .... dark.

KEY POINTS

1 *Will* and *shall* have other meanings. See Units 18 and 19.

2 The Present Continuous is used to describe fixed arrangements, and to ask about social arrangements.
   Are you doing anything this evening?

3 The Present Simple and Present Perfect can also be used to refer to future time.
   *I'll tell you the news **when I see** you.*
   *Call me **when you have finished**.*

4 *Going to* can be used instead of *will* in predictions. For some speakers this seems more colloquial.
   *I'm sure **you're going to enjoy** the film.*
   *I'm sure **you'll enjoy** the film.*

SEE ALSO

Units 18 and 19
for functional uses of *will* and *shall*.
Unit 5
Progress test
Unit 14
Time expressions

15

Unit 4 Present time

Explanations

Present Simple

1   Facts which are always true
    The Present Simple is used to describe facts in science, and geographical descriptions.
    *The light from the Sun **takes** 8 mins 20 secs to reach the Earth.*
    *The River Po **flows** into the Adriatic Sea.*

2   Habitual actions
    The Present Simple is used to describe habitual actions. A frequency adverb is often used.
    *I usually **take** the bus to work.*

3   Plot summaries and historical tables
    The Present Simple is used to describe the events in a narrative, when the events are summarised. It is used to describe what happens in a film or book, or in a table of events.
    *In Chapter One, Susan **meets** David, and **agrees** to go to the school dance with him.*
    *1789. The French Revolution **begins**.*
    *George Washington **becomes** the first president of the USA.*

Present Continuous

1   Actions which are still in progress
    The Present Continuous is used to describe actions which are temporary and not yet finished.
    *I'm **doing** the washing-up.*

2   Habits over a period of time
    The Present Continuous can describe a temporary habit. A time expression is necessary.
    *At the moment **we're sending** all the mail by courier, because the Post Office is on strike.*

3   A repeated temporary event
    The Present Continuous can describe a repeated temporary action. A time expression is necessary.
    *Whenever I see Tom **he's smoking**.*
    *You're **making** the same mistake again!*

4   An annoying habit
    The Present Continuous is used to describe an annoying habit. A frequency adverb is necessary.
    *You're **always borrowing** money from me!*

| Problems with simple and continuous | 1 | Some verbs are not normally used in the continuous, because they describe activities which already extend in time. These are sometimes called 'state' meanings. |

> *be, believe, cost, depend, have, hear, know, matter, smell*
> *suppose, taste, think, understand*

2 Some of these verbs can be used in continuous forms with a change of meaning.

> **Tim is being** *rather difficult at the moment.*   *(Behave)*
> **I'm having** *breakfast.*   *(Eat)*
> **I'm tasting** *the soup, to check if it needs more salt.*   *(Sample)*
> **I'm thinking** *of buying a new car.*   *(Consider)*

3 The difference between simple and continuous can be one of attitude.

> *Do you sleep a lot?*   (Your general habit)
> *Are you sleeping enough?*   (Your situation at the moment)

Both questions could be asked in the same situation.

Activities

1

Choose the most suitable tense.

a) What sort of work do you do/are you doing?
b) I can't talk now. I cook/I'm cooking the dinner.
c) What shall we have? Do you like/Are you liking fish?
d) Can I borrow this typewriter? Or do you use it/are you using it?
e) What do the people here do/are the people here doing in the evenings?
f) Follow that bus. Then you turn/you are turning left.
g) A lot of people think that the Sun goes/is going around the Earth.
h) Excuse me, do you read/are you reading your newspaper? Could I borrow it?
i) Do you wait/Are you waiting for the bus to Newcastle?
j) Andy builds/is building his own house in the country.

2

Put each verb in brackets into either the Present Simple or Present Continuous.

a) There's nobody here, and the door's locked. What (we do) *do we do* now?
b) What (you look) .... at? (I wear) .... the wrong clothes again?
c) I (look after) .... Jack's dog this weekend. (you want) .... to take it for a walk?
d) Who (drive) .... that Mercedes that's parked outside?
e) I (still have) .... a pain in my leg but it (get) .... better.
f) Who (Sue dance) .... with? That's not her brother, is it?
g) Harry (look) .... very untidy! He (wear) .... dirty jeans all the time.
h) I (write) .... in reply to your advertisement in the Daily News.
i) That plant I bought (not grow) .... very much. And I (water) .... it every day.
j) Which hotel (you stay) .... in whenever you (come) .... here?

3

Decide whether the verb underlined refers to present or future time.

a) Where <u>are you staying</u> on Saturday night? *future*
b) George <u>retires</u> at the end of next year. ....
c) What are we doing when the guests <u>arrive</u>? ....
d) <u>I'm trying</u> really hard to understand this book. ....
e) Wait for me here until I <u>get</u> back. ....
f) Sue <u>is leaving</u> in the morning. ....
g) <u>I'm waiting</u> for the bus. ....
h) I'm off now, and <u>I'm taking</u> the car. ....
i) <u>They're showing</u> a Woody Allen film on Channel 4 tonight. ....
j) <u>I'm going</u> for a walk this evening. ....

4

Make *-ing* forms of each verb given, and then complete the spelling rules below.

write	swim	get	admit	annoy
begin	study	like	try	decide

a) If a word ends in vowel + consonant + 'e' (*write*) ....
....
b) If a word ends in vowel + consonant (*swim*) ....
....
c) If a word ends in 'y' (*try, annoy*)..............................
....

5

Rewrite each sentence, replacing the words underlined with a form of the verb in brackets.

a) This flower <u>has</u> a wonderful <u>perfume</u>. (smell)
This flower smells wonderful.
b) I think you <u>are behaving in a</u> very silly <u>way</u>. (be)
....
c) She <u>is expecting</u> a baby in the summer. (have)
....
d) Nancy <u>is considering</u> moving to Scotland. (think of)
....
e) Don't go in. They <u>are holding</u> a meeting. (have)
....
f) I <u>am meeting</u> Janet this evening actually. (see)
....
g) Good clothes <u>are becoming</u> more and more <u>expensive</u>. (cost)
....
h) I <u>am just trying</u> the soup to see if it needs more salt. (taste)
....
i) Helen <u>is taking</u> a bath at the moment. (have)
....
j) I <u>think</u> that you would be happier in another job. (feel)
....

6

Put each verb in brackets into either the Present Simple or Present Continuous.

Dear Aunt Jean,

I (1) *am just writing* (just write) to tell you how much I (2).......... (appreciate) the money you sent me, and to tell you how I (3)......... (get on) in my first term at university. Actually, I (4)......... (really enjoy) myself! I (5)......... (study) quite hard as well, but at the moment I (6).......... (spend) a lot of time just making friends. I(7).......... (still stay) with my friend Sue, and I (8)......... (look for) somewhere of my own to live. Only a few of the first-year students (9).......... (live) in college here, and I (10)......... (seem) to be spending a lot of time travelling backwards and forwards. I (11).......... (go) to lectures every morning, and most afternoons I (12).......... (study) in the library. In fact I (13)........ (write) this letter instead of an essay on 'Hamlet'! I (14).......... (think) I'll buy some new clothes with the money you sent. Everything (15).......... (cost) a lot here, and I (16)........(save) to buy a winter coat. It (17).......... (get) really cold here in the evenings. I (18)......... (know) lots of other students and generally speaking we (19).......... (have) quite a good time socially! I (20)........ (also learn) to drive.

See you soon,

Katherine

KEY POINTS

1 The Present Simple describes facts and habitual actions. The Present Continuous describes actions which are still in progress at the time of speaking.

2 Many verbs which describe states rather than momentary events can only be used in the simple. Many verbs describing mental activities (*understand, know*) are of this kind.

3 Some verbs have both state and event meanings, but the meanings are not the same.

4 When describing a photograph, we usually describe the scene as if it is happening now, and use the Present Continuous.

5 Present tense forms are also used to refer to future time.

6 In situations where some languages use present tenses, English uses the Present Perfect.

SEE ALSO

Unit 3
Future time
Unit 5
Progress test

Unit 5 Progress test

(Units 1, 2, 3, 4)

1
Rewrite each sentence, beginning as shown, so that the meaning stays the same.

a) There's a party at Mary's house next week.
Next week Mary ....

b) When you phoned me, it was my lunchtime.
When you phoned me, I...

c) I started working for this company three years ago.
I've...

d) Our meeting is tomorrow.
We are..

e) I haven't had a Chinese meal for ages.
It's ages...

f) David went home before we arrived.
When we...

g) The arrival time of Helen's flight is 8.00.
Helen's flight..

h) Hurry up! We'll get to the theatre after the beginning of the play.
By the time we get to the theatre, the play......................

i) Oh no! My wallet is missing.
Oh no! I have..

j) I've only recently started wearing glasses.
I didn't...

2
Put each verb in brackets into a suitable tense.

I come from a very large family, and recently my parents (1) .... (decide) that they (2) .... (spend) long enough living in an overcrowded house in Birmingham. 'We (3) .... (move) to the country,' my father (4) .... (announce) one evening. 'I (5) .... (sell) this house, and we (6) .... (live) on a farm.' So last week we (7) .... (load) all our possessions into two hired vans, and for the last few days we (8) ....(try) to organise ourselves in our new home. Yesterday, for example, my three brothers and I (9) .... (start) painting the downstairs rooms. Unfortunately while I (10) .... (mix) the paint, one of my sisters (11) .... (open) the door. Nobody (12) .... (tell) her that we (13) .... (be) in the room, you see. So instead of painting the walls, we (14) .... (spend) all morning cleaning the paint off the floor. But worse things (15) .... (happen) since then. This morning when I (16) .... (wake up), water (17) .....(drip) through the ceiling next to my bed. We (18) .... (spend) today so far repairing the roof. It's not all bad news, though. The school in the village nearby (19) .... (close down) two years ago, and my parents (20) .... (not find) another school for us yet.

20

3

Complete the numbered spaces in the dialogue.

Journalist: Mr Foster, you saw the robbery, didn't you? When the two men burst into the bank, what (1)......................?

Mr Foster: I was counting money behind the counter. I didn't realise what was happening at first. Then I noticed the shotguns.

Journalist: And what (2) ....?

Mr Foster: Well, nothing really. I just stood there.

Journalist: And how long (3) ....?

Mr Foster: The whole robbery was over in about five minutes.

Journalist: And who (4) ....?

Mr Foster: The manager called them. After the men had gone, of course.

Journalist: And (5) ....?

Mr Foster: Yes, of course. Not just me, everybody. They questioned us as soon as they arrived.

Journalist: And what (6) ....?

Mr Foster: The same things I've told you, really. There's not much else to say, is there?

Journalist: Could you give me a few details about yourself? Just for the news story? How long (7) ....?

Mr Foster: Three years. I used to be at the branch in the High Street.

Journalist: And why (8) ....?

Mr Foster: Actually I had to move, they made me. I lost some money, you see. I seem to be rather unlucky ...

4

Rewrite each sentence, beginning as shown, so that the meaning stays the same.

a) Jack left the office before I arrived there.
   When I arrived...

b) Do you have any experience of driving this kind of car?
   Have you ever...

c) This is my first visit to Scotland.
   This is the first time.....................................

d) During dinner, the phone rang.
   While I...

e) Do you have anything fixed for Saturday evening?
   What are..

f) I started this job five years ago.
   I have..

g) Is this car yours?
   Do you..

h) Look at those black clouds! There's rain on the way!
   Look at those black clouds! It's.........................

i) Our twenty-fifth wedding anniversary is at the end of next year.
   By the end of next year we...............................

j) I haven't been to the cinema for two months.
   The last time...

5

Put each verb in brackets into a suitable tense.

I was on time for my dentist's appointment, but the dentist was still busy with another patient, so I (1) .... (sit) in the waiting room and (2) .... (read) some of the old magazines lying there. While I (3) .... (wonder) whether to leave and come back another day, I (4) .... (notice) a magazine article about teeth. It (5) .... (begin): 'How long is it since you last (6) .... (go) to the dentist? (7) .... (you go) regularly every six months? Or (8) .... (you put off) your visit for the last six years?' Next to the article was a cartoon of a man in a dentist's chair. The dentist (9) .... (say): 'I'm afraid this (10) .... (hurt).' I (11) .... (suddenly realise) that my tooth (12) .... (stop) aching. But just as I (13) .... (open) the door to leave, the dentist's door (14) .... (open). 'Next please,' he (15) .... (call), as the previous patient (16) .... (push) past me. 'Actually I'm not here to see you, I (17) .... (wait) for my friend,' I (18) .... (shout), leaving as rapidly as I could. (19) .... (you ever do) this kind of thing? Surely I can't be the only person who (20) .... (hate) the dentist!

6

Use these words and phrases to make complete sentences. The sentences are all part of a letter. Make changes and add any necessary words as in the example.

I/not know/you/be/Brighton.
I didn't know you were in Brighton.

27, Golding Road
London SE20 3HP

Dear Harry,

a) I/ hope / you / remember me.
   ....

b) We/ meet/ last year when you/ be on holiday /Brighton.
   ....

c) I/ be / sorry I /not write/ you since then.
   ....

d) I /work abroad and I / only just get back/ England.
   ....

e) Next week I / come /Bristol, and I /think/ we could meet.
   ....

f) you /remember Shirley, the girl we / meet / Brighton?
   ....

g) We /get married next month, and we /want you /come to the wedding.
   ....

h) I /lose your phone number, but when I / get to Bristol I /try / contact you.
   ....

Best Wishes,
Graham Norris

7
Complete the
letter by using
verbs from the
list in a suitable
tense. Use each
verb once only.

be become change come decide not do go have
live move stay stop tell wait not write

Dear Linda,
I'm sorry I (1) .... to you for so long, but I (2) .... very busy
lately. All last month I (3) .... exams, and I (4) .... anything else
but study for ages. Anyway, I (5) .... studying now, and I (6) ....
for my exam results.
As you can see from the letter, I (7) .... my address and (8) .... in
Croydon now. I (9) .... that I wanted a change from central London
because it (10) .... so expensive. A friend of mine (11) .... me
about this flat, and I (12) .... here about two months ago. When you
(13) .... to London this summer, please visit me. I (14) .... here
until the middle of August. Then I (15) .... on holiday to Scotland.

Please write soon,
Margaret.

Unit 6 Indirect speech

Explanations

With tense changes

1 Summary of tense changes
Tenses are moved into the past after a past tense reporting verb.
The Past Perfect remains the same.
> *I'm leaving.' Jane said* **she was leaving.**
> *'No, I hadn't forgotten.' Greg said that* **he hadn't** *forgotten.*

For Modals (*can, may, must, shall, should*) see Unit 16.

2 Main verb changes only
In complex sentences, only the first verb is changed.
> *'I was walking home when I saw the accident.'*
> *James said he* **had been walking** *home when he saw the accident.*

3 Reference words
Some words referring to persons, place and time change in indirect speech, because the point of reference changes.
> *I'll see you here tomorrow, Jack,' said Mary.*
> *Mary told Jack she would see* **him there the next day.**
> *'I gave you this yesterday.'*
> *John said he had given* **it** *to* **her the day before.**

Other words of this kind are practised in the activity pages.

Without tense changes

1 Present tense reports
If the reporting verb is in the Present tense, there is no change.
> *Brenda* **says** *she's arriving at about 6.00.*

2 Past tense reports
If the reported words are 'always true', there is no change.
> *Harry told me that* **he still likes you.**

If a message is being repeated immediately, there is no change.
> *Mary said* **she's too busy** *to come.*

Questions

1 Indirect questions
Yes/No questions are reported using *if*. The verb is not put into a question form, and there is no question mark.
> *'Do you like hamburgers?' Charles asked me* **if I liked** *hamburgers.*

Wh- questions are reported with the question word. There is no question form.
> *'Where are we going?' I asked Sue* **where we were going.**

2 Embedded questions
These are questions introduced by polite phrases. Note the word order.
> *Could you tell me* **where the station is?'**

In indirect speech, the polite question becomes a reporting verb.
I asked him where the station was.

Commands and requests

1   Commands are reported with *tell* and the infinitive.
    *'Go away!' He told me **to go away**.*

2   Requests are reported with *ask* and the infinitive.
    *'Please help me.' He asked her **to help him**.*

Reporting verbs

The activity pages include practice in common reporting verbs. The grammatical context for each verb should be learned.

Paraphrase

Often it is impossible or unnecessary to report every word spoken.
'Excuse me, do you think you could tell me the time?'
*He asked me **what the time was**.*

Activities

1
Rewrite each sentence as direct speech.

a) Graham told Ian he would see him the following day.
   'I'll see you tomorrow, Ian,' said Graham.

b) Pauline told the children their swimming things were not there.
   ....

c) David told me my letter had arrived the day before.
   ....

d) Shirley told Larry she would see him that evening.
   ....

e) Bill told Stephen he hadn't been at home that morning.
   ....

f) Margaret told John to phone her on the following day.
   ....

g) Tim told Ron he was leaving that afternoon.
   ....

h) Christine told Michael she had lost her lighter the night before.
   ....

2
Rewrite each sentence as indirect speech, beginning as shown.

a) 'You can't park here.'
   The police officer told Jack *that he couldn't park there.*

b) 'I'll see you in the morning, Helen.'
   Peter told Helen ....

c) 'I'm taking the 5.30 train tomorrow evening.'
   Janet said ....

d) 'The trousers have to be ready this afternoon.'
   Paul told the dry-cleaners...

e) 'I left my umbrella here two days ago.'
   Susan told them ....

f) 'The parcel ought to be here by the end of next week.'
Brian said..

g) 'I like this hotel very much.'
Diana told me ....

h) 'I think it's going to rain tonight.'
William said ....

3

Match each question a) to h) with a sentence in indirect speech 1) to 8). Underline the verbs in each sentence.

a) '<u>Does</u> this car <u>belong</u> to you?'
3) *A policeman asked me if the car belonged to me.*

b) 'What time does the next train for London leave?'..............

c) 'Do you like visiting old buildings?'...................................

d) 'Who did you go to the cinema with?'................................

e) 'Is this the right road for Hastings?' ....

f) 'Why do you wear such funny hats?' ....

g) 'Are you doing anything this weekend?'............................

h) 'What time did you get home last night?'...........................

1) Helen asked me if I liked visiting old buildings.
2) Bill asked Mary if she was doing anything that weekend.
3) A policeman asked me if the car belonged to me.
4) I asked Fiona why she wore such funny hats.
5) I asked the ticket collector what time the next train for London left.
6) David asked a passer-by if it was the right road for Hastings.
7) My parents asked me what time I got home the night before.
8) Eddie asked Steve who he had been to the cinema with.

4

Rewrite each question in indirect speech, beginning as shown.

a) 'What time does the film start, Peter?'
I asked *Peter what time the film started.*............................

b) 'Do you watch television every evening, Chris?'
The interviewer asked ....

c) 'Why did you apply for this job?' asked the sales manager.
The sales manager asked me ....

d) 'Are you taking much money with you to France?'
My bank manager wanted to know ....

e) 'When will I know the results of the examination?'
Maria asked the examiner ....

f) 'Are you enjoying your flight?'
The stewardess asked me ....

g) 'How does the photocopier work?'
I asked the salesman ....

h) 'Have you ever been to Japan, Paul?'
Sue asked Paul..

5
Continue reporting each sentence, using only the number of words stated.

a) 'Do you think you could possibly tell me what the time is?'
David asked me *to tell him the time.* (Five words)

b) 'Excuse me, but I wonder if you'd mind opening the window.'
The man sitting next to me asked me....................(Four words)

c) 'You go down this street, turn left, then take the second turning on the right. The cinema is just down the street on the left.'
A passer-by told me how...............................(Five words)

d) 'I want to know how much this bike costs. Can you tell me?'
John asked how.......................................(Four words)

e) 'Look, don't worry, I'll help you if you like.'
Sue said she..(Three words)

f) 'All right, I tell you what, the car's yours for, let's say £500.'
The salesman said I could............................(Five words)

g) 'I hope you don't mind my saying this, but you're being a bit silly, aren't you?'
Peter told me I......................................(Five words)

h) 'It doesn't look as if I'll be arriving until after eight, I'm afraid.'
Jane said she probably...............................(Six words)

6
Rewrite each sentence, beginning as shown, so that the meaning stays the same.

a) What time does the next boat leave?
Do you think you could tell me *what time the next boat leaves*?

b) Where can I change some money?
Can you tell me ....?

c) Where is the toilet?
Could you possibly tell me ....?

d) How much does this pullover cost?
I'd like to know ....?

e) How do I get to Victoria Station?
Can you explain ....?

f) Does this train go to Gatwick Airport?
Could you tell me ....?

g) Where do you come from?
Would you mind telling me ....?

h) What do you think of London?
Do you think you could tell me...............................?

7
Put a form of either *say, tell* or *ask* in each space.

a) I *told* you that you had to be on time. Why are you late?

b) When you .... her if she'd work late, what did she .... ?

c) I think that Alan ...... us a lie about his qualifications.

d) When I .... him what he was doing there, he .... me it was none of my business.

e) I ...... I would help you, so here I am.

f) Did you hear what Sheila .... about her new job?

g) What did Carol .... you about her holiday?

h) There, you see! I ...... you the bus would be on time.

8
Put a form of one of the verbs from the list into the space in each sentence.

accuse	agree	decide	insist	refuse
admit	apologise	deny	offer	remind
advise	confess	doubt	promise	suggest

a) 'No, it's not true, I didn't steal the money!'
Jean *denied* stealing the money.

b) 'Why don't we go to the cinema this evening?'
Peter .... going to the cinema.

c) 'Yes, of course, I'll give you a lift, Helen.'
Liz .... to give Helen a lift.

d) 'I've broken your pen. I'm awfully sorry, Jack.'
David .... for breaking Jack's pen.

e) 'Don't forget to post my letter, will you, Sue?'
Diana .... Sue to post her letter.

f) 'Let me carry your suitcase, John.'
Harry .... to carry John's suitcase.

g) 'All right, it's true, I was nervous.'
The leading actor .... that he had been nervous.

h) 'I don't think Liverpool will win.'
Vanessa .... whether Liverpool would win.

i) 'If I were you, Bill, I'd buy a mountain bike.'
Stephen .... Bill to buy a mountain bike.

j) 'Don't worry, Martin, I'll bring your book back.'
Leslie .... to bring Martin's book back.

k) 'You murdered Lord Digby, didn't you, Colin!'
The inspector .... Colin of murdering Lord Digby.

l) 'No, no, you really must have another drink!'
Dick .... on my having another drink.

m) 'It was me who stole the money,' said Jim.
Jim .... to stealing the money.

n) 'Right. I'll take the brown pair.'
Andrew .... to take the brown pair.

o) 'No, sorry, I don't want to lend you my camera.'
Alex .... to lend me his camera.

9
Rewrite each sentence, beginning as shown, so that the meaning stays the same.

a) 'Sue, can you remember to buy some bread?'
Paul reminded *Sue to buy some bread.*

b) 'I don't really think it'll snow tomorrow.'
I doubt...

c) 'I'm sorry I didn't phone you earlier.'
Jill apologised...

28

d) 'I really think you should see a doctor, Chris.'
William advised ....

e) 'No, I'm sorry, I won't work on Saturday. Definitely not!'
Catherine refused ....

f) 'Let's go out to the pub for lunch, shall we?'
Wendy suggested...

g) 'It's not true! I have never been arrested.'
Larry denied...

h) 'If you like, I'll help you do the decorating, Bob.'
Ann offered...

i) 'I'll definitely take you to the park on Saturday, children.'
Tom promised his...

j) 'Yes, all right, I'll share the bill with you, Dave.'
Brenda agreed ....

KEY POINTS

1 Tense changes are usually necessary after a past tense reporting verb.

2 Words referring to time and place also change in indirect speech.

3 Indirect questions are of two types. Yes/No questions are reported with *If,* and *Wh-* questions are reported with the question word. The verb is not put into a question form in an indirect question.

4 Indirect speech is often introduced by a reporting verb. These are followed by a variety of grammatical constructions. A good dictionary will include this information.

5 Indirect speech may also involve paraphrasing the main points of what was said.

SEE ALSO

Unit 10
Progress test
Unit 17
Modals: Past

Unit 7 Conditionals

Explanations

Real situations: Conditional 1

1 **With *if* and *can***
This kind of sentence describes a real situation. Although a present tense is used after *if*, the time referred to is not present.
*If you **fall**, I **won't be able** to catch you!*
This means that there is a real possibility this will happen as we are actually in the situation described. *Going to* can be used in place of *will*.
*If it rains, **we're going to get** wet.*
Modal *can* is common in Conditional 1 sentences.
*If the cases **are** too heavy, I **can help** you carry them.*

2 ***unless, provided, as long as***
Unless introduces a clause which tells us about an exception to the point made in the main clause.
*Unless you **leave** at once, **I'll call** the police.*
Provided and *as long as* can also introduce a condition.
*Provided you **leave** now, **you'll catch** the train.*

3 **With the imperative**
It is common to use the imperative instead of *if*.
***Get** me some cigarettes, and **I'll pay** you later.*

4 **With *should***
Should makes the action less likely. It is stressed in speech.
*If you **should** see John, can you give him a message?*

Unreal situations: Conditional 2 (present/future)

1 **With *if***
This kind of sentence describes an imaginary or unreal situation. Although the Past Simple tense is used after *if*, the time referred to is not past but imaginary.
*If you **fell**, you **would hurt** yourself.*
This means that I am imagining a situation and its result. We could both be in a dangerous situation, or I could be imagining the whole situation. The past tense form does not refer to past time.

2 ***Were, might, could***
Were is often used instead of *was* in formal language. Note that *were* is not stressed.
*If I **were** taller, **I'd join** the basket-ball team.*
*If I **were** you, **I'd leave** now. (I and you are stressed.)*
*Modals **might** and **could** are common in this kind of sentence.*
*If you **became** a millionaire, you **might be** unhappy.*

3 *Were to*
Were to is another way of expressing a Conditional 2 sentence.
> *If they **were to offer** me the job, **I'd turn** it down.*

Unreal situations: Conditional 3 (past)

1 With *if* and *might*
This kind of situation describes an imaginary or unreal situation. The time referred to is past time.
> *If you **had written** more, you **would have got** better marks.*

Might is common in this kind of sentence.
> *If you **had tried** harder, you **might have succeeded**.*

2 Mixed conditions
For past events which have a result continuing in the present, it is possible to mix Conditionals 2 and 3.
> *If you **had saved** some money, you **wouldn't be** so hard up.*

if sentences

Not all *if* sentences are conditional sentences, and *if* can mean *whenever* or *if it is true that*.
> *If (whenever) it **rains**, we **play** football indoors instead.*
> *If (it is true that) you **have** a job like that, you **are** very lucky.*
> *If (it is true that) nothing **happened**, you **were** lucky.*

Activities

1
Choose the most suitable tense.

a) If the machine ⟨stops⟩/will stop, you ⟨press⟩/will press this button.
b) I can't understand what he sees in her! If anyone treats/will treat treated me like that, I am/will be/would be extremely angry!
c) If you help me/helped me with this exercise, I will do/would do the same for you one day.
d) According to the timetable, if the train leaves/left on time we will/would arrive at 5.30.
e) If it is/it will be fine tomorrow, we go/we will go to the coast.
f) If we find/found a taxi, we will get/would get there before the play starts.
g) It's quite simple really. If you take/will take/took these tablets every day, then you lose/will lose/lost/would lose weight.
h) I don't like this flat. I think I am/I will be/I'd be happier if I live/I will live/I would live/I lived in a house in the country.
i) I can't play football, but I'm sure that if I will/do/did, I play/ will play/would play a lot better than anyone in this awful team!
j) If I phone/will phone/phoned you tonight, are you/will you be/would you be in?

2

Choose the most suitable tense.

a) Why didn't you tell me? If you told/(had told) me,
   I had/(would have) helped you.

b) If Bill didn't steal/hadn't stolen the car, he wasn't/wouldn't be/
   hadn't been in prison now.

c) If Ann wasn't driving/didn't drive/hadn't driven so fast, her car
   didn't crash/wouldn't crash/wouldn't have crashed into a tree.

d) Let me give you some advice. If you smoked/would smoke/had smoked
   less, you didn't feel/wouldn't feel/wouldn't have felt so tired.

e) What bad luck! If Alan didn't fall/hadn't fallen/wouldn't fall over,
   he won/would win/would have won the race.

f) If you invited/had invited me last week, I was able/had been able/
   would have been able to come.

g) I'm sure your letter hasn't arrived yet. If it came/had come I'm sure
   I noticed/had noticed/would have noticed it.

h) We have a suggestion to make. How do you feel/would you feel if we
   offered/would offer/had offered you the job of assistant manager?

i) If you lent/had lent us the money, we paid/would pay/had paid you
   back next week.

j) Terry never catches anything when he goes fishing. And if he catches/
   caught/had caught a fish, he throws/would throw it back!

3

Put each verb in brackets into a suitable tense.

a) Why didn't you phone? If I (know) *had known* you were coming, I (meet)
   .... you at the airport.

b) It's a pity you missed the party. If you (come) .... you (meet) .... my
   friends from Hungary.

c) If we (have) .... some tools, we (be able) .... to repair the car, but we
   haven't got any with us.

d) Thank you for your help. If you (not help) ....me, I (not pass) .... the
   examination.

e) It's a beautiful house, and I (buy) .... it if I (have) .... the money, but
   I can't afford it.

f) I can't imagine what I (do) .... with the money if I (win) .... the
   football pools or a lottery.

g) Mark isn't a serious athlete. If he (train) .... harder, he (be) .... quite a
   good runner.

h) If Claire (listen) .... to her mother, she (not marry) .... David in
   the first place.

i) It rained every day on our holiday. If we (not take) .... the television
   with us, we (not have) .... anything to do.

j) Jim is so untidy! If he (buy) .... some new clothes, he (not look)...........
   so bad!

4

Choose the most appropriate caption for each picture.

a)

1) If she falls, she'll land in the safety net.
2) If she fell, she'd land in the safety net.
3) If she had fallen, she would have landed in the safety net.

b)

1) It's worse if we order soup.
2) It would be worse if we ordered soup.
3) It would have been worse if we'd ordered soup.

c)

1) If I own a dog like that, I'll keep it on a lead.
2) If I owned a dog like that, I'd keep it on a lead.
3) If I had owned a dog like that, I'd have kept it on a lead.

d)

1) I like it more if it looks like someone I know.
2) I'd like it more if it looked like someone I knew.
3) I'd have liked it more if it had looked like someone I knew.

e)

1) If we hurry, we won't miss the train.
2) If we hurried we wouldn't miss the train.
3) If we had hurried, we wouldn't have missed the train.

5

Rewrite each sentence, beginning as shown, so that the meaning stays the same.

a) I didn't have an umbrella with me and so I got wet.
   I wouldn't *have got wet if I had had an umbrella with me.*.

b) I'll call the police if you don't leave me alone!
   Unless ....

c) In the snowy weather we don't go to school.
   If...

d) Without Jack's help, I wouldn't have been able to move the table.
   If...

e) You drink too much coffee, that's why you can't sleep.
   If you ....

f) You press this button to stop the machine.
   If...

g) Make me some coffee, and I'll give you one of my biscuits.
   If...

h) If you hadn't told me about Sue's hair, I wouldn't have noticed.
   Unless...

i) If you see Peter, tell him he should be here at 8.00.
   If you should...

j) I wouldn't accept if you asked me to marry you!
   If you were...

6

Rewrite each sentence with all possible written contractions.

a) If I had known, I would have told you.
   If I'd known, I'd have told you..

b) Tony would not have crashed if he had been more careful.
   ....

c) If you asked me, I would tell you.
   ....

d) If I had had my credit card with me, I would have bought the coat.
   ....

e) You would not have got lost, if you had taken the map.
   ....

f) If you had asked me for a loan I could have given you one.
   ....

g) If Graham had not lost his watch he would not have missed his plane.
   ....

h) If you had not told me her name I would have found out from someone.

   ....

i) If I were you I would try getting up earlier.

   ....

j) No-one would have realised if Peter had not told them.

   ....

KEY POINTS

1 The present tense form in Conditional 1 sentences does not refer to present time.

2 The past tense form in Conditional 2 sentences does not refer to past time.

3 The difference between Conditional 1 and 2 sentences can depend on the attitude of the speaker.
   If she falls, she'll land in the safety net.
   (This means that there is a real possibility that she will fall.)
   If she fell she would land in the safety net.
   (I am commenting on an imaginary situation, and I probably do not think that she is likely to fall.)

4 Modal auxiliaries are common in conditional sentences when we may be uncertain about our predictions.
   *If you leave now you **might catch** the train.*
   *If you asked him nicely, he **might agree**.*
   *If you'd gone through the red light, you **might have hit** another car.*

5 Mixed conditions are possible, especially where a past event has a present result.
   *If Brenda **hadn't stolen** the money, she **wouldn't be** in prison.*

6 *Unless, provided*, and *as long as* can introduce conditions.

7 Many sentences beginning *If* . . . are not true conditional sentences.
   If the police arrested him, they must suspect him.
   Here *if* means *since*.

SEE ALSO

Unit 10
Progress test
Unit 17
Modals
Unit 18
Functions

Unit 8
Hypothetical and unreal tenses

Explanations

Wishes

1   Wishes about present states
    These wishes use the form of the Past Simple after the verb *wish*. The time referred to is an imaginary or 'unreal' present.
        *I wish I **knew** the answer to this question.*
    (In this case, I do not know the answer.)
        *I wish I **didn't have** so much work to do.*

2   Wishes about past events
    These wishes use the form of the Past Perfect after the verb *wish*. The time referred to is past time.
        *I wish I **had gone** to your party last week.*
    (In this case, I did not go.)

3   Wishes about future events: *could* and *have to*
    Wishes using *could* refer to ability or to future time.
        *I wish I **could drive**.*   (Ability)
        *I wish June **could meet** me next week.*   (Future time)
    Wishes with *have to* can also refer to future time.
        *I wish I **didn't have to get up** early tomorrow.*

4   Wishes about future events: *would* (annoying habits)
    These wishes use *would* after the verb *wish*. They often take the form of a complaint about a bad habit.
        *I wish Peter **wouldn't chew** gum all the time.*
    There is very little difference of use between this kind of wish and the wishes in 1. This kind of wish may also refer to a specific action which you would like to happen.
        *I wish the police **would do** something about these people!*

If only

1   *If only* is used instead of *wish* to make emphatic wishes.
        If only I knew the answer to this question!
        If only I had gone to your party last week!

2   In speech, *only* is often heavily stressed.

It's time

1   *It's time* followed by a person is followed by an unreal past tense.
        *Sorry, but it's time **we went** home.*
    This has a similar meaning to a Conditional 2 sentence:
        If we went home, it would be better.

36

2   *High* can be added for extra emphasis.
     It's **high time you learned** to look after yourself!

3   Both meanings suggest that an event is supposed to happen.
     It's time you started work!   (You are being lazy)
     It's time to start work.   (A statement of fact)

I'd rather   1   *I'd rather* followed by a person is followed by an unreal past tense.
                     *I'd rather **you didn't tell** John about this.*
                     This has a similar meaning to a Conditional 2 sentence:
                     If you didn't tell John about this, it would be better.

                2   *I'd sooner* can be used in the same way and has the same meaning.
                     *Actually, I'd sooner **we left** now.*

Suppose and   Both words can be used to introduce unreal situations.
imagine   *Suppose **you lost** your keys. What would you do?*
                    *Imagine **you were** rich. How would you feel?*

Activities

1

Choose the most
suitable tense.

a) I wish Peter doesn't live/didn't live/wouldn't live so far away from the
   town centre. We'll have to take a taxi.
b) I feel rather cold. I wish I brought/had brought my pullover with me.
c) What a pity. I wish we don't have to/didn't have to/wouldn't have to leave.
   I've just started to enjoy myself.
d) I wish you tell/told/had told me about the test. I haven't done any revision.
e) I wish the people next door hadn't made/wouldn't make/couldn't make so
   much noise. I can't hear myself think!
f) Darling, I love you so much! I wish we are/had been/would be/could be
   together always!
g) I'm sorry I missed your birthday party. I really wish I come/came/had
   come/I would come.
h) I like my new boss but I wish she gave/would give/could give me some
   more responsibility.
i) Having a lovely time in Brighton. I wish you are/were/had been here. Love,
   Sheila.
j) This car was a complete waste of money. I wish I didn't buy it/hadn't
   bought it.

2

Put each verb in
brackets into a
suitable tense.

a) This train journey seems endless! I wish we (go) *had gone* by car.
b) I wish I (have)............ the money to buy some new clothes, but I can't afford
   it at the moment.
c) I wish the government (do) .... something about the pollution in this
   city.

d) I'm getting really soaked! I wish I (not forget) .... my umbrella.

e) I wish you (not do) .... that! It's a really annoying habit.

f) That was a lovely meal, but I wish I (not eat) .... so much.

g) I wish (I study) .... harder for my exams. I don't think I'm going to pass.

h) I wish you (not leave) .... your dirty shoes in your bedroom!

i) I'm afraid I have no idea where Diana has gone. I wish I (know) ....

j) I really enjoyed our trip to the theatre. I wish we (go) .... more often.

3
Choose the most suitable tense.

a) A cheque is all right, but I'd rather you pay/(paid) me cash.

b) Imagine you live/lived in New York. How would you feel?

c) If only I have/had/would have a screwdriver with me.

d) If you want to catch the last train, it's time you leave/left.

e) I'd rather you don't tell/didn't tell anyone about our conversation.

f) I've got a terrible hangover. If only I didn't drink/hadn't drunk that fourth bottle of wine.

g) If you don't mind, I'd sooner you practised/had practised/would practise your violin somewhere else.

h) It's high time you learn/learned to look after yourself.

i) Jean thinks that everyone likes her. If only she knows/knew what people say behind her back!

j) I'd rather we stay/stayed at home this Christmas for a change.

4
Put each verb in brackets into a suitable tense.

a) What can we do to get in touch with Robert? If only we (know) *knew* his phone number.

b) Come on children! It's time you (be) .... in bed.

c) Actually I'd rather you (not smoke) .... in here.

d) Suppose you (see) .... a ghost. What would you do?

e) I'm so annoyed about my car accident. If only I (be) .... more careful!

f) It's high time you (start) .... working more seriously.

g) I'd rather you (not put) .... your coffee on top of my book.

h) I've no idea where we are! If only we (have) .... a map.

i) Your hair is rather long. Don't you think it's time you (have) .... a haircut?

j) Visiting museums is interesting I suppose, but I'd sooner we (go) .... swimming.

5
Rewrite each sentence, beginning as shown, so that the meaning stays the same.

a) It would be nice to be able to fly a plane.
   I wish I *could fly a plane.* ....

b) Please don't eat in the classroom.
   I'd rather ....

c) I think we should leave now.
   I think it's time ....

d) What a pity we ate all the food.
   If only we ....

e) It's a shame we don't have a video.
   I wish ....

f) Don't shout all the time, it's so annoying!
   I wish ....

g) I don't want you to buy me a present.
   I'd sooner ....

h) I don't like being so tall.
   I wish I ....

i) We ought to start work now.
   It's time ....

j) I regret not going to university.
   I wish I ....

KEY POINTS

1 Past tense forms are used in imaginary (hypothetical) situations after *it's time* and *I'd rather* when followed by a person.
   *It's time we **left**.*

2 Wishes about the present use a past tense form, and wishes about the past use a Past Perfect form.

3 Wishes with *would* refer either to annoying habits, or to possible future changes.

4 *Wish* and *hope* cannot be used in the same way. Wishes can be for impossible things, but hopes only for possible things.
   With a person: *I hope you have a good time.*
                  I hope you won't be late.
   Wish cannot be used in this way.

   With the infinitive: *I hope **to see** you next week.*
   Wish with the infinitive means *want* (a polite meaning).
       *I wish **to see** you next week.*
   Note also the formal expressions:
       We wish you a happy New Year/every happiness/luck.

SEE ALSO

Unit 10
Progress test

Unit 9 Passive voice

Explanations

Uses

1 Transitive and intransitive
Only verbs with an object (transitive) can be made passive.
> *They sent the letter.*   *The letter **was sent**.*
> *They arrived late.*   (Cannot be made passive.)
Verbs with both direct and indirect object can be made passive in two ways:
> *They sent me the letter.*   *I **was sent** the letter.*
> *The letter **was sent** to me.*

2 *Like* and *love*
Some verbs which are transitive cannot be made passive in some uses.
> *I like this place.*   (A passive form of this sentence would not be acceptable.)

3 Contexts
By placing the object at the beginning of the sentence, the passive can change the focus of interest in a sentence.
> *United were beaten by Arsenal.* (We are more interested in United)
The passive is used in a variety of contexts.
Impersonal statements.   *Students **are asked** not to smoke.*
When the agent is unknown.   *My bike **has been stolen**!*
(This avoids using *someone* or *they*.)
When the agent is obvious.   *Mr Jones **will be arrested**.*
How something was done.   *The box **was opened with a knife**.*

Reporting verbs

1 The Passive is often used with *say, believe, understand, know* and similar verbs used in reporting to avoid an impersonal *they* or *people*.
> *People say that John Wilson lives in New York.*
> *John Wilson **is said to live** in New York.*

2 The Past tense and continuous verbs can also be reported in this way.
> *John Wilson is said **to be travelling** in Africa.*
> *John Wilson is said **to have arrived** in Australia.*

To have or get something done

1 Causative *have* describes services done for us by someone else.
> *Last year I **had** new tiles **put** on the roof.*

2 The same construction can describe misfortunes which happen to us, caused by an unspecified person.
> *Peter **had** his car **stolen** last week.*
> *And then he **had** his leg **broken** playing football.*

3 Using *get* instead of *have* can suggest managing to do something.
> *It was difficult but we **got** the painting **done** in the end.*

Needs doing	This is an idiomatic way of expressing some passive sentences, usually about things or people which need some kind of service. *The floor is filthy. It **needs scrubbing**.*
Verbs and prepositions	If a verb is followed by a preposition and object, the preposition stays with the verb in a passive sentence. *People shouted at the Prime Minister during his speech.* *The Prime Minister **was shouted at** during his speech.*

Other problems

1   A passive form in one language is not necessarily translated by a passive form in another.
    *I **was born** near London.*

2   *Make* (when meaning *force*) is followed by *to* in the passive.
    *They made David work hard. David **was made to** work hard.*

3   The agent is not always included for reasons given in Uses: **3** above.

Activities

1
Underline the verb forms which are not possible.

a) My car has being stolen.
b) Jack was borned on a Thursday.
c) Then I realised that none of the guests had been sent an invitation.
d) Mary's car is being serviced today.
e) Your order will been sent as soon as possible.
f) The hole in the road was being repaired when I came home.
g) This swimming pool is used by over a thousand people each week.
h) When was this church built?
i) An address is writing on the back of the envelope.
j) Customers are request to ask for a receipt.

2
Choose the most suitable tense.

a) Their new house hasn't been finished/wasn't finished yet.
b) The robbers were arrested/have been arrested as soon as they left the bank.
c) Sue told us her baby is born/had been born two weeks earlier than expected.
d) If there is too much snow, the match has been cancelled/will be cancelled.
e) By the time we got there, the rain had stopped/had been stopped.
f) When were you told/have you been told about the new rules?
g) Most of the passengers were swimming/were swum easily to the shore.
h) The winning horse was ridden/was riding by Pat Murphy.
i) I looked again for the old man, but he was vanished/had vanished.
j) I don't think that you will be asked/are being asked to show your passport.

3
Put each verb in brackets into a suitable passive tense.

a) I'm sorry, madam, but this carpet (already sell) *has already been sold*.
b) The old house on the corner (knock down)..................last year.
c) When exactly (John give) .... his prize?

d) Most people agree that America (not discover) .... by Christopher Columbus.

e) All complaints about products (deal with) .... by our customer services department.

f) Police confirmed that the murder weapon (since discover) .... in a nearby lake.

g) It (announce) .... yesterday that the government has decided not to raise income tax.

h) Good news! I (ask) ....to take over as the new managing director.

i) I don't believe that this play (write) .... by Shakespeare.

j) Ann really likes (invite) .... to dinner parties.

4

Rewrite each sentence, putting the verb underlined in the passive where this is possible.

a) I really <u>like</u> this hotel.
not possible ....

b) People <u>ate</u> most of the food at the party.
....

c) Jane <u>won</u> the poetry competition.
....

d) Peter's new car <u>cost</u> over £20,000.
....

e) Martin always <u>wears</u> casual clothes.
....

f) One of our visitors <u>lost</u> this cigarette lighter.
....

g) They <u>haven't decided</u> the exact time of the match yet.
....

h) Most of the guests <u>had left</u> the hotel by midday.
....

i) Some parents <u>read</u> to their children every night.
....

j) This bike <u>belongs</u> to my sister.
....

5

Rewrite each sentence, beginning as shown, so that the meaning stays the same. Include the agent where this is necessary.

a) Last Thursday we appointed a new marketing manager.
A new *marketing manager was appointed last Thursday.*

b) Smith Ltd are supplying our company with new office furniture.
Our company ....

c) William the Conqueror built the castle in the 11th century.
The castle...

d) No decision has yet been made.
Nothing...

e) People believe that someone murdered Mr Stone.
It is...

f) Your hair is long, you ought to get it cut.
Your hair is long, it ....

g) The police were following the suspects.
The suspects ....

h) No-one has seen Peter since the day of the party.
Peter ....

i) We put up a notice about the trip on the notice board yesterday.
A notice ....

j) People think that an apple a day is good for you.
An apple a day ....

6
Rewrite each sentence so that it contains a form of *have something done*. Do not include the agent.

a) A painter painted our house last month.
We had our house painted last month.

b) The hairdresser is cutting my hair this afternoon.
....

c) Someone has stolen my motorbike.
....

d) The dentist has taken out all of Ricky's teeth.
....

e) I haven't been to the car-wash for a long time.
....

f) The men are coming to put in the new central heating on Saturday.
....

g) Someone broke Harry's nose in a fight.
....

h) Isn't it time someone fixed your television?
....

i) Helen's publishers have just published her book.
....

j) The police towed away Nigel's car.
....

7
Rewrite each sentence so that it contains a passive form, and does **not** contain the words underlined.

a) <u>Apparently</u>, Freddie has a wife in Scotland.
Freddie is said to have a wife in Scotland.

b) <u>Nobody</u> knows <u>anything</u> about Brenda's family.
....

c) <u>People</u> think that <u>someone</u> started the fire deliberately.
....

d) You should <u>ask</u> a doctor to see to that cut.
....

e) <u>People</u> say that Chris was in the army.
....

f) My trousers <u>need</u> to be pressed before I leave.
....

g) <u>No-one</u> has signed this letter.
....

43

h) Mary's hair still <u>needs</u> cutting.

....

i) <u>People</u> believe that Norma is living in Paris.

....

j) <u>The director of the school</u> has decided that smoking is no longer allowed.

....

KEY POINTS

1   Not all verbs can be made passive. You can check in a dictionary whether the verb is transitive or intransitive.

2   The agent is only included if this information is needed.

3   Passive forms are often used to give an impersonal view.

4   It is not usually possible to change from passive to active without changing the meaning. A passive form may be more suitable in some contexts but unsuitable in others.

5   Passive forms tend to be used more often in writing, especially in scientific and technical language.

6   In some languages, verbs can have passive forms but active meanings. This may mislead you into giving the verb a passive form in English.

> **SEE ALSO**
>
> **Unit 10**
> Progress test

Unit 10 Progress test

(Units 6, 7, 8, 9)

1
Choose the most suitable caption for each picture.

a)

1) He's had his hair cut.
2) He's going to have his hair cut.
3) He had his hair cut.

b)

1) I've been robbed!
2) I've been stolen!
3) I've had myself robbed!

c)

1) I'd rather your not smoking.
2) I'd rather you didn't smoke.
3) I'd rather you not smoke.

d)

1) My car has vanished!
2) My car has been vanished!
3) Someone has vanished my car!

2
Rewrite each sentence, beginning as shown, so that the meaning stays the same.

a) What a pity I don't have curly hair.
   I wish my ....
b) I didn't know your number, so I didn't call you.
   If I ....
c) What time do we get to Paris?
   Could you tell me...
d) I regret not visiting the Louvre the last time I was in Paris.
   I wish..

45

e) Put more salt in or you won't be able to taste it.
Unless ....

f) I think we should go now.
It's time ....

g) 'If I were you, Harry, I wouldn't take the job,' said Brenda.
Brenda advised ....

h) Please give me money instead of a present.
I'd rather you ....

i) Lucky you were here, or the house would have caught fire.
If ....

j) Someone broke into Peter's house last week.
Peter had ....

3
Rewrite each sentence so that it contains the word given in capitals, and so that the meaning stays the same. The word cannot be changed in any way.

a) Please don't open the window.   RATHER
....

b) Fiona wanted to know the time.   WHAT
....

c) We won't go out if the weather is bad.   UNLESS
....

d) I would like you to be here!   WISH
....

e) Catherine refused to let me go.   COULDN'T
....

f) If I were you I'd try to get some sleep.   ADVISE
....

g) What a pity we didn't see the match.   WISH
....

h) The old man introduced himself.   TOLD
....

i) David told me the time of the next train.   LEFT
....

j) The police inspector said I had killed Mrs Burns.   ACCUSED
....

4
Rewrite each sentence, beginning as shown, so that the meaning stays the same.

a) 'When are you leaving for Rome, Maria?' asked Diana.
Diana asked Maria ....

b) Someone robbed Malcolm as he was parking his car.
Malcolm ....

c) People think that train-robber Dave Briggs has escaped.
Train-robber Dave Briggs ....

d) Nobody knows anything about Pam's past life.
Nothing ....

e) 'Do you think you could possibly carry this bag, David?'
Jean asked David to ....

f) They've stolen something, but we don't know what.
Something ....

g) This house was specially built for my uncle.
My uncle ....

h) 'Don't forget to buy some bread, Mum,' said Pauline.
Pauline reminded..

i) Does this camera belong to you?
Do ....

j) 'It's not true, I didn't make any long-distance calls,' said Sue.
Sue denied ....

5
Put each verb in brackets into a suitable tense.

Last week I (1) .... (walk) home after playing tennis when it (2) .... (start) raining very heavily. 'Oh no, I (3) .... (get) soaked before I (4) .... (reach) home,' I thought. 'I wish I (5) .... (remember) to bring my raincoat.' But unfortunately I (6) .... (leave) it at home. 'How stupid of me! I (7) .... (always forget) to bring it with me. 'Luckily just then a friend of mine passed in her car and offered me a lift. '(8) .... (you go) home?' she asked, 'or (9) .... (you want) to go for a drink?' 'I think I'd rather you (10) .... (take) me home,' I said, 'If I (11) .... (not change) my clothes, I know I (12) .... (fall) ill, and then I (13) .... (not be able) to play in the tennis tournament next week. And I (14) .... (practise) hard for the last month.' I (15) (wait) for you to change if you (16) .... (like),' she told me. 'I think it's time you (17) .... (relax) for a change. You (18) .... (worry) too much about things lately. And people who (19) .... (worry) too much (20) .... (fall) ill more easily. It's got nothing to do with the rain!'

6
Rewrite each sentence so that it contains the word given in capitals, and so that the meaning stays the same. The word cannot be changed in any way.

a) Is somebody serving you? — BEING
....

b) Can you give me a lift? I'll be late otherwise. — UNLESS
....

c) The painters painted our house last month. — HAD
....

d) It's a pity that Charles is always complaining. — WOULDN'T
....

e) Someone will meet you at the airport. — BE
....

f) Please don't leave your motorbike outside the back door. — DIDN'T
....

g) I'm sorry that I didn't see Ruth before she left. — WISH
....

h) Have you received your salary yet? — PAID
....

i) I think I'll manage to finish the letters by 4.00. — GET
....

j) My parents made me study every night. — WAS
....

47

7

Put each verb in brackets into a suitable tense.

Packet sugar from the supermarket (1) .... (extract) from either sugar cane or sugar beet. These products (2) .... (mix) with hot water, which (3) .... (dissolve) their natural sugar. Sugar (4) .... (also find) in fruit some of which, such as dates and grapes, (5) .... (contain) very high amounts of sugar. To be a little more scientific, sugar should (6) .... (call) sucrose. Sucrose (7) .... (make up) of two substances, glucose, which (8) .... (use) for instant energy, and fructose, which (9) .... (last) longer as a source of energy. The sugar in fruit is mainly fructose. So when we (10) .... (eat) fruit, we (11) .... (also eat) quite large amounts of natural sugar. Some scientists (12) .... (believe) that too much sugar (13) .... (eat) in sweets, cakes and biscuits. It (14) .... (say) to be generally bad for the health, although nothing (15) .... (definitely prove) so far. However, it (16) .... (know) that sugar (17) .... (cause) tooth decay. As one expert put it: 'If other foods (18) .... (damage) our body as much as sugar (19) .... (damage) our teeth, they (20) .... (ban) immediately.'

8

Complete the missing parts of the dialogue.

Harry: Hello Julie, I haven't seen you for ages.

Julie: I've been away on holiday actually.

Harry: Lucky you. Where (1) ....?

Julie: To Brazil. I had a great time.

Harry: Brazil? How fantastic. I (2) ....

Julie: It was my first too. But next month (3) ....

Harry: Again? Doesn't (4) ....?

Julie: Yes, it is rather expensive, but it's a business trip.

Harry: That's very convenient! I wish (5) ....

Julie: It is a good job, it's true.

Harry: I never go on any exciting business trips in my job.

Julie: Well, perhaps it's time you (6) ....

Harry: Maybe you are right. I must admit (7) ....

Julie: They're looking for an accountant in my company, actually. I'm sure you (8) .... if you applied.

Unit 11 Relative clauses

Explanations

Subject or object

1 Subject and Object
Relative clauses give extra information about a noun in the main clause. They can refer to this as subject or object.
That's the woman who bought my car.
*The **woman** (Subject) bought my car.*
That's the car that I used to own.
*I used to own **the car**. (Object)*

2 Combining sentences
Note how sentences are combined.
Subject: *This is Jean. She bought my car.*
Jean is the person who bought my car.
(*She* is not repeated, as *the person* is the subject.)
Object: *That is Jean's car. I used to own it.*
That's the car that I used to own.
(*It* is not repeated, as *the car* is the object.)

Defining or non-defining

1 Defining
Defining clauses give important information which tells us exactly what is being referred to.
That book which you lent me is really good.

2 Non-defining
Non-defining clauses add extra information, separated by commas in writing, and intonation in speaking.
The book, which I hadn't read, was still on the shelf.

Omitting the relative pronoun

1 Object clauses
The relative pronoun can be left out in object clauses in both speaking and writing, provided these are defining.
That's the car I used to own.

2 Non-defining clauses
The relative pronoun cannot be left out in a non-defining clause.

Which, who and *that*

1 *That* instead of *which*
That is often used instead of *which* in speech.
Is this the house that you bought?

2 *That* instead of *who*
That can also refer to people in everyday speech.
Have you met the boy that Sue is going to marry?

3   *Which* in non-defining clauses
    That cannot be used to introduce a non-defining clause.
      The hotel, which was a hundred years old, was very comfortable.

4   Prepositions
    That cannot be used after a preposition.
      This is the car (that/which) I paid £2000 for.   (Everyday Speech)
      *This is the car **for which** I paid £2000.*   (Formal)

Whose and *whom*   1   *Whose* means *of whom*, and usually refers to people.
      This is Jack. His sister is staying with us.
      This is Jack, whose sister is staying with us.

      2   *Whom* is the object form of *who*, and has to be used after prepositions.
      This is the person I sold my car to.   (Everyday Speech)
      *This is the person **to whom** I sold my car.*   (Formal)

Activities

1
Underline any
relative pronouns
that can be left
out in these
sentences.

a) I think that my boss is the person <u>who</u> I admire most.
b) Harry, who was tired, went to bed very early.
c) We're taking the train that leaves at 6.00.
d) Have you seen the book that I left here on the desk?
e) The film which we liked most was the French one.
f) My radio, which isn't very old, has suddenly stopped working.
g) The clothes which you left behind are at the reception desk.
h) The couple who met me at the station took me out to dinner.
i) Last week I ran into an old friend who I hadn't seen for ages.
j) Don't cook the meat that I put in the freezer, it's for the dog.

2
Replace the
relative pronoun
underlined with
that, where
possible.

a) This is the magazine <u>which</u> I told you about.
    This is the magazine that I told you about.
b) John's flat, <u>which</u> is in the same block as mine, is much larger.
    ....
c) The girl <u>whose</u> bag I offered to carry turned out to be an old friend.
    ....
d) The policeman <u>who</u> arrested her had recognised her car.
    ....
e) I work with someone <u>who</u> knows you.
    ....
f) We don't sell goods <u>which</u> have been damaged.
    ....
g) Brighton, <u>which</u> is on the south coast, is a popular holiday resort.
    ....
h) I don't know anyone <u>whose</u> clothes would fit you.
    ....

i) There's a pub near here <u>which</u> serves very good meals.

....

j) People <u>who</u> park outside get given parking tickets.

....

3
Decide whether each sentence contains a defining or a non-defining relative clause.

a) Everyone who got to the sales early found excellent bargains. *Defining*

b) Leave the questions which you can't answer until the end.

....

c) Helen picked up the book, which had a green cover.

....

d) The guests who were late didn't have enough to eat.

....

e) Sue, who was extremely hungry, decided to cook some spaghetti.

....

f) The person I spoke to before said the repair would be free of charge.

....

g) My bedroom, which was rather small, looked out on a noisy street.

....

h) David's sister, who likes cats, offered to take one of the kittens.

....

i) The person who finishes first will be the winner, of course.

....

j) Smith, who had earlier missed a penalty, scored after twenty minutes.

....

4
Choose the most suitable word in each sentence.

a) My friend Jack, <u>that/who/whose</u> parents live in Glasgow, invited me to spend Christmas in Scotland.

b) Here's the computer program <u>that/whom/whose</u> I told you about.

c) I don't believe the story <u>that/who/whom</u> she told us.

d) Peter comes from Witney, <u>that/who/which</u> is near Oxford.

e) This is the gun with <u>that/whom/which</u> the murder was committed.

f) Have you received the parcel <u>whom/whose/which</u> we sent you?

g) Is this the person <u>who/which/whose</u> you asked me about?

h) That's the girl <u>that/who/whose</u> brother sits next to me at school.

i) The meal, <u>that/which/whose</u> wasn't very tasty, was quite expensive.

j) We didn't enjoy the play <u>that/who/whose</u> we went to see.

5
Put a suitable relative pronoun in each space, or leave the space blank wherever possible.

a) The person *whose* fingerprints are on the gun was the person .... killed Dr Martin.

b) My bike, ... I had left at the gate, had disappeared.

c) The shoes ...... I finally bought were the ones ...... I tried on first.

d) The bag in .... the robbers put the money was found outside the bank.

e) The medicine .... the doctor gave me had no effect at all.

f) Peter, ... couldn't see the screen, decided to change his seat.

g) The present .....you gave me was the one ...... I gave you last year!

h) I really liked that tea .... you made me this morning.

i)   What was the name of your friend .... tent we borrowed?

j)   The flight ...... Joe was leaving on was cancelled.

6

Make *one* new sentence from each pair of sentences, beginning as shown, and using the word given in capitals.

a)   Brenda is a friend. I went on holiday with her.   WHO
     Brenda is *the friend who I went on holiday with.*...........

b)   This is Mr Smith. His son Bill plays in our team.   WHOSE
     This is Mr Smith ....

c)   Her book was published last year. It became a best seller. WHICH
     Her book ....

d)   This is the bank. We borrowed the money from it.   WHICH
     This is the bank from ....

e)   I told you about a person. She is at the door.   WHO
     The person ....

f)   Jack's car had broken down. He had to take a bus.   WHOSE
     Jack, ...

7

Make *one* sentence from each group of sentences, beginning as shown.

a)   The hotel was full of guests. The hotel was miles from anywhere.
     The guests had gone there to admire the scenery.
     The hotel, which *was miles from anywhere, was full of guests who had gone*
     there to admire the scenery.

b)   I lent you a book. It was written by a friend of mine. She lives in France.
     The book I ....

c)   A woman's jewels were stolen. A police officer was staying in the same
     hotel. The woman was interviewed by him.
     The woman whose ....

d)   A goal was scored by a teenager. He had come on as substitute.
     This goal won the match.
     The goal which ....

e)   I was sitting next to a boy in the exam. He told me the answers.
     The boy I ....

f)   My wallet contained over £100. It was found in the street by a schoolboy.
     He returned it.
     My wallet, ...

g)   My friend Albert has decided to buy a motor-bike. His car was stolen last
     week.
     My friend Albert, ...

h)   Carol is a vegetarian. I cooked a meal for her last week. She enjoyed it.
     Carol, ...

8

Put one suitable word in each space, or leave the space blank wherever possible.

Murder At The Station by Lorraine Small. Episode 5. *Trouble on the 6.15*.
The story so far: Jane Platt, (1) *who* is travelling to London because of a
mysterious letter, is the only person (2) .... witnesses a murder at Victoria
Station. The detective to (3) .... she gives her statement then disappears. Jane
goes to an office in Soho to answer the letter (4) .... she had received. There
she discovers that her uncle Gordon, (5) .... lives in South America, has sent
her a small box (6) .... she is only to open if in trouble. Jane,

(7) .... parents have never mentioned an Uncle Gordon, is suspicious
of the box, (8) .... she gives to her friend Tony. They go to
Scotland Yard and see Inspector Groves, (9) .... has not heard of
the Victoria Station murder, (10) .... was not reported to the
police. Jane gives Inspector Groves the murdered man's ticket (11) ....
she found beside his body. Then Jane and Tony decide to go to Redhill,
(12) .... was the town (13) ....the murdered man had come from.
On the train they meet a man, (14) .... face is somehow familiar to
Jane, (15) .... says he knows her Uncle Gordon. Now read on.

9

These sentences
are all
grammatically
possible, but not
appropriate in
speech. Rewrite
each sentence so
that it ends with
the preposition
underlined.

a) Margaret is the girl <u>with</u> whom I went on holiday.
    Margaret is the girl I went on holiday with...................

b) The golf club is the only club <u>of</u> which I am a member.
    ....

c) That's the girl <u>about</u> whom we were talking.
    ....

d) It was a wonderful present, <u>for</u> which I was extremely grateful.
    ....

e) This is the school <u>to</u> which I used to go.
    ....

f) Is this the case <u>in</u> which we should put the wineglasses?
    ....

g) Can you move the chair <u>on</u> which you are sitting?
    ....

h) That's the shop <u>from</u> which I got my shoes.
    ....

i) Is that the person <u>next to</u> whom you usually sit?
    ....

j) This is Bill, <u>about</u> whom you have heard so much.
    ....

10

Make *one*
sentence from
each group of
sentences,
beginning as
shown.

a) I got on a train. I wanted to go to a station. The train didn't stop there.
    The train *I got on didn't stop at the station I wanted to go to.*........

b) I read a book. You recommended a book to me. This was the book.
    The book I ....

c) The ship hit an iceberg and sank. Warning messages had been sent to it. The
    ship ignored these.
    The ship, ...

d) The postman realised I was on holiday. You had sent me a parcel.
    The postman left it next door.
    The postman, ...

e) I used to own a dog. People came to the door. The dog never barked at them.
    The dog I ....

    f) I bought my car from a woman. She lives in a house. You can see the house over there.

       The woman I ....

    g) We went to a beach on the first day of our holiday. It was covered in seaweed. This smelled a lot.

       The beach we... .

    h) My neighbours have three small children. The children make a lot of noise. My neighbours never apologise.

       My neighbours, ...

    i) I bought a new typewriter. It cost me a lot of money.

       The new ....

    j) I lost my wallet last week. It was found by a workman. He was digging a hole in the street outside our house.

       The wallet ....

KEY POINTS

1   Long and complex sentences with relative clauses are not usual in speech. It is more usual in speech to join shorter clauses with conjunctions.

2   Relatives are usually left out in object clauses in speech.
      This is the book I told you about.

3   In speech it is common to end relative clauses with a preposition.
      That's the girl I live next door to.

SEE ALSO

Unit 15
Progress test

Unit 12 Prepositions

Explanations

Movement

Prepositions used with verbs of motion (*come, go, run* etc.) show the direction of the movement.

> *Jack ran **out of** the room. Sue moved **towards** the door.*

Other examples: *to, into, across, around, along, up, down, past.*

Position and place

Prepositions also show position.

> *Ted was sitting **next to** Janet. The bank is **opposite** the cinema.*

Other examples: *before, below, beside, in front of, near, on top of, under.*

Prepositions also show place.

> *I live **in** France. Sue lives **on** an island. John is **at** school.*

See below for problems of usage.

Other uses

1   Prepositions are also used in time expressions (See Unit 14.)

2   Prepositions also cover a wide range of meanings.
> *This book is **about** Napoleon. I can't drink tea **with/without** sugar.*

Problems of use

1   *At* and *to*
    At is not used with verbs of motion.
> *We went **to** the cinema. We arrived **at** the cinema.*

2   *Near* and *next to*
    Next to means the same as *beside*. *Near* means *not far away from*, which can be a matter of opinion.
> *Peter always sits **next to** Mary.*
> *I live **near** the sea, it's only ten miles away.*

3   *Above* and *over*
    Both mean 'higher than', but *over* suggests closeness or touching. There may be little difference in some contexts.
> *There was something written **above/over** the door.*
> *There was a plane high **above** them. Put this blanket **over** you.*

4   *In* and *at*: Places
    In refers to towns, countries and the 'inside' of places.
> *She lives **in** Paris. They arrived **in** Peru. He's **in** the kitchen.*
    At refers to points with a particular purpose rather than 'inside'.
> *She lives **at** home.*
> *They met **at** the cinema. (Place) They met **in** the cinema. (Inside)*

5   Prepositions at the end of a sentence
    Study these common examples:
> *Who are you waiting **for**?*   (Question)

55

> *You are very difficult to live **with**!* (Infinitive)
> *That's the company that I work **for**.* (Relative clause)

Prepositions which are also adverbs	Some prepositions can be used as adverbs without an object. *Ted was walking **along**, whistling.* Examples: *around, along, behind, opposite.*
Prepositions with more than one word	Examples: *according to, on behalf of, by means of.* Other examples are included in the activities.
Prepositional phrases	There are many fixed phrases containing prepositions. Examples: *by mistake, on purpose, out of order.* Other examples are included in the activities.

Activities

1

Choose the most suitable preposition.

a) I got at/to the station just in time to see Jack getting from/off the train.
b) The pub is among/between the chemist's and the butcher's and across/opposite the library.
c) Sue lives at/in Wales, which is a country at/in the west of Britain.
d) I was brought up in/on an island near/next to the coast of Scotland.
e) Travelling by/in your own car is better than going by/on foot.
f) Jack was leaning by/against the wall with his hands in/into his pockets.
g) Ann had a hat on/over her head and a veil above/over her face.
h) We arrived at/in England at/in Gatwick Airport.
i) I left my bags at/from the station at/in a left luggage locker.
j) Peter came running into/to the room and threw his books at/onto the floor.

2

Complete each sentence with one word or phrase from the list. Use each word or phrase once only.

according to	because of	in common with	instead of
apart from	by means of	in favour of	on behalf of
as for	in case of	in front of	regardless of

a) I think I'd rather have coffee *instead of* tea.
b) ....danger, Paul ran back into the burning house.
c) .... fire, smash the glass and push the button.
d) Personally, I am .... banning cigarette smoking completely!
e) I would like to thank you, ... everyone who was rescued.
f) .... you, no-one else knows that I have escaped.
g) .... Steve, he believes that we should stay where we are.
h) Jim managed to climb into the house .... a ladder he found.
i) .... the rain the match was postponed.
j) .... the timetable, the next train isn't for two hours.
k) Julie has nothing .... Bill. They are quite different.
l) A large black car suddenly drew up .... the house.

56

3

Decide whether
it is possible to
leave out the
words
underlined,
so that the
remaining words
make sense.

a) Most people were wandering around <u>the streets</u>, taking photos. *possible*
b) I gave my bike to <u>my little sister</u>, when it became too small for me. ....
c) The people who live in the house opposite <u>our house</u> are Italian. ....
d) I left my coat on <u>the bed in here</u> but it seems to have disappeared. ....
e) I'll wait for you outside <u>the cinema</u>, on the pavement. ....
f) Peter took a deep breath, and then went under <u>the water</u> again. ....
g) Don't worry, the hotel's quite near <u>to where we are now</u>. ....
h) The children can sit behind you in the back seats. ....
i) We travelled all day and arrived at <u>our destination</u> in the evening. ....
j) I drove past <u>the house at the end of the street</u> but I didn't notice anything wrong. ....

4

Complete each
sentence by using
a word from the
list. Use each
word once only.

at	by	for	in	on
off	out of	to	under	without

a) Police officers don't have to wear uniform when they are *off* duty.
b) I feel very tired. .... times I consider giving up work.
c) The children were all upset, and some were .... tears.
d) This factory needs modernising. Everything here is .... date.
e) Don't worry, everything is .... control.
f) Sorry, I seem to have taken the wrong umbrella .... mistake.
g) Please hurry. We need these documents .... delay.
h) That wasn't an accident! You did it .... purpose.
i) We thought the two films were very similar .... a great extent.
j) We decided to take a holiday in Wales .... a change.

5

Choose the most
suitable phrase.

a) I can't disturb John now. He's <u>at bed</u>/<u>in bed</u>.
b) Tony always arrives exactly <u>in time/on time</u> for his lesson.
c) Two pounds for each ticket, that makes £12 <u>in all/with all</u>.
d) I can't pick that last apple. It's <u>out of hand/out of reach</u>.
e) Joe and I met on the plane completely <u>by chance/by surprise</u>.
f) The children spend most of their time <u>out of doors/out of place</u>.
g) I'm sorry but Jane isn't here <u>at present/at a time</u>.
h) How can Sam love Lucy? They have nothing <u>in common/in general</u>.
i) They should be here soon. They are <u>in the way/on the way</u>.
j) Terry isn't here. He's away <u>in business/on business</u>.

6

Complete each
sentence with a
suitable word
from the list. Use
each word once
only.

breath	fail	impression	secret	strike
costs	hurry	return	stock	words

a) This is important. You must catch the two men at all *costs*.
b) He says he's ill. Or in other ...., he doesn't want to come.
c) I was under the .... that you enjoyed working here.
d) Sorry, I can't stop. I'm in a ....
e) Please hand your work in on Tuesday, without ....

f) We can't go by train. The train-drivers are on ....

g) Martin is supposed to have given up smoking, but he smokes in ....

h) I'm afraid we don't have your size, we are out of ....

i) If I give you the information, what will you give me in ...... ?

j) I ran for the bus, and now I'm out of ....

7
Complete each
sentence with a
suitable word
from the list. Use
each word once
only.

average	force	particular	profit	sight
detail	himself	practice	public	whole

a) Harry managed to sell his house at a *profit*.

b) What was he doing here all by ....?

c) Larry is so famous that he doesn't appear in .... very often.

d) That was a terrible shot! I'm rather out of ....

e) How many cars do you sell, on ...., every week?

f) The police are coming! Stay out of .... until they leave.

g) I might be able to help you. What do you want to know in ....?

h) I suppose I enjoyed my holiday on the ....

i) Can you tell me about the plans in ....?

j) The gun had to be taken away from David by ....

8
Complete each
sentence with
one of the
phrases from the
list. Use each
phrase once only.

by heart	in difficulties	in turn	on holiday	out of work
by sight	in pain	in two	on sale	without a doubt

a) When I sat on the pencil, it broke *in two*.

b) Most of the people in the office are .... at the moment.

c) This is .... the best washing machine on the market.

d) Graham has been .... ever since he came to London.

e) I know her ...., but I don't know her name.

f) The lifeguard dived in to save a swimmer ....

g) John learned his first speech ....

h) Why don't you share the bike? You can ride it ....

i) You could tell he was .... by the way he kept groaning.

j) Cigarettes and ice-cream are .... in the foyer.

9
Complete each
sentence with
one of the
phrases from the
list. Use each
phrase once only.

at any rate	by surprise	in person	out of danger	out of tune
by all means	from now on	in private	out of order	under orders

a) Jim's excuse was that he was acting *under orders* from his boss.

b) Things have changed. ...., no-one will leave before 5.00.

c) Thank goodness. All the passengers are now ....

d) The president would like to meet you and thank you ....

e) Your violin sounds awful! I think it's ....

f) It's a warm country. We won't need our pullovers, ...

g) Excuse me, but I'd like to have a word with you ....

h) You can't use the phone. It's ....

i) The news about Shirley took me completely ....

j) Yes, of course. Take the chairs, ...

KEY POINTS

1 There is a group of prepositions used with verbs of motion.
   across, along, around, down, into, out of, past, to, towards, up

2 Some prepositions can be used without an object as adverbs.
   Jean lives opposite.

3 A sentence can end with a preposition.
   Paul didn't have a chair to sit on.

SEE ALSO

Unit 14
Time expressions
Unit 15
Progress test

Unit 13
Expressing purpose, result, and contrast

Explanations

Purpose

1 *So (that)*
   So that is usually followed by *can, could, will* or *would*.
   The police locked the door **so (that)** *no-one could get in.*

2 Infinitive of purpose
   The person in the main clause, and the person referred to by the infinitive, must be the same.
   Jack went to England **to study** *engineering.*

3 *In order to, so as to*
   These are more formal ways of expressing purpose.
   Scientists used only local materials, **in order to** *save money.*
   There are also negative forms: *in order not to, so as not to*.
   The soldiers moved at night, **so as not to** *alarm the villagers.*

4 *For*
   This describes how something is used.
   This button is **for starting** *the engine. This is* **for the lights.**

Result

1 *So/such + (adjective) + (that)*
   Jim was **so tall (that)** *he hit his head on the ceiling.*
   Helen is **such a busy person (that)** *she never feels bored.*
   Such is used with adjective and noun. Note also this formal use:
   Helen is **so busy a person (that)** *she never feels bored.*

2 *So much/many/few/little + (noun) + (that)*
   There were **so many passengers (that)** *we couldn't find a seat.*

3 *Too + (adjective) + to*
   The table was far **too heavy to** *lift.*
   This can be explained as:
   The table was far too heavy (for me) to lift.

4 *Not (adjective) enough*
   The table was **not light enough** *to lift.*

Contrast

1 *Although, though, even though, while, whereas*
   Although often becomes *though* in speech. *Though* can come at the end of a sentence, *although* cannot.

60

> *Although I asked her, she didn't come.*
> In speech this might be:
> *I asked her, (but) she didn't come, **though**.*
> Or ***Though** I asked her, she didn't come.*
> *Even though is a more emphatic form of although.*
> ***Even though** I asked her, she didn't come.* (which was surprising)
> *While* and *whereas* are more common in writing and formal speech. They contrast opposite ideas.
> ***While** United were fast and accurate, City were slow and careless.*

2 *However*
   However is more common in formal speech or writing. It can go at the beginning or end of the sentence.
> *It's cheap. **However**, I don't like it./I don't like it, **however**.*

3 *Nevertheless*
   This is a very formal way of expressing *however*.
> *Smith says he is poor. **Nevertheless**, he has bought a new car.*

4 *Despite* and *in spite of*
   These are followed by nouns (or gerunds), and not by clauses.
> ***Despite** losing, we celebrated.*   ***In spite of** the rain, we went out.*

Activities

1
Choose the most suitable word or phrase underlined in each sentence.

a) Janet went out so that she bought/~~to buy~~ Harry a present.
b) This food is much too hot <u>to eat/to be eaten</u>.
c) <u>However/Though</u> it was late, I decided to phone Brian.
d) <u>Although/Despite</u> the car was cheap, it was in good condition.
e) Let's check once more, <u>for being/so as to be</u> sure.
f) We could go to the club. Is it worth it, <u>even though/though</u>?
g) It was <u>so windy/such a windy</u> that half the trees were blown down.
h) The batteries were <u>not enough small/too small</u> to fit the radio.
i) Despite <u>of the weather/the weather</u>, we went sailing.
j) Bill had <u>so much/so that</u> fun that he stayed another week.

2
Rewrite each sentence so that it contains the word given in capitals, and so that the meaning stays the same. The word cannot be changed in any way.

a) Sue went shopping so she could buy herself a new television. TO BUY
   Sue *went shopping to buy herself a new television.*................
b) You use this to open wine bottles. FOR
   This..
c) I put the food in the fridge because I wanted it to get cold. SO
   I..
d) Harry left early because he didn't want to miss the bus. SO AS
   Harry..
e) I saved up some money to buy a motorbike. COULD
   I..

   f) Jane gave up smoking because she wanted to save money. ORDER
    Jane ....

   g) I came here so that I could see you. TO
    I ....

   h) Use this money to buy the tickets. FOR
    This ....

   i) I picked up the vase carefully, so as not to break it. WOULDN'T
    I ....

   j) We put up a fence to prevent the rabbit escaping. COULDN'T
    We ....

3
Rewrite each sentence, beginning as shown, so that the meaning stays the same.

 a) Sam lost his job because he was lazy.
  Sam was so *lazy that he lost his job.*

 b) I couldn't buy the house because it was expensive.
  The house was too ....

 c) The book was so interesting that I couldn't put it down.
  It was ....

 d) There was too much noise, so we couldn't hear the speech.
  There was so ....

 e) The house was too small to live in comfortably.
  The house wasn't ....

 f) William never makes mistakes because he is a careful reader.
  William is so ....

 g) We can't eat now because there isn't enough time.
  There is too ....

 h) I can't come to your party because I'm too busy.
  I'm too ....

 i) The class was cancelled because there weren't enough students.
  There were so ....

 j) It's such a lovely day today that I feel like taking a walk.
  It's so ....

4
Complete each sentence with *one* suitable word.

 a) I couldn't run fast *enough* to catch the shop-lifter.
 b) There were .... good roads that we could drive at high speed.
 c) It was .... dark that I couldn't see a thing.
 d) The trousers were .... long enough to fit Jean.
 e) We had .... a good time that we decided to go there again.
 f) It was .... late that we couldn't get a bus home.
 g) I took a taxi as it was .... far to walk.
 h) There were .... many dishes that I couldn't make up my mind.
 i) The ladder wasn't tall .... to reach the window.
 j) There are .... lovely fish that you don't feel like eating meat.

5
Rewrite each
sentence,
beginning as
shown, so that
the meaning stays
the same. Two
sentences should
be rewritten as
one.

a) Despite the cold weather, we all went for a walk.
   Although *it was cold, we all went for a walk.*
b) John has done well in French, but not so well in Maths.
   While ....
c) I tried to persuade her. I didn't succeed, however.
   Although ....
d) It was raining, but I went swimming anyway.
   In spite of ....
e) I like fish, but I don't like catching them myself.
   Although ....
f) Ann felt ill, but insisted on going to work.
   Despite ....
g) I rang the doorbell. Nobody answered, though.
   Although ....
h) In spite of his early lead, Hudson lost the race.
   Although ....
i) I'm not going to pay, although I know that I should.
   While ....
j) We expected Larry to accept the job, but he didn't.
   Even though Larry ....

6
Explain what
each object is for,
using one of the
verbs in the list.
Use each verb
once only.

boil	cut	lock	paint	stick
clean	keep	open	put	wash

a) brush
   It's for painting things.
b) scissors
   ....
c) glue
   ....
d) kettle
   ....
e) fridge
   ....
f) sink
   ....
g) dustbin
   ....
h) toothbrush
   ....
i) corkscrew
   ....
j) key
   ....

KEY POINTS

1 The infinitive of purpose must refer to the same person as the main clause.
   I went to the shops. I wanted to buy some fruit.
   I went to the shops to buy some fruit.

2 *In order to* is more common in formal speech and writing.

3 Contrasts with *while*, *whereas* and *nevertheless* are used in formal speech and writing.

SEE ALSO

Unit 15
Progress test
Unit 32
Text organisers

Unit 14
Time expressions

Explanations

This page focuses on problem areas. Other time expressions are included in the activities.

Present time

Nowadays and *these days*
Both contrast the present with the past.
What are you up to these days? Nowadays more women have careers.

Future time

1 *In*
In can refer to future time.
*I'll be there **in a moment**. I'll be back **in a week**.*

2 Calendar references
If today is Monday:
*Wednesday is **the day after tomorrow** or **the day after next**.*
*Wednesday is also **in two days' time**.*
*Next Monday is **this time next week**.*

3 *Eventually* and *in the end*
Both refer to what will happen after a long period.
*I think that our side will win **in the end/eventually**.*

4 *Presently*
This means 'in a few moments'.
*Just a minute. I'll be with you **presently**.*

Past time

1 *Once*
This can mean 'in the past'. It can also mean 'from the time when'.
*I lived here **once**. (in the past) **Once** she gets here, we can leave. (when)*

2 Periods of the day
Last is not normally used with *morning, afternoon* or *evening*.
*They left **yesterday morning** and came back **last night**.*

3 Calendar references
If today is Monday:
*Saturday was **the day before yesterday** or **the day before last**.*

4 *In those days* and *at that time*
Both refer to a past time already referred to.
*I met Janet in 1980. **In those days** I was a keen dancer.*

5 *After, later* and *afterwards*
   After needs an object.
   > *I'll see you **after the holidays**.*
   Afterwards means 'after this or that'.
   > *The film is starting now. I'll tell you afterwards.*
   Later means 'at a later time'.
   > *I'm busy now. I'll call you back later.*

Other problems

1 *In:*   *In January, In 1968, In the morning/afternoon/evening*
   On: *On Thursday*
   At: *At six o'clock, At night, At midday/midnight*

2 *For:*   *I lived there for ten years.* (for a period of time)
   Since: *I have lived here since 1986.* (since a point in time)
   Ago: *Edward died two years ago.* (how long ago in the past)

3 *By:*   *I'll be home by 6.00.* (not later than 6.00)

4 *At last:*   *At last you have arrived!* (expressing relief)
   In the end: *We waited for ages, and in the end/finally we left.*
   At the end: *I left at the end of the film.*

5 *On time:*   *Bill is never late, he's always on time.* (not late)
   In time: *Luckily the police arrived in time to help.* (early enough)

Activities

1

Choose the most suitable word or phrase underlined.

a) I haven't seen Jim before/(since) we worked together in London.
b) I'll finish the letter now and you can post it after/later.
c) What were you doing last evening/yesterday evening when I called?
d) Did you live here in/since 1987?
e) Diana hasn't finished her course already/yet.
f) What do you usually do in the afternoon/this afternoon?
g) Have you seen Jean and Chris nowadays/recently?
h) Helen arrived here at Thursday night/on Thursday night.
i) It's really ages since/when I saw you last.
j) Ann is going to be famous once/one day.

2

Put *one* word in each space.

a) Graham came to see us over a week ago, the Friday before *last*.
b) Is it very warm here .... the winter?
c) No thanks, I've had some tea ....
d) Don't worry, it won't hurt and I'll .... be finished.
e) I liked the book. I didn't know what was going to happen ....
f) I think that people had much more spare time in the ....
g) This is very urgent. Please send it at ....
h) Harry isn't here. He left about five minutes ....
i) The film doesn't start until 7.30. We're half an hour ....
j) Would you mind waiting for .... a moment, please?

3

Complete each sentence with a word or phrase from the list. Use each word or phrase once only.

afterwards	eventually	in the end	nowadays	soon
early	immediately	lately	once	yet

a) There is far too much traffic on the roads *nowadays*.
b) Never mind. I'm sure we'll find what we are looking for ....
c) I haven't seen you for ages. What have you been doing ....?
d) Jack hasn't left. He hasn't finished his work ....
e) Take some notes in the meeting, and we'll discuss them ....
f) If you don't mind waiting, Brenda will be back ....
g) I considered taking a new job, but decided against it ....
h) Norman and I worked for the same company ....
i) You didn't fool me! I recognised you ....
j) You can get more work done if you get up ....

4

Put *one* word in each space.

a) You will receive your salary *at/before* the end of the month.
b) I feel really tired. I think I'll go to bed early ....
c) The weather has been terrible so far .... month.
d) I'll see what David says, and .... I'll come back and tell you.
e) I'm a bit busy ...., but I can talk to you later.
f) If you haven't finished ...., don't worry.
g) Are you doing anything .... Friday evening?
h) Where's Brian? He should be here .... now.
i) We cannot accept applications sent .... the closing date.
j) .... upon a time, there were three bears.

5

Complete each sentence with the most suitable word or phrase.

a) Jean bought an expensive watch, but regretted it *B* .
   A) at the end   B) later   C) then   D) after
b) Lunch will be ready .... the time you get back.
   A) at   B) during   C) in   D) by
c) I haven't been feeling well ...., doctor.
   A) recently   B) afterwards   C) suddenly   D) at last

d) Long ...., the valley you can see was actually a lake.
   A) past   B) ago   C) since   D) before

e) We ran into the station and caught the train .... in time.
   A) right   B) just   C) early   D) already

f) I haven't had dinner with them for ....
   A) long   B) it's ages   C) years   D) the summer

g) I've cleaned all the parts, but the motor .... doesn't work.
   A) at last   B) now   C) always   D) still

h) .... you get used to the job, it won't seem so bad.
   A) since   B) while   C) once   D) as

i) I haven't .... decided where to go on holiday.
   A) yet   B) already   C) still   D) just

j) The first time I noticed something wrong was .... I got home.
   A) since   B) when   C) for   D) until

6

Complete each
sentence with
one of the words
or phrases from
the list.
Use each phrase
once only.

all night long	from time to time	one at a time
all the time	in a few moments	over and over again
all the year round	in the nick of time	the other day
for hours on end	once and for all	this time next week

a) Don't carry the boxes all together. We'll move them *one at a time* .
b) I've told you ...., don't leave your bag here!
c) It's time you stopped biting your nails ....
d) Sheila grabbed Bill .... before he could fall into the water.
e) Hurry up! The bomb will go off ....
f) We shouldn't have trusted Michael. He was lying ....
g) Gerry sits staring at the television ....
h) .... I'll be lying on the beach, not working in the office!
i) The swimming pool on the common is open ....
j) I met your friend Janet in the pub ....
k) Dave isn't a keen fisherman, but he goes fishing ....
l) The party finished at dawn after we had danced ....

7

Replace the word
or phrase in
italics with one of
the words or
phrases given, so
that the meaning
stays the same.

a) The weather was bad at first, but it cleared up *in the end. B*
   A) at last   B) eventually   C) lately

b) Jane was leading the race, but *all at once* she fell over. ....
   A) suddenly   B) one by one   C) after that

c) Have you been swimming *recently*? ....
   A) lately   B) already   C) yet

d) I enjoy going skiing *every now and again*. ....
   A) frequently   B) immediately   C) occasionally

e) I saw Terry in the street *the other day*. ....
   A) recently   B) yesterday   C) last night

f) I think we've solved this problem *once and for all*. ....
   A) in the end   B) for ever   C) temporarily

g) Kath told Martin that she was leaving *for good.* ....
   A) for ever   B) for a while   C) early

h) We arrived *in good time* for the train. ....
   A) on time   B) at the right moment   C) with time to spare

i) I believe we met *on a previous occasion.* ....
   A) once before   B) the last time   C) completely by chance

j) The political situation seems to be changing *minute by minute.* ....
   A) from time to time   B) time after time   C) very rapidly

KEY POINTS

1 Some time expressions are connected with particular tenses.
   (See Units 1 to 5.)

   *Claire **arrived** an hour ago.*
   *I've **been living** here **since 1977.***
   *John **worked** there **for two years.***
   *Sally **has been studying** French **for six months.***
   *I **haven't been** to the theatre **for ages.***
   *Terry **will have left** by then.*

2 *For* can sometimes be left out.
   *Sandra **waited three hours** in freezing weather.*

SEE ALSO
Units 1 to 5 (Tenses) **Unit 15** Progress test

Unit 15 Progress test

(Units 11, 12, 13, 14)

1

Put *one* suitable word in each space.

When John saw the large crowd (1) .... had gathered (2) .... the street, he wasn't sure (3) .... first what had happened. There were (4) .... many people blocking the way into the hotel, that he had to push his way (5) .... them to get (6) .... the door. At the door he found two policemen (7) .... were trying, (8) .... great difficulty, to hold the crowd back. 'What (9) .... earth is going on?' he asked them. 'Where have you been (10)........?' they replied, '(11) .... the moon?' Then John noticed that some of the crowd were holding placards (12) .... read: 'We love you Sally.' (13)......... course, that was it. Sally Good was a footballer, the first woman to play for England. (14) .... John wasn't really interested (15) .... sport he decided to join the crowd and wait (16) .... she appeared. About ten minutes (17) ...., a smiling woman appeared and waved to the crowd. John was taken completely (18) .... surprise when she took his arm and said, 'Remember me? I'm the girl (19) .... used to sit (20) .... to you at school.'

2

Rewrite each sentence, beginning as shown, so that the meaning stays the same.

a) Jack's parents were here last week and gave us a present.
Jack's parents, ...

b) Although Sue felt tired, she stayed up late talking to Jill.
Despite ....

c) I'm afraid that Tony has gone to bed.
I'm afraid that Tony is ....

d) It was a hot day so we had lunch outside in the garden.
It was such ....

e) A week ago today we were in Venice.
This ....

f) You'll be paid on Friday.
You won't ....

g) It's ages since I last saw a good cowboy film.
I haven't ....

h) Jean hasn't finished her work yet.
Jean is ....

i) I told Paula about this hole in the ceiling.
This is ....

j) I've been working for this company for ten years.
I started ....

3

Put *one* suitable word in each space.

a) ...... the time you've done the shopping, I'll be ready.

b) I'm going home now, but I'll phone you ....

c) Harry has been working very hard ....

d) I'll write to you ...... the end of the week.

70

e) I waited for you .... 6.00, but then I left.
f) Peter sometimes goes walking .... hours.
g) I won't be long. I'll be ready .... a moment.
h) .... upon a time, there was a beautiful princess.
i) Guess who I saw the .... day? My old English teacher!
j) I'm not a regular swimmer but I go .... and again.

4

Put *one* suitable word in each space.

a) This is the book I told you ....
b) There's someone outside .... car has broken down.
c) Sue won the gold medal .... having a bad leg.
d) I suppose I agree with you .... a great extent.
e) The police, from .... I learned nothing, are being secretive.
f) Excuse me, but your bicycle is .... my way.
g) She bought me a present, ... I told her not to bother.
h) Tony knows most of Shakespeare .... heart.
i) The letter was addressed: 'To .... it may concern.'
j) There are no letters today. The post office is .... strike.

5

Rewrite each sentence so that it contains the word given in capitals, and so that the meaning stays the same.

a) I bought my car from that man. WHOM
....
b) That boy's sister sits behind me at school. WHOSE
....
c) Bill's typewriter had broken and he had to use a pencil. WHOSE
....
d) The girls were hungry and decided to have a meal. WHO
....
e) I live in Croydon, it's near London. WHICH
....
f) Did you borrow this book? THAT
....
g) This is Brenda, she lives upstairs. WHO
....
h) You gave me a very useful present. WHICH
....
i) The car was in good condition and wasn't expensive. WHICH
....
j) Someone found the money and was given a reward. WHO
....

6

Put *one* preposition in each space.

a) The plane landed .... Athens Airport, which is .... the sea.
b) He was cold .... bed so his mother put a blanket .... him.
c) I'm not ..... favour of nuclear power ...... case of accidents.
d) When Peter sheltered ...... a tree an apple fell ...... his head.
e) Sorry, I'm ...... a hurry. Come with me, we can talk ..... the way.
f) Quite .... chance I noticed that the house was ...... sale.
g) Can we discuss this ...... private? Alone, ... other words.

71

h) I went to Naples .... business, but not .... myself.

i) If you're .... difficulties with money, I'll help you .....all means.

j) Hearing she was ...... of work took me .... surprise.

7

Rewrite each pair of sentences as one sentence, which must contain the word or words given in capitals.

a) I liked the shoes. However, I didn't buy them.   ALTHOUGH
....

b) Joe had financial problems. He bought a new motorbike.   DESPITE
....

c) I couldn't drink the soup. It was too hot.   TO
....

d) Susan was tired. She decided to go to bed.   THAT
....

e) We spoke in whispers. We didn't want to wake the baby.   SO AS
....

f) I kept looking for my missing watch. I knew it was no use.   EVEN
....

g) There were a lot of people in front of me. I couldn't see.   SO MANY
....

h) The weather is fine. My flowers haven't come out, though.   SPITE
....

i) It was a cold night. We stayed indoors.   SUCH
....

j) The swimming pool wasn't deep. You couldn't dive into it.   ENOUGH
....

8

Put *one* suitable word in each space.

Stephen arrived in Bluffville (1) .... the early evening, and walked (2) .... the bus station through the town centre, looking for somewhere to stay. There was a huge old-fashioned hotel, (3) .... it was obviously closed. The windows (4) .... street level were covered (5) .... sheets of corrugated iron. (6) .... there must have been many travellers passing (7) .... Bluffville, but now the motorway (8) .... the south passed the town several miles (9) .... , and so very few people stopped. Stephen found a telephone (10) .... a run-down bar, and called the nearest motel, (11) .... turned out to be seven miles away on the motorway. He asked the barman, (12) .... was reading a comic book, how (13) .... a taxi would cost to take him (14) .... the motel. The man stared hard at Stephen (15) .... he said, 'No taxis here, haven't been any (16) .... more than ten years.' Stephen suddenly realised that he should have listened (17) .... the bus driver's warning about the town. In (18) .... of his curiosity to find the person (19) .... had sent him the mysterious letter, Stephen felt (20) .... miserable that if there had been a bus back to New York, he would have taken it.

Unit 16
Modal auxiliaries, present and future: ability, certainty, obligation

Explanations

Ability

Can and *be able to*
Be able is used in situations where *can* does not have the necessary grammatical form.
> *I'd like **to be able to swim**. **Not being able to swim** is annoying.*

Certainty and uncertainty

1 *Must* and *can't*
These are used to make deductions, when we are more or less certain about something, especially with the verb *to be*.
> *You **must be** tired after your journey.* (I suppose you are)
> *That **can't be** Sue. She's in Brazil.* (I'm sure it's impossible)

2 *May*, *might* and *could*
These all express uncertainty or possibility. They are usually stressed in speech. *Might* is less likely than *may*. *Could* is not used with *not* in this meaning.
> *It **may not rain**. I **might go out**, I don't know. I **could get wet!***

3 *Be bound to*
This refers to the future, whereas *must* refers to the present.
> *You're **bound to see** Paula if you go there.* (I'm sure you will)
> *You **must see** Paula if you go there.* (An obligation)

Obligation

1 *Must* and *have to*
Have to describes obligations made by someone else, while *must* is used to describe a personal obligation. There may be no difference.
> *You **must start** working harder!* (I say so)
> *You **have to turn** left here.* (It's the law)
> *Sorry, I **must leave/have to leave** now.* (No difference)

2 *Mustn't* and *don't have to*
Mustn't describes something which is not allowed. *Don't have to* describes something which is not necessary.
> *You **mustn't leave** any bags here.* (It's against the rules)
> *You **don't have to apply** yet.* (It's not necessary)

3   *Should* and *ought to*
    These have the same meaning. They describe 'what is a good idea' and can
    be used to give advice, or polite instructions.
    > *I think you **should see** a doctor. You **ought not to continue**.*
    > *You **should send in** your application by July 18th.*

4   *Should* as expectation
    Should can also describe actions we expect to happen.
    > *Brenda **should be** home by now.*   (She is expected to be.)

5   *Had better*
    This refers to present or future time, and gives advice about how to stop
    something going wrong.
    > *I think **you'd better leave** now.*   (Before it is too late)
    > *You'd better not drive.*   (It might be dangerous)

6   *Is/Are to*
    This is used in formal instructions. *Not* is stressed.
    > *No-one **is to leave** the room. You **are not to leave** the room.*

Activities

1

Choose the most suitable word or phrase underlined.

a) There's someone at the door. It <u>can be/must be</u> the postman.
b) Don't worry, you <u>don't have to/mustn't</u> pay now.
c) I think you <u>had better/would better</u> take a pullover with you.
d) Jones <u>could be/must be</u> president if Smith has to resign.
e) Sorry, I can't stay any longer. I <u>have to go/might go</u>.
f) It was 5.00 an hour ago. Your watch <u>can't be/mustn't be</u> right.
g) It's a school rule, all the pupils <u>have to wear/must wear</u> a uniform.
h) I suppose that our team <u>must win/should win</u>, but I'm not sure.
i) Let's tell Diana. She <u>could not/might not</u> know.
j) In my opinion, the government <u>might do/should do</u> something about this.

2

Rewrite each sentence so that it contains the word given in capitals, and so that the meaning stays the same. The word cannot be changed in any way.

a) I think you should give up smoking immediately.   HAD
    I think you had better give up smoking immediately.

74

b) I expect we will get there by 5.00, if there isn't too much
   traffic.   SHOULD
   ....

c) Is it necessary for me to bring my passport?   HAVE
   ....

d) I am sure that the cat is in the house somewhere.   MUST
   ....

e) An aerial is not required with this radio.   HAVE
   ....

f) It is very inconvenient if you can't drive.   ABLE
   ....

g) I am sure that John is not the thief.   CAN'T
   ....

h) I am certain that Norman will be late.   BOUND
   ....

i) All students should report to the main hall at 9.00.   ARE
   ....

j) I thought that you would know better!   OUGHT
   ....

3

Choose the most
suitable word or
phrase
underlined.

a) We can't be lost. It isn't allowed/I don't believe it.
b) Jane is bound to be late. She always is/She must be.
c) Late-comers are to report to the main office. It's a good idea/It's
   the rule.
d) You don't have to stay unless it's necessary/if you don't want to.
e) Astronauts must feel afraid sometimes. They're supposed to/It's only
   natural.
f) You can't come in here. It isn't allowed/I don't believe it.
g) All motorcyclists have to wear crash helmets. It's a good idea/It's
   the rule.
h) I ought not to tell Jack. It's not a good idea/It's the rule.
i) We should be there soon. I expect so/It's absolutely certain.
j) You'd better take an umbrella. It's raining/It might rain.

4

Complete each
sentence so that it
contains *might,
might not, must,
mustn't, can* or
can't. More than
one answer may
be possible.

a) Don't stand up in the boat! You *might* fall in the river!
b) Sue says she's stuck in the traffic and she .... be late.
c) You really .... start spending more time on your work.
d) Tell Peter he .... stay the night here if he wants to.
e) That's a really stupid idea! You .... be serious, surely!
f) You .... realise it, but this is very important to me.
g) Don't be silly. You .... expect me to believe you!
h) We're not sure but we .... go to Prague for Christmas this year.
i) Me learn to fly! You .... be joking!
j) Bill cooked the lunch, so you .... expect anything special!

5

Rewrite each sentence so that it contains *can, could, must, have to* or *should* (including negative forms).

a) I'm sure that Helen feels really lonely.
   Helen must feel really lonely...

b) You're not allowed to park here.
   ....

c) It would be a good idea if Harry took a holiday.
   ....

d) I'm sure that Brenda isn't over thirty.
   ....

e) Do I need a different driving licence for a motorbike?
   ....

f) What would you advise me to do?
   ....

g) Mary knows how to stand on her head.
   ....

h) You needn't come with me if you don't want to.
   ....

i) It's possible for anyone to break into this house!
   ....

j) The dentist will see you soon. I don't think he'll be long.
   ....

6

Choose the most suitable caption for each picture.

a)

1) He should be exhausted!
2) He must be exhausted!

b)

1) We mustn't pay to go in.
2) We don't have to pay to go in.

c)

1) I'm afraid we have to operate.
2) I'm afraid we should operate.

d)

1) Mind out, you could drop it!
2) Mind out! You can drop it!

76

e)

f)

1) Thanks, but I'd better not!
2) I don't have to, thanks.

1) We must be here for hours!
2) We're bound to be here for hours!

KEY POINTS

1 Most modal auxiliaries have more than one meaning. You may have to think carefully about the context, or tone of voice, to understand the meaning.

2 The negative forms *mustn't* and *don't have to* have different meanings.
    *You **mustn't** go.* (It is against the rules)
    *You **don't have to** go.* (It isn't necessary)

3 *Should* is a weaker obligation than *must* and *have to*, but is used as a polite way of expressing an obligation, in formal speech or in writing.
    *Passengers for Gatwick Airport **should change** at Reading.*

SEE ALSO
Unit 17 Modal auxiliaries: past **Unit 20** Progress test

Unit 17 Modal auxiliaries, past: ability, certainty, obligation

Explanations

Past ability

1 *Could*
Could describes past ability.
> *When I was young, I **could run** very fast.*

2 *Could* and *was able to*
Was able to describes the actual performance of an action.
> *Mary **was able to help** us.*   (She actually helped us)
> *Mary **could help** us.*   (But perhaps she didn't)

Certainty and uncertainty

1 *Must have* and *can't have*
These are used to make deductions about past actions. The *have* form does not change.
> *I **must have left** my wallet in the car.*   (I am sure I did)
> *Jim **can't have noticed** you.*   (I am sure he didn't)

2 *May have, might have* and *could have*
These express possibility or uncertainty about past actions. The *have* form does not change.
> *Jean **might have missed** the train.*   (Perhaps she did)
> *He **may not have received** the letter.*   (Perhaps he didn't)
> *You **could have been killed**!*   (It was a possibility)

3 *Was/Were to have*
This describes something which was supposed to happen, but didn't.
It is formal in use. The *have* form does not change.
> *He **was to have left** yesterday.*   (He was supposed to leave, but he didn't)

Obligation

1 *Had to*
Had to is generally used as the past form of *must*.
> *Sorry I'm late, I **had to take** the children to school.*
The question form is *Did you have to?*
> ***Did you have to work** late yesterday?*

2 *Should have* and *ought to have*
These express the speaker's feeling that a mistake was made. The *have* form does not change.

78

*You **should have posted** the letter yesterday.*   (You made a mistake)
*You **shouldn't have told** me the answer.*   (You were wrong)

3 *Needn't have* and *didn't need to*
Needn't have describes an action which happened, but was unnecessary.
The *have* form does not change.

*I **needn't have bought** more sugar.*   (I did, but we had enough)
*I **didn't need to buy** more sugar.*   (I didn't, because we had enough)

Pronunciation and writing

Have is unstressed or weakly stressed in the past infinitive forms on this and the previous page, and cannot be abbreviated in writing.

Indirect speech

Must, shall and *should*
Must is reported as *had to* or *must*. *Shall* with future reference is reported as *would*. Other uses of *shall* are reported as *should*.

'*You must go.*'   *He told me I **had to go**. He told me **I must go**.*
'*I shall be there.*'   *He told us he **would be** there.*
'*Shall I help?*'   *He asked if he **should help**.*

Activities

1
Choose the most suitable response to each comment or question.

a) A: What did I do wrong?
   B: (1) You shouldn't have connected these two wires.
      2) You didn't have to connect these two wires.
b) A: Why is the dog barking?
   B: 1) It should have heard something.
      2) It must have heard something.
c) A: Why are you home so early?
   B: 1) I needn't have worked this afternoon.
      2) I didn't have to work this afternoon.
d) A: Why did you worry about me? I didn't take any risks.
   B: 1) You must have been injured.
      2) You could have been injured.

e) A: You forgot my birthday again!
   B: 1) Sorry, I should have looked in my diary.
      2) Sorry, I had to look in my diary.
f) A: We had a terrible crossing on the boat in a storm.
   B: 1) That didn't have to be very pleasant!
      2) That can't have been very pleasant!
g) A: Where were you yesterday? You didn't turn up!
   B: 1) I had to go to London.
      2) I must have gone to London.
h) A: What do you think about the election?
   B: 1) The Freedom Party had to win.
      2) The Freedom Party should have won.
i) A: There's a lot of food left over from the party, isn't there?
   B: 1) Yes, you couldn't have made so many sandwiches.
      2) Yes, you needn't have made so many sandwiches.
j) A: What do you think has happened to Tony?
   B: 1) I don't know, he should have got lost.
      2) I don't know, he might have got lost.

2
Rewrite each sentence so that it contains the word given in capitals, and so that the meaning stays the same. The word cannot be changed in any way.

a) It wasn't necessary for me to go out after all. HAVE
   I needn't have gone out after all.
b) There was a plan for Jack to become manager, but he left. WAS
   ....
c) It was a mistake for you to buy that car. SHOULD
   ....
d) I don't think that Sally enjoyed her holiday. CAN'T
   ....
e) It's possible that Bill saw me. MAY
   ....
f) I'm sure that Karen was a beautiful baby. MUST
   ....
g) Perhaps Alan didn't mean what he said. MIGHT
   ....
h) It's possible that I left my wallet at home. COULD
   ....
i) I think you were wrong to sell your bike. SHOULDN'T
   ....
j) The only thing I could do was run away! HAD
   ....

3
Choose the most suitable phrase underlined.

a) We should have turned left. We've missed the turning/We followed the instructions.
b) We didn't have to wear uniform at school. But I never did/That's why I liked it.
c) The butler must have stolen the jewels. He was ordered to/There is no other explanation.

80

d) You could have phoned from the station. <u>I'm sure you did/Why didn't you?</u>

e) You needn't have bought any dog food. <u>There isn't any/There is plenty</u>.

f) Ann might not have understood the message. <u>I suppose it's possible/ She wasn't supposed to.</u>

g) You can't have spent all the money already! <u>You weren't able to/ I'm sure you haven't.</u>

h) I shouldn't have used this kind of paint. <u>It's the right kind/It's the wrong kind.</u>

4

Rewrite each sentence so that it contains: *can't, might, must, should* or *needn't.*

a) I'm sure that David took your books by mistake.
   David must have taken your books by mistake.

b) It was a mistake to park outside the police station.
   ....

c) It was unnecessary for you to clean the floor.
   ....

d) I'm sure that Liz hasn't met Harry before.
   ....

e) Ann possibly hasn't left yet.
   ....

f) I'm sure they haven't eaten all the food. It's not possible!
   ....

g) Jack is supposed to have arrived half an hour ago.
   ....

h) Perhaps Pam and Tim decided not to come.
   ....

i) I think it was the cat that took the fish from the table!
   ....

j) It was a waste of time worrying, after all!
   ....

5

Choose the most suitable caption for each picture.

a)

1) You must have read the notice.
2) You should have read the notice.

b)

1) We can't have worn our raincoats.
2) We needn't have worn our raincoats.

c)

1) He must have hit him in the right spot!
2) He should have hit him in the right spot!

d)

1) You must have caused an accident!
2) You might have caused an accident!

e)

1) Sorry, I had to go to the dentist's.
2) Sorry, I should have gone to the dentist's.

f)

1) You shouldn't have stroked the lion!
2) You didn't have to stroke the lion!

KEY POINTS   1   There is a difference between *didn't have to* and *needn't have done.*
         I didn't have to pay. (I didn't pay)
         I needn't have paid. (I paid but it was unnecessary)

    2   *Have* is unstressed in past infinitive forms.
         You shouldn't have done it.

    3   *Have* in past infinitive forms cannot be abbreviated in writing.

SEE ALSO
Unit 20 Progress test

Unit 18
Language functions 1

Explanations

1   What are functions?
    Language is usually divided up into the parts of its grammatical system. It is
    also possible to describe language according to what it is used for.

    If I were you, I'd leave now.   Conditional 2 (Grammatical)
    If I were you, I'd leave now.   Giving Advice (Function)

2   How do we choose what to say?
    What we say can be influenced by the situation we are in, the person we
    are talking to, and by what we are talking about.
    Asking Permission - from a friend:
        Is it all right if I use the phone?
    Asking Permission - from the same person, but a more serious topic:
        Do you think I could possibly phone Australia?
    Asking Permission - from a stranger:
        Do you mind if I open the window?
    What we say can depend on whether we want to be polite or not, or on how
    we feel. Although there are no exact rules about what we should say in any
    situation, there are *polite* ways of speaking which are generally used when
    we talk to strangers, to people who have higher status, and when we are
    talking about sensitive topics.

3   This unit practises the following functions. (Others are practised in Unit
    19.) The responses made are also included.
    There may be other ways of expressing these functions which are not
    included in the activities.

    Asking for and giving advice
    Agreeing and disagreeing
    Apologising
    Complaining
    Ending a conversation
    Asking for and giving directions
    Greeting
    Asking how someone is
    Asking for information
    Introducing yourself and other people
    Inviting
    Accepting and declining invitations
    Offering something
    Offering to do something

Activities

1

Match each sentence a) to j) with a functional label from 1) to 10).

a) That's very kind of you, I'd love to. ....*4*....
b) Well, it's been nice talking to you, but I'm afraid I have to go. ....
c) Could you tell me how to get to the post office? ....
d) You might have told me you were having a party! ....
e) Shall I carry this bag for you? ....
f) What do you think I should do? ....
g) Actually, I don't think that's right. ....
h) Would you like to come round for a drink later? ....
i) Jack, this is my brother, Mark. ....
j) Could you tell me what time the bank opens? ....

1) Complaining.
2) Inviting.
3) Asking for information.
4) Accepting an invitation.
5) Asking for advice.
6) Asking for directions.
7) Introducing other people.
8) Offering to do something.
9) Disagreeing.
10) Ending a conversation.

2

Match each sentence a) to j) with a functional label from 1) to 10).

a) Would you like some more tea? ....*6*....
b) I think you'd better phone the police. ....
c) I'd love to come, but I'm already going out that evening. ....
d) Good morning, I'm Brenda Watson, the Marketing Manager. ....
e) I'm sorry I'm late, it won't happen again. ....
f) Would you like me to do the washing up? ....
g) Excuse me, but is the bus station anywhere near here? ....
h) Hi, Sally, how are you? ....
i) I think that's the point exactly. ....
j) It's at the end of this street, opposite the church. ....

1) Declining an invitation.
2) Introducing yourself.
3) Greeting a friend.
4) Offering to do something.
5) Asking for directions.

6) Offering something.
7) Agreeing.
8) Apologising.
9) Giving directions.
10) Giving advice.

3

Choose the most
suitable response.

a) Do you feel like going to the cinema this evening?
  1) That would be great.
  2) Thank you very much for your kind invitation.
b) I'm awfully sorry about your carpet, you must let me pay to have it cleaned.
  1) Don't worry, it's all right I think.
  2) Forget it.
c) More coffee anybody?
  1) Would it be all right if I had some more?
  2) I'd love some.
d) Excuse me, but is it far from here to Anglesham?
  1) Just keep going along this road.
  2) Yes, it is.
e) I wish you wouldn't smoke in here!
  1) I don't agree, I'm afraid.
  2) Sorry, shall I open the window?
f) Well, it was nice talking to you, but I have to dash.
  1) Yes, I enjoyed talking to you too.
  2) OK, see you.
g) Could you tell me whether this train stops at Hatfield?
  1) I believe I could.
  2) I believe it does.
h) Shall I collect the tickets for you?
  1) That would be a real help.
  2) Yes, I think you shall.
i) What would you do in my situation?
  1) I think you should ask for a loan from the bank.
  2) I thought you would ask for a loan from the bank.
j) How do you do, I'm Bill Thompson.
  1) Very well thank you.
  2) How do you do.

4

Rewrite each
sentence,
beginning as
shown, so that
the meaning stays
the same.

a) Can I offer you a lift home?
  Would *you like a lift home?* ....
b) What time does the next train leave?
  Could ....
c) I think you should sell your car.
  If I ....
d) Shall I mow the lawn?
  Would ....

e) Am I going the right way for Downwood?
Is ....

f) Do you have to make so much noise!
I wish ....

g) What's your advice?
What do ....

h) Let's go for a pizza.
How ....

i) I'm sorry, I'm to blame.
I'm sorry, it ....

j) I advise you not to go.
I don't ....

KEY POINTS

1 What we say depends on the situation, our relationship with the person we are talking to, and what we are talking about.

2 Giving an appropriate response depends on judging how someone is talking to us. People may not respond fully if we do not use polite forms.

SEE ALSO

Unit 20
Progress test

Unit 19
Language functions 2

Explanations

This unit practises the following functions. (Others are practised in Unit 18).
The responses are also included.
There may be other ways of expressing these functions which are not included
in the activities.

Things to say on special occasions or at special moments
Asking for and giving an opinion
Pausing to think
Asking for permission
Giving and refusing permission
Expressing preferences
Promising
Reassuring
Recommending
Refusing to do something
Making and responding to a request
Suggesting
Thanking

Activities

1

Match each
sentence a) to j)
with a functional
label from 1) to
10).

a) Wait a minute, let me see. ....5....
b) What did you think of the film, then? ....
c) I'll definitely bring your camera back tomorrow. ....
d) Would it be all right if I left a bit early today? ....
e) Sorry, no, I won't do it. ....
f) Could you possibly turn on the air conditioning? ....
g) I think I'd rather have fish, actually. ....
h) Why don't we have a party next weekend? ....
i) That's very kind of you, I appreciate it. ....
j) Don't worry, everything will turn out all right. ....

1) Promising.
2) Refusing.
3) Suggesting.
4) Expressing a preference.
5) Pausing to think.
6) Making a request.

7) Thanking.
8) Asking for an opinion.
9) Reassuring.
10) Asking permission.

2

Match each sentence a) to j) with an explanation from 1) to 10).

a) Congratulations! ....*4*....
b) Look out! ....
c) Oh bother! ....
d) Whoops! ....
e) Well done! ....
f) Excuse me! ....
g) Pardon? ....
h) Bless you! ....
i) Cheers! ....
j) You poor thing! ....

1) Praising someone's performance.
2) Expressing annoyance.
3) Wishing someone good health when drinking.
4) Expressing happiness at someone's success.
5) Attracting attention or asking someone to move out of your way.
6) Expressing sympathy.
7) Expressing that something has/has nearly gone wrong.
8) Giving a warning.
9) Showing that you have misheard or misunderstood.
10) Said when another person sneezes.

3

Choose the most suitable response.

a) What do you think of my new car?
   1) It's all right I suppose.
   2) I think a lot.
b) Do you promise to pay me back at the end of the month?
   1) I'll pay.
   2) I promise.
c) Can I use your phone?
   1) You may not.
   2) Of course.
d) Where do you suggest I stay?
   1) I recommend the Hilton.
   2) Let's stay at the Hilton.

e) Do you want beer or wine?
   1) I'd prefer beer, please.
   2) I'd rather beer, please.

f) I can't stop worrying about my exam tomorrow.
   1) That's all right, never mind.
   2) I'm sure you'll do well.

g) Janet, make us some tea, will you?
   1) No I won't, I'm afraid.
   2) I can't, I'm afraid.

h) Would you mind moving your bag from the seat?
   1) Oh, sorry.
   2) No, I wouldn't.

i) How kind, you really shouldn't have bothered.
   1) It was nothing, really.
   2) Don't worry, I didn't bother.

j) Is it all right if I use your bike?
   1) Please accept it with my best wishes.
   2) Sure, go ahead.

4

Rewrite each sentence, beginning as shown, so that the meaning stays the same.

a) What's your opinion of Roger's new book?
What do *you think of Roger's new book?*

b) Thank you very much for your help.
I am ....

c) May I leave my bag here?
Is it ....

d) Let's go to the beach tomorrow.
Why ....

e) I like going sailing more than going swimming.
I'd ....

f) Could you open the window?
Do you ....

g) Is it all right if you take care of the children?
Do you ....

h) I recommend going by train.
I think you ....

i) Excuse me, I can't get past you!
Excuse me, you are ....

j) 'You've passed your driving test, Ron! Well done!' said Carol.
Carol congratulated ....

KEY POINTS

1 What we say depends on the situation, our relationship with the person we are talking to, and what we are talking about.

2 Giving an appropriate response depends on judging how someone is talking to us. People may not respond fully if we do not use polite forms.

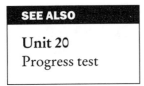

SEE ALSO

Unit 20
Progress test

Unit 20 Progress test

(Units 16, 17, 18, 19)

1

Put *one* suitable word in each space.

Have you ever tried asking people for directions? I (1) .... to go to London on business recently, and I soon realised that I (2) .... have bought a street map. Whenever I followed the (3) .... of passers-by, I got lost. 'You can't (4) .... it, ' they would say. 'Carry straight (5) .... , it's opposite the bank.' After walking for half an hour, I would realise that I (6) .... have gone wrong somewhere. '(7) .... you tell me where the bank (8) .... , please?' I would ask someone. I (9) .... to have known that this was a mistake. 'Which bank do you mean? I think you (10) .... go back to the station...' I now see that I (11) .... have taken a taxi. After all, London taxi drivers (12) .... to pass a test on their knowledge (13) .... its streets. But of course, whenever I thought of this, I (14) .... find a taxi. They had (15) .... simply vanished. In the end I found a solution. I (16) .... up to the first tourists I saw and asked if I (17) .... look at their tourist map. They (18) .... out to be from Scotland, and they (19) .... me very detailed directions. The only problem was that I wasn't (20) .... to understand exactly what they said.

2

Rewrite each sentence, beginning as shown, so that the meaning stays the same.

a) How much does this umbrella cost?
    Could you tell me..

b) Please don't leave all the lights on, it's very annoying.
    I wish you..

c) Can I invite you to the pub for a drink?
    Would..

d) I'm sorry I broke your typewriter.
    I do apologise..

e) I would advise you to take travellers cheques.
    I think..

f) Can you give me directions for the station?
    Could you tell me how..

g) Peter, let me introduce you to Diana.
    Peter, this..

h) Can I offer you some tea?
    Would..

i) If I were you, I wouldn't buy a dog.
    I don't think..

j) Why don't I do the shopping for you?
    Shall..

3

Rewrite each sentence so that it contains the word given in capitals, and so that the meaning stays the same. The word cannot be changed in any way.

a) I'm sure that Jack hasn't left home yet.   CAN'T

....

b) I suppose that is Trafalgar Square.   MUST

....

c) Perhaps Jean's plane was delayed.   MIGHT

....

d) You were wrong to get up so late!   HAVE

....

e) It was unnecessary for you to come early today.   HAVE

....

f) It's time for me to go.   HAVE

....

g) Tony is supposed to be here by now.   HAVE

....

h) I suppose that I left my keys at home.   MUST

....

i) It was a mistake not to bring your umbrella.   HAVE

....

j) Perhaps this is the answer.   COULD

....

4

Use these words and phrases to make complete sentences. The sentences are all part of a letter. Make changes and add any necessary words as in the example.

I/not hear/you/ages.
I haven't heard from you for ages....

Dear Brenda,

a) Thanks/reply/quickly/my last letter.

....

b) I/be/glad/you/able/put up/when/I/come/London.

....

c) You/must/surprised/receive/letter/me.

....

d) I/really/look forward/see/again/after so long

....

e) I/meet/someone/recently/tell/you/take/job.

....

f) You/work/Brooks Bank/long?

....

g) I/think/should/go/university/instead.

....

h) Why/you decide/take/job?

....

i) This time next year I/finish/university.

....

j) Soon/I/have to/start/write/thesis!

....

Best Wishes,
Sheila

93

5

Choose the most suitable expression for each situation.

a) You want to invite someone you have just met to go to the theatre with you.
   1) May I go to the theatre?
   2) Would you like to come to the theatre?
   3) Do you think you should go to the theatre?

b) You are recommending a new restaurant to a friend.
   1) You really must try the new Italian restaurant in Green Street.
   2) You had better try the new Italian restaurant in Green Street.
   3) You would try the new Italian restaurant in Green Street.

c) Your boss suggests that you work overtime on Saturday, but you don't want to.
   1) You must be joking!
   2) It's nice of you to ask, but I refuse.
   3) Sorry, but I have something already arranged.

d) You want to ask the waiter to bring you another drink.
   1) I'd like another beer, please.
   2) Excuse me, but do you think I could take another beer?
   3) You can bring me a beer if you like.

e) You want someone to move out of your way.
   1) Look out!
   2) Excuse me!
   3) Pardon!

f) You greet a friend you haven't seen for a few weeks.
   1) Hello Pauline, how do you do?
   2) Hello Pauline, what's going on?
   3) Hello Pauline, how are you?

g) You are sitting on a bus and want the person in front of you to shut the window.
   1) Could you shut the window, please?
   2) May I shut the window, please?
   3) Do you want to shut the window, please?

h) You want to know how to get to the station, and you ask a stranger.
   1) Tell me, where is the station?
   2) Do you mind telling me where the station is?
   3) Could you tell me the way to the station, please?

i) You want some advice from a friend.
   1) What do you think I should do?
   2) Tell me what I must do.
   3) What could you do if you were me?

j) You ask your boss for permission to leave work early.
   1) Do you mind leaving early?
   2) Is it all right if I go now?
   3) I'm off now, bye!

Unit 21 Countables and uncountables. Problems with plurals

Explanations

1 Concept

Countable:	Singular	Plural
	a shoe	*(some) shoes*
Uncountable:	Singular	No Plural
	advice, some advice	

2 Change of Meaning
Some words have different meanings in countable and uncountable forms.

Countable	*an iron*	(domestic appliance)
	a wood	(small area of trees)
	a paper	(newspaper)
Uncountable:	*some iron*	(substance)
	some wood	(a substance)
	some paper	(a substance)

There is a similar contrast between:
Material: *coffee*   Item: *a coffee* (= a cup of coffee)

3 Uncountable and Types
Some uncountables can be used as countables to describe a 'type' in a technical sense:
Uncountable: *fruit* Technical type: *a fruit*

4 Food and Portions

Uncountable:	*chicken* (the meat) *some chicken* (a portion)
Countable:	*a chicken* (the animal)

5 Others with change of meaning

business (in general)	*a business* (a company)
gossip (talking)	*a gossip* (a person)
hair (all together)	*a hair* (a single example)
help (in general)	*a help* (a helpful person/thing)
toast (grilled bread)	*a toast* (formal words before drinking)
work (in general)	*a work* (a work of art/engineering)

6   Typical uncountables
    Substances: *plastic, iron, paper*
    Liquids and gases: *water, oxygen*
    Abstract ideas: *happiness, anger*
    Mass/Collection: *furniture, luggage*
    Other words are practised in the activities.

7   Plural form, singular verb
    Some words, ending in 's', have no singular form, but are used with a
    singular verb.
        The news is very bad today.   Billiards is an interesting game.

8   No singular form
    Some words have no singular form.
        My trousers are too tight.   The stairs are very steep.
    Other common examples are:
        clothes, goods, jeans, means, outskirts, surroundings, thanks

9   Groups of people
    Some words which refer to groups of people can have a singular verb if
    we think of the group as a unit, and a plural if we think of the group
    as a number of people.
        I think the government is/are wrong.
    Other common examples:
        army, audience, class, company, crew, crowd, family, staff, team
    Some group words only take a plural verb: *cattle, police, people*

Activities

1
Choose the most
suitable word
underlined.

a) Different countries have different (weather)/weathers.
b) All areas of the skin are in fact covered in tiny hair/hairs.
c) We've looked at the menu and we'd all like chicken/chickens.
d) Jack is a millionaire and owns a lot of business/businesses.
e) Have you a copy of the complete work/works of Dante?
f) None of the passengers had insured their baggage/baggages.
g) During the afternoon there will be thunder and lightning/thunders
    and lightnings in many areas.
h) Students must pass their paper/papers to the front.
i) I'd like coffee, toast/toasts, and marmalade please.
j) I'm afraid we can't find cheap accommodation/accommodations for all of
    you.

2
Complete each
sentence with *a/an,*
some or by leaving
the space blank.

a) When the play ended, there was .... lengthy applause.
b) I can't come out tonight. I have .... homework to do.
c) What shall we do tomorrow evening? How about .... dancing?
d) There is .... very beautiful countryside near here.
e) Sue received .... excellent education.

96

f) My trousers need pressing. Can you lend me .... iron?

g) My friends bought me .... coffee maker for my birthday.

h) David has just bought .... new furniture.

i) Let me give you .... advice.

j) The inside is strengthened with .... steel frame.

3

Choose the most suitable word underlined.

a) I would love to go on a long (journey)/travel by train.

b) What's the latest news? Can I look at your paper/journal?

c) I want to know about trains to Leeds. Can you give me a/an information/timetable?

d) Here's your ticket. Do you have any luggage/suitcase?

e) Don't forget to buy a sliced bread/loaf.

f) Why don't we leave the car in this car-park/parking?

g) I can't come to work today. I have a bad cold/flu.

h) Excuse me sir, but do you have a licence/permission for this gun?

i) Brighton has quite a good beach/seaside.

j) I'm going out tonight with a few of my company/friends.

4

Put *one* suitable word in each space.

a) I'm looking for *accommodation*. Do you know anywhere I can stay?

b) Take my ...., don't go out alone after dark.

c) The government plans to improve .... by paying teachers more.

d) Can you lend me some ......? I want to type a letter.

e) I need some .... about language schools. Can you help me?

f) Richard is unemployed, and he is looking for a ....

g) Could I have some ....? Those apples and oranges look nice.

h) I used to have long ......, but I had it cut.

i) I can't do this on my own. Could you give me some ......?

j) If you can't undo the knot, cut the string with some ....

5

Complete each sentence with the most suitable word or phrase.

a) I like your new trousers. Where did you buy *B*?

　　A) it　B) them　C) them both　D) them all

b) There is always a very large .... at the church I go to.

　　A) congregation　B) audience　C) spectator　D) company

c) The local .... has agreed to repair the road outside our house.
   A) government   B) people   C) council   D) jury
d) When the police arrived, we were pleased to see ....
   A) him   B) him or her   C) it   D) them
e) The car turned over, but luckily it didn't suffer serious ....
   A) damage   B) injury   C) damages   D) injuries
f) Sorry, I'm late, but I had a lot of .... to do.
   A) job   B) work   C) task   D) labour
g) Julie bought herself a complete new .... for winter.
   A) outfit   B) cloth   C) clothing   D) wear
h) I feel like going out tonight. Let's go to a/an ....
   A) dancing   B) night   C) club   D) entertainment
i) Thanks for a great weekend! We really had a/an ....
   A) fun   B) enjoyment   C) hospitality   D) good time
j) In order to prove Smith is guilty, we must find some ....
   A) information   B) evidence   C) knowledge   D) means

6

Choose the most appropriate meaning for each sentence.

a) You mustn't lose heart.
   1) Don't have an operation.   ②) Don't give up hope.
b) Where's my glass?
   1) I need a drink.   2) I can't see.
c) Jack has a new post.
   1) The postman has delivered a letter.   2) He has a different job.
d) All goods must be paid for in advance.
   1) Nothing enjoyable in life is free.   2) You have to pay for these things first.
e) I've joined a new company.
   1) I have a new job.   2) I have some new friends.
f) This hotel has class.
   1) You can study hotel management here.   2) It is a good quality hotel.
g) I don't have the means to help you.
   1) I'm not able to help.   2) I can't understand what help you need.
h) I'd like some china.
   1) I want to go abroad.   2) I need some cups and plates.
i) Do you have any cash?
   1) Do you only have a cheque?   2) Isn't there a place to pay in this shop?
j) They have a business in Leeds.
   1) They have to go there to do a job.   2) They own a company there.

7
Rewrite each sentence so that it contains the word given in capitals, and so that the meaning stays the same. The word cannot be changed in any way.

a) This island has a large population.   PEOPLE
There are a lot of people on this island.

b) Do you own these things?   BELONGINGS
....

c) The weather was good on our holiday.   HAD
....

d) There were a lot of cars on the road to Manchester.   TRAFFIC
....

e) Gerry is a very strong person.   STRENGTH
....

f) There are pieces of paper all over the floor!   LITTER
....

g) There is definitely improvement in your work.   PROGRESS
....

h) Can I park my car here?   PARKING
....

i) These machines are very expensive.   MACHINERY
....

j) Could you get some bread from the supermarket?   LOAF
....

8
Complete each sentence with one suitable word from the list. Use each word once only.

blade	flight	item	piece	sheet
clap	head	lump	set	slice

a) Let me give you a *piece* of advice.
b) There is an interesting .... of news in the paper.
c) A .... of stairs takes you to the top of the house.
d) Could I have another .... of paper, please?
e) Put another .... of coal on the fire.
f) Helen has a lovely .... of hair.
g) Do you want another .... of toast?
h) We bought Mike and Lynn a .... of cutlery for a wedding present.
i) There was not a single .... of grass left standing.
j) The lightning was followed by a .... of thunder.

9
Complete each sentence with *one* suitable word from the list. Use each word once only.

accommodation	bread	cookery	lightning	spelling
advice	cash	information	luggage	parking

a) I can't cut this loaf. Do you have a proper *bread* knife?
b) I'm afraid that 'neice' is a .... mistake.
c) There's usually a/an .... space opposite the church.
d) We need a/an .... box to keep the money in.
e) The tourist board have built a/an .... centre near the castle.
f) We decided to put a/an .... conductor on the roof.
g) Marjorie used to write a/an .... column in a magazine.
h) These suitcases are heavy. We must find a/an .... trolley.

       i)   I must rush. I'm going to a/an .... lesson.

       j)   Julie found her flat through a/an .... agency.

KEY POINTS

1   Check in a dictionary to be sure whether a word is countable or uncountable.

2   The meaning of a word may change depending on whether it is used in a countable or uncountable sense.

3   Note that not all words ending in 's' have singular form, and that some words ending in 's' take a singular verb.

SEE ALSO

Unit 22
Articles
Unit 25
Progress test

Unit 22 Articles

Explanations

Zero article

1 With uncountables and abstract or general ideas, and plurals (not previously mentioned and not post-modified: see below).
   I like orange juice. Give peace a chance. I hate wasps.

2 With most proper names (see below).
   We live in France. I'll see you in January.

3 With names of meals when they refer to routine times.
   It's time for lunch. What's for dinner?

4 With unique jobs or roles (definite article is also possible).
   Jim is (the) chairman of the company.

5 With prepositions of place, when the place plays a special role.
   Sally is in prison.(She's a prisoner)
   Sally is in the prison.(A visitor to the building)
   Similar are: *church, hospital, school, university*

6 With general means of transport.
   We went there by car.
   But if *in* or *on* is used: *We went there in a car/on a bus.*

Definite article

1 Previously mentioned items.
   *There is a bedroom and a living room. **The bedroom** is large.*

2 Single items, whose reference is clear.
   *Can you pass **the marmalade**? What happened after **the war**?*

3 Unique objects.
   ***The moon** is full tonight.*

4 Items which are followed by a descriptive phrase, which makes them definite (post-modification).
   *This is **the man I told you about.***
   This category includes names:
   London Bridge but ***the** Tower of London* (post-modified)

5 National groups.
   ***The British** drink far too much tea.*

6 Classes of people.
   ***The rich** get richer and **the poor** get poorer.*

7 Individual items which represent a class.
   ***The lion** is fast disappearing.*

101

8 Names of musical instruments and ability to play.
   *I can't play **the piano** but I can play **the guitar**.*

9 Some geographical names.
   Plural countries, or where the name contains a noun:
   ***The** Netherlands. **The** People's Republic of China.*
   Names of rivers and oceans, and regions:
   ***The** Thames flows into **the** North Sea. **The** Arctic.*

10 Superlatives, ordinals, the same, the only.
   *This is **the best**. You are **the first**. This is **the only one**.*

11 Media.
   *What's on **(the) television**? I went to **the cinema**.*

Indefinite article   1 Describing jobs.
   *Peter is **a lorry driver**.*

2 With singular fractions, group numbers and large numbers.
   *One and **a half** kilos. **A dozen** eggs. **A hundred** envelopes.*

3 Meaning *per*.
   *He was doing ninety miles **an hour**.*
   *Julie earns £500 **a week**.*

Activities

1

Put *a/an* or *the* in each space, or leave the space blank.

a) We went by .... train to *the* west of England.
b) .... people who live in .... Netherlands are called .... Dutch.
c) .... judge sent me to .... prison for .... ten years.
d) .... Columbus was one of .... first people to cross .... Atlantic.
e) As .... captain of .... ship, I have .... complete authority.
f) David learned to play .... violin when he was at .... university.
g) .... Trafalgar Square is near .... Charing Cross Station.
h) Did you read .... book I lent you .... last week?
i) We'll put up .... shelves and then go to .... pub for .... drink.
j) Is that .... present Bill gave you for .... Christmas?

2

Choose the most suitable phrase underlined.

a) Is this a person/the person you told me about?
b) This is the only cinema/an only cinema in the area.
c) Philip has just bought the Thames barge/a Thames barge.
d) Here is a thousand pounds/the thousand pounds I owe you.
e) Are you going to church/the church on Sunday?
f) Do you have a milk jug/milk jug?
g) The Prime Minister/Prime Minister will give a speech this afternoon.
h) The computer/Computer has already changed our lives dramatically.
i) I haven't been to an open-air theatre/open-air theatre before.
j) I'm going to the British Museum/British Museum this afternoon.

3

Complete each sentence with the most suitable word or phrase.

a) The butler was ..C.. I suspected.
   A) last person   B) a last person   C) the last person   D) some last person

b) Where .... you borrowed last week?
   A) is scissors   B) are the scissors   C) is some scissors   D) are scissors

c) Why don't we go to the park ......?
   A) in the car   B) with a car   C) with car   D) by the car

d) Too much rubbish is being dumped in ....
   A) sea   B) the sea   C) a sea   D) some sea

e) Let's go on holiday to ....
   A) Greek Islands   B) the Greece Islands   C) islands of Greece
   D) the Greek Islands

f) This is exactly .... I was looking for.
   A) job   B) a job   C) some job   D) the job

g) Of all these cars, I think I prefer ....
   A) a Japanese   B) some Japanese   C) the Japanese one   D) a Japanese one

h) Interest on this account is only .... per cent.
   A) a four and a quarter   B) four and a quarter   C) four and quarter
   D) four quarter

i) I try to go jogging at least four times ....
   A) the week   B) of the week   C) a week   D) of a week

j) Sally spent six months out of ....
   A) work   B) a work   C) the work   D) some work

4

Complete each sentence a) to j) with one of the endings 1) to 10). More than one answer may be possible.

a) Some people say that the ..9..

b) Most people think that a/an ....

c) I don't agree that ....

d) I feel that a ....

e) I don't believe that a/an ....

f) I didn't realise that the ....

g) It's incredible to think that a/an ....

h) I didn't know that ....

i) I think it's quite unfair that the ....

j) Nobody nowadays thinks that ....

1) .... good job is an important part of life.

2) .... single injection can protect you from so many diseases.

3) .... hundred miles an hour is too fast even on a motorway.

4) .... the unemployed should receive more help from the state.

5) .... queen of England doesn't pay any income tax.

6) .... tiger may well become extinct very soon.

7) .... third of a person's income should be paid in tax.

8) .... women should just stay at home and look after the children.

9) .... English are difficult to get to know at first.

10) .... the Tower of London was built by William the Conqueror.

5
Put *a/an* or *the* in each space, or leave the space blank.

a) Neil Armstrong made *the* first footprint on *the* moon.
b) There was .... accident yesterday at .... corner of .... street.
c) I need .... time to think about .... offer you made me.
d) .... recipe for .... success is .... hard work.
e) .... people who live in .... glass houses shouldn't throw ...... stones.
f) .... worst part of .... living in a caravan is .... lack of space.
g) .... book you ordered .... last week is now in .... stock.
h) .... dancing is .... more interesting activity than .... reading.
i) .... people we met on .... holiday in .... north of England sent us .... postcard.
j) .... little knowledge is .... dangerous thing.

6
Rewrite each sentence, beginning as shown, so that the meaning stays the same.

a) There is only one problem, the weather.
The weather *is the only problem.*
b) There are no good films on this week.
There is nothing ....
c) Can't you swim faster than that?
Is that ....
d) I haven't been here before.
This is ....
e) A lot of wine is drunk in France.
The ....
f) If you drive faster, it is more dangerous.
The ....
g) It is difficult to discover what is true.
The ....
h) Are you a good pianist?
Can you ....
i) Please do not enter the room all together.
Please enter the room one ....
j) I saw a television film of *Hamlet*.
I saw a film of *Hamlet* ....

7
Choose the most suitable phrase underlined.

a) I was under an impression/under the impression that you had left.
b) I have to go. I'm in a hurry/in hurry.
c) I managed to sell the old painting at a profit/at profit.
d) I think I prefer the other restaurant on the whole/on whole.

e) How many hours do you work, <u>on average/on the average</u>, every week?

f) I was <u>in pain/in a pain</u> after I twisted my ankle.

g) Jack recovered from his accident and is now <u>out of danger/out of the danger</u>.

h) Excuse me, but you're <u>in the way/in a way</u>.

i) Sue felt seasick on <u>the cross-channel ferry/a cross the channel ferry</u>.

j) The burglar hit me on <u>my back of the neck/the back of my neck</u>.

8

Put *a/an* or *the* in each space, or leave the space blank.

a) What's *the* use in taking .... medicine for ..*a*.. cold?

b) Is .... happiness of .... majority more important than .... rights of .... individual?

c) It's .... long way by .... train to .... north of .... Scotland.

d) .... philosophers seem to think that .... life is .... mystery.

e) .... most cars start badly on .... cold mornings.

f) There was .... time when I enjoyed .... skating.

g) Do you have .... reason for .... arriving late?

h) By .... time I arrive .... home I feel .... sense of .... relief.

i) .... end of .... book is .... by far .... best part.

j) .... friend always tells me .... answers to .... homework we have.

KEY POINTS

1 Meaning can change, depending on what kind of article is used.
   *Helen is **at the school**.* (At the building, we don't know why)
   *Helen is **at school**.* (She is a student or a teacher)

2 The context of meaning is also important, particularly where an item has been, or has not been, mentioned before:
   *The BBC reported that **the two men** have since been recaptured. (The two men must have been mentioned before, and so this is an extract from a longer text)*

3 Many uses of the articles are idiomatic, and should be learned as part of a phrase.
   *Diana works as **a** graphic designer.*

> **SEE ALSO**
>
> **Unit 21**
> Countables and uncountables
> **Unit 23**
> Determiners

Unit 23
All, no, each, every, either, neither, none

Explanations

All

1   As a quantity word, *all* can be followed by *of* before *the* and a noun.
    Jim was there all (of) the time.

2   It can also emphasise a plural personal pronoun or a noun or noun
    phrase. Note the position of *all* in these examples.
    They all wore white shorts and shirts.
    Those stamps you bought me have all disappeared.

3   It can also stand alone, when it tends to mean 'the only thing'.
    All I want is some peace and quiet.
    Compare the use of 'everything', meaning 'all the things':
    Everything has gone wrong!
    All would not be appropriate in this sentence.

No

1   As a quantity word, *no* can be used meaning *not any*.
    There are no plates left. No new students have joined the class.

2   *No* can also be used as an adverb.
    I suppose we are no worse off than before.
    There were no less than 500 applications for the job.

3   *No* is not normally used alone before an adjective. Compare:
    There are no interesting parts in this book. It is not interesting.
    There is an idiomatic use of *no* with *good*:
    I tried hard but it was no good, I couldn't reach. (useless)
    Another common idiomatic use is with -ing forms:
    Remember, no cheating! No smoking, please.

Each, every, all

1   *Each* refers to single items in a group of items, one at a time.
    Each member of the team received a medal.
    They were given £10 each.
    All refers to the team as a whole.
    All the team played well.
    Each can refer to only two items, while *every* cannot.
    She kissed him on each cheek.

2   *Each* can be followed by *of* and a noun or pronoun.
    When the team won the cup, each of them was given a medal.

106

3   *Each* can also follow a noun or pronoun.
    *My two brothers were **each** chosen to act in the play.*
    *On the first night, they **each** forgot their lines.*

4   Repeated actions are generally described with *every*.
    *I practise the violin **every day**.*

Either, neither

1   *Either* and *neither* both refer to choices between two items.
    *I didn't like **either** of those films.*
    ***Neither** of the films was any good.*

2   *Either* can also mean *both*.
    *On **either** side of the house there are shops.*

None

1   *None* can mean *not one*.
    ***None** of us can ride a horse.*

2   *None* can also mean *not any*. It is followed by a singular verb, especially in formal speech or writing.
    ***None** of the members of the committee **has arrived** yet.*
    In everyday speech, a plural verb is often used.
    ***None** of these telephones **work**.*

Activities

1
Rewrite each sentence so that it contains the word in capitals, and so that the meaning stays the same.

a) This is the only money I have left.   ALL
   This is all the money I have left.................................

b) There wasn't anyone at the meeting.   NO
   ....

c) Both singers had bad voices.   NEITHER
   ....

d) All of the cups are dirty.   NONE
   ....

e) Everyone was cheering loudly.   ALL
   ....

f) You both deserve promotion.   EACH
   ....

g) I read both books, but I liked neither of them.   EITHER
   ....

h) Whenever I cross the Channel by boat I feel seasick.   EVERY
   ....

i) I only ate a sandwich for lunch.   ALL
   ....

j) Both sides of the street have parking meters.   EITHER
   ....

107

2

Rewrite each sentence, beginning as shown, so that the meaning stays the same.

a) Everyone in the office was given a personal parking space.
Each *person in the office was given a personal parking space*.

b) This town doesn't have any good hotels.
There are ....

c) Love is the only thing that you need.
All ....

d) These two pens don't write properly.
Neither ....

e) We are all responsible for our own actions.
Each ....

f) All of us feel lonely sometimes.
We ....

g) All of the shops are closed.
None ....

h) Both jobs were unsuitable for Helen.
Neither ....

i) All the cakes have been eaten.
The cakes ....

j) Unfortunately, the meal was the same as usual.
Unfortunately the meal was no ....

3

Complete each sentence with the most suitable word or phrase.

a) Jack walked into the room with a gun in either ..C.. .
A) side   B) door   C) hand   D) one

b) I had .... a hundred offers for my house.
A) neither   B) each   C) all   D) no less than

c) I feel so tired this evening. I've been working hard ....
A) all day   B) every day   C) each day   D) day by day

d) The two cars for sale were in poor condition, so I didn't buy ....
A) either of them   B) both of them   C) neither of them   D) each of them

e) I tried to lift the heavy trunk but it was ....
A) not good   B) no less than good   C) neither good   D) no good

f) The room was full of people and .... were speaking.
A) neither of them   B) all of them   C) none of them   D) each of them

g) .... spent more time walking a century ago.
A) People all   B) All persons   C) Each people   D) All

h) My friend Jonathan has a gold earring in ....
A) his two ears   B) each ear   C) every ear   D) the ears

i) I looked everywhere for my pen and it was here ....
A) none of the time   B) every time   C) all the time   D) each time

j) People say that there is .... like show business.
A) all business   B) no business   C) not business   D) all business

4

Put the most suitable word from the list into each space.

all	each	either	every	neither	no	none

a) Is *either* of you interested in working on Saturday this week?
b) I am afraid there are .... vacancies in the company at present.
c) I think we should be given at least £50 .... .
d) .... other Saturday we watch our local hockey team.
e) Let's start now. There's .... time like the present!
f) .... you are interested in doing is going to the pub!
g) There are two beds. You can sleep in .... one, it doesn't matter.
h) Sally gave a present to .... and every one of us!
i) And the star of our show is .... other than Dorothy Rogers!
j) My company has treated me well, and given me .... chance to succeed.

5

Rewrite each sentence, beginning as shown, so that the meaning stays the same.

a) I always go to the cinema on Thursdays.
   Every *Thursday I go to the cinema.*
b) This has nothing to do with you!
   This is none ....
c) There aren't any empty seats at the front.
   All ....
d) Lorries are not allowed to go through the town centre.
   No ....
e) The days get colder and colder.
   Each day ....
f) Both questions were impossible to understand.
   I couldn't understand ....
g) You only want to listen to rock music!
   All ....
h) As many as 20,000 people are thought to have attended the concert.
   No ....
i) Each child was given £100.
   The children ....
j) We cannot waste any time!
   There is ....

KEY POINTS

1   If *all* is the subject of a sentence, it means 'the only thing'. Otherwise *everything* is used. Compare:
    All we need now is a new car.
    Everything is missing, I'm afraid.

2   Note these idiomatic uses of *no*:
    No parking. No smoking.
    It's no use. It's no good.

3   *Each* refers to single items in a group one at a time. It is followed by a singular verb.
    Each of these books has its interesting points.

109

4   *Either* and *neither* refer to two items, separately, and are followed by a singular verb.

   Neither of these hotels is very comfortable.

5   *None* (not one) is followed by a singular verb in formal speech and writing.

   None of these answers is correct.

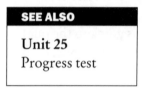

SEE ALSO

Unit 25
Progress test

Unit 24
Making comparisons

Explanations

Forming comparatives and superlatives of adjectives

1   Comparatives with -er.
    One-syllable words, and two-syllable words ending in -y generally add -er to make the comparative form (with -y changing to -i). Words ending in -e add only -r.
        late, later   early, earlier

2   Comparatives with *more* or *less*.
    Other two-syllable words, and words of more than two syllables, use *more* or *less*.
        more modern   less interesting

3   Two-syllable words.
    Some two-syllable words are used with either -er or *more*. Examples are:
        clever   common   narrow   simple

4   Irregular comparatives.
    Some irregular comparatives are:
        *This is my **elder** sister.* (This cannot be used to make a comparison.)
        *How much **further/farther** do we have to go?*   (Meaning *more far*)
        *I can't really advise you any **further**.*   (Meaning *more*)

5   Superlatives.
    Superlatives ending in -est or with *(the) most* follow the same rules outlined in **1** and **2**.
        the latest   the earliest   the most modern

Comparatives of adverbs

1   These are normally made with *more* and *less*.
        more quickly   less carefully

2   Some adverbs, which are not formed from adjectives, have a comparative formed with -er. Examples are:
        faster   harder

Making comparisons

1   The simplest kind of comparison is with a comparative and *than*.
        *You don't look **older than** your brother.*

2   Comparatives can be repeated to suggest continuing change.
        *This lesson seems to be getting **longer and longer**.*
        *Jim started feeling **more and more tired**.*

3   Comparatives can be made stronger by using these words:
    much   far   a lot   a little
    *This book is **much/far/a lot/a little** more expensive.*

4   Comparatives can be used in parallel constructions with *the*.
    ***The faster** you drive, **the more** petrol you use.*

5   Expressions with best:
    *Sorry, but this is **the best** I can do. I tried **my best**.*
    May the best one win.

Comparative clauses

1   With *than*.
    *Food here is **more expensive than** I thought.*

2   With *not as/so...as*.
    *Being a nurse is **not as** interesting **as** being a doctor.*

3   With *(just) as...as*.
    *Living in the country is **just as** expensive **as** living in London.*

4   With *such ...as*.
    *I've never been to **such** a good party **as** that one.*

5   Parts of the comparison that repeat the main verb can be left out, though
    auxiliaries (e.g. *can, be, have, will*) are repeated and the verb can be replaced
    by a form of *do*.
    *You paid more for your house **than I did**.*
    *Jack can swim a lot better **than I can**.*

Activities

1
Put *one* suitable word in each space.

a) My brother is two years older *than* me.
b) The train takes just .... long as the bus.
c) I've never tasted such delicious apples .... these.
d) I thought the second hotel we stayed in was .... more friendly.
e) Unfortunately we are .... well-off than we used to be.
f) Marion doesn't feel so happy there .... she did at first.
g) Do you think you could make a .... less noise?
h) These exercises seem to be getting harder and .... .
i) Jean doesn't need as much help as Harry .... .
j) David didn't enjoy the match as much as I .... .

2
Rewrite each sentence beginning as shown, so that the meaning stays the same.

a) Jill can run faster than Peter.
    Peter *can't run as fast as Jill (can).*......................

b) I thought this journey would last longer than it did.
This journey didn't ....

c) I didn't arrive as early as I expected.
I arrived ....

d) You are working too slowly.
You'll have to ....

e) I have a brother who is older than me.
I have an ....

f) Martin thought the second part of the film was more interesting.
Martin didn't think the first ....

g) Paula's work is less careful than before.
Paula has been working ....

h) There aren't any trains earlier than this one.
This is ....

i) All other pubs are further away.
This pub ....

j) Is this the best price you can offer?
Can't you ....

3
Complete each sentence by choosing the most suitable word or phrase.

a) I really think that apologising is ..C.. you can do.
A) not as much as   B) a little   C) the least   D) as far as

b) I can't stand this weather. It's getting ....
A) more and more   B) worse and worse   C) coldest and coldest
D) further and further

c) Although Brenda came last, everyone agreed she had .... her best.
A) done   B) made   C) had   D) got

d) I wish Charles worked as hard as Mary ....
A) did   B) can   C) will   D) does

e) The more you water this plant, the .... it will grow.
A) best   B) tall   C) wetter   D) faster

f) From now on, we won't be able to go out as much as we ....
A) were   B) had   C) used to   D) will

g) I've never owned .... independent cat as this one!
A) a more than   B) such an   C) a so   D) as much an

h) Brian has been working .... since he was promoted.
A) much harder   B) as harder   C) just as hardly   D) more hardly

i) I've been feeling .... tired lately, doctor.
A) such a   B) the most   C) more and more   D) much

j) This exercise will give you .... practice.
A) farther   B) much more   C) as better   D) a lot

4
Put *one* suitable word in each space, beginning with the letter given.

a) Is William feeling any *better* today?
b) Everyone ate a lot, but Chris ate the m.......... .
c) What's the l.......... news about the situation in India?
d) I'd feel a lot h.......... if you let me help.
e) Graham has been sinking d.......... into debt lately.

113

f) It's 35 degrees today! It must be the h.......... day so far this year.

g) Only £45? Is that all? Oh well, it's b.......... than nothing.

h) I'll have to wait a f.......... two months before I get my promotion.

i) Ruth wore her b.......... dress to her sister's wedding.

j) Harry has got over the w.......... of his cold.

5
Rewrite each sentence, beginning as shown, so that the meaning stays the same.

a) That's the best meal I've ever eaten.
I've never eaten a *better meal*.

b) Fish and meat are the same price in some countries.
Fish costs just ....

c) I've never enjoyed myself so much.
I've never had ....

d) If you run a lot, you will get fitter.
The more ....

e) The doctor can't see you earlier than Wednesday I'm afraid.
Wednesday is ....

f) I must have a rest. I can't walk any more.
I must have a rest. I can't go ....

g) Home computers used to be much more expensive.
Home computers aren't ....

h) I don't know as much Italian as Sue does.
Sue knows ....

i) I thought that learning to drive would be difficult, but it isn't.
Learning to drive is ....

j) Barbara can skate just as well as John can.
John isn't ....

6
Rewrite each sentence so that it contains the word given in capitals, and so that the meaning stays the same. The word cannot be changed in any way.

a) Your car was cheaper than mine.   COST
Your car cost less than mine did....................

b) I'm not as good at maths as you are.   BETTER
....

c) Keith is slightly taller than Nigel.   LITTLE
....

d) Bill was growing angrier all the time.   AND
....

e) Sally tried as hard as she could.   BEST
....

f) I thought this film would be better.   AS
....

g) This is the bumpiest road I've ever driven along!   SUCH

    ....

h) When you eat a lot, you get fat.   MORE

    ....

i) George said he couldn't do any better.   COULD

    ....

j) This year's exam and last year's exam were equally difficult.   JUST

    ....

KEY POINTS

1 Check spelling and formation rules for comparative and superlative adjectives.

2 Some adverbs have the same forms as adjectives, and form comparatives and superlatives like adjectives.
   fast   faster   fastest

3 In comparative clauses, auxiliaries are often used instead of repeating the verb a second time.
   *Wendy works twice as hard **as I do**.*

> **SEE ALSO**
> **Unit 25**
> Progress test

Unit 25 Progress test

(Units 21, 22, 23, 24)

1
Put *one* suitable word in each space.

Somehow I always have problems when I go away on holiday. (1) ..... year my travel agent promises me that my holiday will be (2) ..... best I have ever had, but none of these promises has ever (3) ..... true. This year I got food poisoning (4) ..... day I arrived. (5) ..... must have (6) ..... the fish I ate at the hotel (7) ..... evening. In (8) ..... morning I felt terrible, and I was seen by two doctors. (9) ..... of them spoke English, (10) ..... didn't help. It took me (11) ..... of the first week to recover, and I (12) ..... most of the time sitting next to (13) ..... hotel swimming pool reading newspapers. (14) ..... the time I felt better, (15) ..... weather had changed, but I was determined to go sight-seeing, and do (16) ..... swimming. Unfortunately (17) ..... of the museums was open, as there was (18) ... strike, and it was far too cold to go for (19) ..... swim. I would have enjoyed myself (20) ...... if I had stayed at home.

2
Rewrite each sentence, beginning as shown, so that the meaning stays the same.

a) That's the worst film I've ever seen.
   I've never seen ....
b) There aren't any sandwiches left, I'm afraid.
   I'm afraid all ....
c) I thought that Martin's last novel was more interesting.
   Martin's latest novel ....
d) I talked to neither of Harry's sisters.
   I didn't ....
e) Bob is a much better swimmer than George.
   George can't ....
f) If you walk slowly, it takes longer to get there.
   The more ....
g) Calling the police isn't any good.
   It's ....
h) I phoned Norman last of all.
   Norman was ....
i) We were pleased to see the police arrive.
   When the police arrived ....
j) I thought this meal would cost more than it did.
   This meal didn't ....

3
Complete each sentence with one suitable word. Do not use the word *piece*.

a) Would you like another ...... of cake?
b) There is another ...... of stairs after this one.
c) What a lovely ...... of hair you have.
d) Put up your hand if you need another ...... of paper.
e) There was an interesting ...... of news about Japan in the paper.
f) Could you put a few ...... of coal on the fire?

g) Pour me a ...... of water, would you?

h) They gave me a very large ...... of potatoes with my dinner.

i) There was a terrible flash of lightning and a ...... of thunder.

j) Oh bother, I've split my new ...... of shorts.

4
Rewrite each sentence so that it contains the word given in capitals, and so that the meaning stays the same. The word cannot be changed in any way.

a) You are not allowed to park here.   PARKING
....

b) There aren't any tables, chairs or beds in the house.   FURNITURE
....

c) This city seems very crowded.   PEOPLE
....

d) Can you tell me about guided tours of the city?   INFORMATION
....

e) The people in the theatre were enthusiastic.   AUDIENCE
....

f) I like maths best.   SUBJECT
....

g) There are a lot of cars on this road today.   TRAFFIC
....

h) Sue has gone to see a play.   THEATRE
....

i) I'm looking for somewhere to stay.   ACCOMMODATION
....

j) Jim is out of work at the moment.   JOB
....

5
Use these words and phrases to make complete sentences. The sentences are all part of a letter. Make changes and add any necessary words as in the example.

I/decide/buy/new car.
I have decided to buy a new car......................................

Dear Sir
I/write/complain/about/work/your company/do/last week/my house.

a) ....

Three men/arrive/Monday/paint/inside walls.

b) ....

They use/wrong colour/and spill paint/over/carpets.

c) ....

They also break/valuable vase.

d) ....

Foreman/assure me/they/repaint/walls.

e) ....

I go away/on business/and not return/until Friday.

f) ....

All walls/still/same colour.

g) ....

Foreman also promise/company/pay for/damage to/vase.

h) ....

I enclose/bill/for this.

i) ....

I not pay/your bill/decorating/until/house/painted properly.

j) ....

Yours faithfully,
Martin Spruce

6

Rewrite each sentence, beginning as shown, so that the meaning stays the same.

a) Jim teaches French.
Jim works as ....

b) Neil Armstrong stepped on the moon first.
Neil Armstrong was ....

c) Can't you do better than that?
Is that ....

d) I haven't eaten lobster before.
This is ....

e) Is Julia a good violinist?
Can Julie ....

f) The only thing you need is a screwdriver.
All ....

g) Both of the lifts were out of order.
Neither ....

h) David always goes shopping on Fridays.
Every ....

i) Both cases were too heavy to lift.
I couldn't lift ....

j) George's annual salary is £15,000.
George earns ....

7

Put one word in each space.

a) My trousers are creased. I must iron ..... .

b) Could you give me ..... information about the Arts Festival?

c) I can't come out tonight. I have ..... work to do.

d) Look at your hair! You must have ..... cut!

e) I've decided to buy ..... new furniture.

f) The news ..... on at nine o'clock.

g) Thank you very much. You've been ..... great help.

h) Is this ..... pub you told me about?

i) Chris was ..... last person to leave the room.

j) Don't ..... English drink a lot of tea!

Unit 26 Phrasal verbs 1

Explanations

1 Verbs with three parts

The object always follows these verbs, and cannot be put between any of the parts. Verbs marked * can be used intransitively without the final preposition.

> *I've decided to **cut down on** smoking. I've decided to **cut down**.*

A selection of verbs is listed here with examples. Others, and other meanings of those listed here, are included in the activities.

Cut down on *
> *I've decided to **cut down on** smoking.*   (reduce the amount of)

Catch up with *
> *They are too far ahead for us to*   (reach the same place as)
> ***catch up with** them.*

Come up against
> *I'm afraid we've **come up against***   (meet)
> *a problem we can't solve.*

Come up with
> *Have you **come up with** an answer yet?*   (discover)

Drop in on *
> *I **dropped in on** Bill and Sheila*   (visited)
> *on my way home.*

Face up to
> *You must **face up to** reality!*   (accept, deal with)

Feel up to
> *You must **feel up to** going to work.*   (feel fit to do)

Get away with
> *Jack stole the money and*   (avoid capture)
> ***got away with** it.*

Get along/on with *
> *Do you **get along with** your new boss?*   (have good relations)

Get on with
> *Stop talking and **get on with** your work!*   (continue with)

Get out of
> *I managed to **get out of** working late.*   (avoid a responsibility)

Get round to
> *I haven't **got round to** decorating yet.*   (find time to do)

Get up to
> *What has young Bill been **getting up to**?*   (do, often something wrong)

Go in for
> *Do you **go in for** sailing?*   (have as a hobby)

Grow out of
> *Julie has **grown out of***   (become too old for)
> *playing with dolls.*

Keep up with *

> *You're going too fast! I can't*
> **keep up with** *you!*   (stay in the same place as)

Look down on

> *Our neighbours* **look down on**   (feel superior to)
> *anyone without a car.*

Look up to

> *I really* **look up to** *my teacher.*   (respect)

Look forward to

> *We are* **looking forward to** *our holiday.*   (think we will enjoy)

Make up for

> *The wonderful dinner* **made up for**   (compensate for)
> *the bad service.*

Put up with

> *I can't* **put up with**
> *these screaming children!*   (bear)

Run out of *

> *Oh dear, we've* **run out of** *petrol!*   (have no more of)

Stand up for

> *You must learn to* **stand up for** *yourself!*   (defend)

2 Verbs with two parts: transitive and inseparable

These verbs take an object, but the object cannot be put between verb and preposition.
I can't **do without** *coffee in the morning!*

Ask after

> *Jim* **asked after** *you yesterday.*   (asked for news of)

Call for

> *I'll* **call for** *you at six.*   (come and collect)

Call on

> *I* **called on** *some friends in Plymouth.*   (visited)

Come across

> *Joe* **came across** *this old*   (find by chance)
> *painting in the attic.*

Come into

> *Sue* **came into** *a large sum of money.*   (inherit)

Count on

> *I'm* **counting on** *you to help me.*   (depend on)

Deal with

> *How would you* **deal with**   (take action about)
> *the traffic problem?*

Do without

> *We'll have to* **do without**   (manage without)
> *a holiday this year.*

Get at

> *What are you* **getting at**?   (suggest)

Get over
> *Barry has **got over** his illness now.*   (recover from)

Go over
> *Let's **go over** our plan once more.*   (discuss the details)

Join in
> *Try to **join in** the lesson*   (contribute to)
> *as much as you can.*

Live on
> *They **live on** the money*   (have as income)
> *her father gives them.*

Look into
> *The government is **looking***   (investigate)
> ***into** the problem.*

Look round
> *Let's **look round** the town today.*   (look at everything)

Make for
> *Where are you **making for** exactly?*   (go in the direction of)

Pick on
> *My teacher is always **picking on** me.*   (choose a person to punish)

Run into
> *I **ran into** Steve in the*   (meet by chance)
> *supermarket yesterday.*

See about
> *We'll have to **see about***   (arrange)
> *getting you an office.*

See to
> *Can you **see to** the dog's food?*   (attend to, take care of)

Stand for
> *I won't **stand for** such rudeness!*   (tolerate)
> *Andrew is **standing for** parliament.*   (be a candidate)

Take after
> *Helen **takes after** her mother.*   (have the same characteristics)

Activities

1
Rewrite each sentence so that it contains the phrasal verb given, in a suitable form.

a) Sorry, but I haven't found time to fix your bike yet.   (get round to)
Sorry, but I haven't got round to fixing your bike yet.

b) Oh bother, we don't have any milk left.   (run out of)
....

c) It took me a long time to recover from my illness.   (get over)
....

d) Peter is just like his father!   (take after)
....

e) I think we've found an answer to the problem.   (come up with)
....

f) I don't think I'm well enough to play football today.   (feel up to)

....

g) Ann is someone I really respect.   (look up to)

....

h) I must arrange to have the kitchen painted.   (see about)

....

i) Please help me. I'm relying on you.   (count on)

....

j) Julie must be too old to bite her nails.   (grow out of)

....

2

Rewrite each sentence so that it contains the word given in capitals, and so that the meaning stays the same. The word cannot be changed in any way.

a) Quite by chance, Brenda met Philip at the station.   RAN
   Brenda ran into Philip at the station.
b) You'll just have to learn to accept the facts!   FACE

....

c) It's time that more women defended their rights!   STOOD

....

d) How can you bear so much traffic noise?   PUT

....

e) Charles cheated in his exams, and didn't get caught.   GOT

....

f) I visited a few friends while I was in Manchester.   CALLED

....

g) What are you trying to say?   GETTING

....

h) I must go to the dentist, and get my teeth taken care of.   SEEN

....

i) Do you have a good relationship with your in-laws?   GET

....

j) You're so lucky to have inherited all that money!   COME

....

3

Complete each
sentence with
one of the words
from the list. Use
each word once
only.

| across against for in into on round to up with |

a) I'll send someone to call *for* the parcel on Thursday.
b) You'll have to work hard to keep .... with the rest of the class.
c) Jean didn't expect to come up ...... such difficulties.
d) It's not fair. You're always picking ...... me.
e) Terry sang the first verse and then everyone joined ....
f) I came ...... one of your novels in a second-hand bookshop.
g) I'm not interested in buying anything. I'm just looking ....
h) Don't you think the manager should deal .... this problem?
i) George came .... a lot of money when his uncle died.
j) You look very guilty! What have you been getting up ....?

4

Complete each
sentence with the
most suitable
word or phrase.

a) There isn't any sugar, I'm afraid. You'll have to .C... .
   A) run out   B) put up with   C) do without   D) make for
b) How much money do you manage to ....?
   A) come into   B) go in for   C) deal with   D) live on

c) The weather was fine, and everyone was .... the coast.
   A) going in for   B) making for   C) joining in   D) seeing about
d) I was passing their house, so I .... Claire and Michael.
   A) dropped in on   B) came up with   C) got on with   D) ran into
e) I don't really .... winter sports very much.
   A) deal with   B) face up to   C) go in for   D) get round to
f) Losing my job was a great shock, but I think I'm .... it.
   A) seeing to   B) putting up with   C) standing for   D) getting over
g) Sheila's gone to .... having a new phone installed.
   A) see about   B) deal with   C) get round to   D) ask after
h) I've had to .... a lot of insulting behaviour from you!
   A) look down on   B) put up with   C) stand up for   D) get on with
i) The hotel was terrible, but the wonderful beach .... our disappointment.
   A) got over   B) faced up to   C) saw to   D) made up for
j) Jack has decided to .... the time he spends watching television.
   A) run out of   B) see to   C) cut down on   D) come up with

5

Choose the most suitable ending for each sentence. Other meanings of verbs listed above (possibly in a different category) are included here.

a) I can't put up with ..*B*..

   A) you if you should come to London.   B) people who smoke all the time.   C) the plates onto the top shelf.

b) The chairperson of the committee then called on Tony ....

   A) but his line was engaged.   B) to make a speech in reply.
   C) so that his voice could be heard above the crowd.

c) Mary has been chosen to stand for ....

   A) the bad behaviour of her colleagues.   B) herself in future.
   C) Parliament in the next election.

d) After my holidays it takes me a few days to catch up with ....

   A) the people running in front of me.   B) all the news I've missed.
   C) a really bad cold.

e) Small children soon grow out of ....

   A) their shoes.   B) all the good food they eat.   C) the habits they have when they get older.

f) I've decided to go in for ....

   A) eating fruit for breakfast.   B) a few days rest in the country.
   C) a photography competition in *Photographer's Weekly*.

g) I'm afraid that our plans to open a new factory have run into ......

   A) some old friends.   B) a tree by the side of the road.   C) a few unexpected difficulties.

h) We find that this type of tyre makes for ....

   A) safer driving in wet weather.   B) the first place it can stop.   C) all smaller types of car.

i) I saw my old friend John last week. I couldn't get over.......

   A) my cold before I saw him, though.   B) near enough to talk to him though.   C) how young he looked.

j) In this part of town, people are only worried about keeping up with ....

   A) others who are faster.   B) late-night television programmes.
   C) the Joneses.

KEY POINTS

1 Check any new phrasal verb with a dictionary, to be sure what type it is.

2 Bear in mind that many phrasal verbs have more than one meaning.

3 Phrasal verbs tend to be more common in spoken language and informal written language.

> **SEE ALSO**
>
> **Unit 30**
> Progress test

Unit 27 Phrasal verbs 2

Explanations

1 Verbs with two parts: transitive and separable

These verbs take an object, and the object (especially *it* and *them*) can be put between the verb and the preposition. Object phrases tend to be put after the preposition. The pronouns *him, her, it, us, them* are put after the verb. Verbs marked* have an intransitive form with a different meaning.

> *We **brought up** this child. We **brought** her **up**.*
> *Call back* and *show around* always put the object between the verb and the preposition.

Other meanings of the verbs listed here are included in the activities.

Bring up
> *We **brought up** this child.*   (look after and educate)

Carry out
> *You haven't **carried out** my instructions.*   (act upon)

Call off
> *We have decided to **call off** the match.*   (cancel)

Clear up*
> *Could you **clear up** your room please?*   (make tidy)
> *The weather is **clearing up***.   (improve)

Fill in*
> *Can you **fill in** this form please?*   (complete)
> *Our teacher was ill, so Mrs Frost **filled in***.*   (take someone's place)

Find out
> *I want to **find out** what happened.*   (learn about)

Give away
> *The millionaire **gave** all his money **away**.*   (make a gift of)
> *Jill asked me not to **give** her secret **away**.*   (make something known)

Give up*
> *I've decided to **give up** eating meat.*   (stop)
> *After trying hard, George finally **gave up**.*   (stopped trying)

Hold up
> *Two masked men **held up** the bank.*   (rob)

Knock out
> *The blow on the head **knocked** me **out**.*   (make unconscious)

Leave out
> *I always **leave out** the difficult exercises.*   (not include)

Look up*
> *I have to **look** this word **up** in my dictionary.*   (locate)
> *Things are **looking up***.   (appear better)

Make up*
> *I think you **made** this story **up**.*   (invent)
> *The couple quarrelled but then **made up**.*   (become friends again)

125

Pick up
> *I'll **pick** you **up** at six.*   (collect)

Put aside
> *Harry **puts** money **aside***   (save)
> *every week for his holiday.*

Put off
> *They **put** the meeting **off** until Thursday.*   (postpone)
> *The smell of fish **put** me **off** my tea.*   (discourage from)

Put up
> *If you come to Florence I can **put** you **up**.*   (provide
>   accommodation)

Show around
> *Let me **show** you **around** the new building.*   (give a guided tour)

Take over*
> *A German company **took** us **over** last year.*   (buy a company)
> *If you are tired, I'll **take over***.*   (take someone's place)

Take up
> *I've decided to **take up** tennis.*   (start a hobby)

Tear up
> *Wendy **tore up** Alan's letters.*   (tear into pieces)

Think over
> *Please **think over** our offer.*   (consider)

Try out
> *Have you **tried out** the new computer?*   (use for the first time)

Turn down
> *Paul was offered the job but he **turned** it **down**.* (refuse an offer)

Wear out
> *All this work has **worn** me **out**.*   (make tired)

Work out
> *This is a difficult problem, I can't **work** it **out**.*   (find a solution)

2

Verbs with two
parts: intransitive

These verbs have no object. Verbs marked* have a transitive form with a
different meaning. There are other meanings, not included here.
> *The car **broke down** on the motorway.*

Break down
> *The car **broke down** on the motorway.*   (stop working)

Break out
> *The war **broke out** unexpectedly.*   (begin suddenly)

Come out
> *Her new book **came out** last week.*   (be published)

Draw up*
> *Suddenly an ambulance **drew up** outside.*   (come to a stop)
> *My lawyer is **drawing up** a contract for us*.*   (write a legal document)

Fall out
> *Charles and Maria have **fallen out** again.*   (quarrel)

Get away
> *The bank robbers **got away** in a stolen van.*   (escape)

Give in
> *She pleaded with me, and I finally **gave in.***   (yield)

Go off
> *Everyone panicked when the bomb*   (explode)
> ***went off**.*

Look out
> ***Look out!** There's a car coming!*   (beware)

Set in
> *I think the rain has **set in** for the day.*   (begin as if to continue)

Show off
> *You always **show off** at parties.*   (behave to attract attention)

Take off
> *Your plane **takes off** at 6.00.*   (leave the ground)

Turn up*
> *Guess who **turned up** at our party?*   (arrive, often unexpectedly)
> *Can you **turn up** the sound*?*   (increase)

Wear off
> *When the drug **wears off** you may feel pain.*   (fade away)

Activities

1

Rewrite each sentence so that the meaning stays the same, and using one of the verbs in the list in a suitable form. Use each verb once only.

call off	draw up	give in	look up	put aside
put up	turn down	turn up	wear off	work out

a) Jack always arrives late for work.
   Jack always turns up late for work. ....

b) See if their number is in the phone directory.
   ....

c) I'm saving up to buy a new bike.
   ....

d) A large black limousine stopped outside the house.
   ....

e) I'm afraid the match has been cancelled.
   ....

f) The government refused to yield to the demands of the terrorists.
   ....

g) We offered them £100,000 for the house but they refused our offer.
   ....

h) You can stay with us if you come to Cambridge.
   ....

i) I can't calculate how much the whole trip will cost.
   ....

j) After a few days the pain in Dave's leg went away.
   ....

2

Put *one* word in
each space.

a) Why don't you let me show you *round* London?
b) Jane is coming to pick us .... after work.
c) Have you found .... what time the train leaves?
d) We had to wait for an hour before the plane took ....
e) Harry was brought .... by his grandparents.

f) A shelf fell on my head and knocked me ....
g) I was so angry when I saw the parking ticket that I tore it ....
h) A fire has broken .... in an office block in central London.
i) Julian always talks loudly and shows ....
j) If you don't like this part you can leave it ....

3

Rewrite each
sentence so that it
contains the
word given in
capitals, and so
that the meaning
stays the same.

a) I think it's going to rain all day.   IN
   I think the rain has set in for the day.
b) I don't know what to write on this form.   IN
   ....
c) I started doing this job when Janet left.   OVER
   ....
d) This story of yours isn't true!   UP
   ....
e) I haven't decided about the job, but I'm considering it.   OVER
   ....
f) We believe that it was you who robbed the Post Office.   UP
   ....
g) Oh no! The car doesn't work!   DOWN
   ....
h) It would be a good idea to stop drinking coffee.   UP
   ....
i) Ruth's party has been postponed until next week.   OFF
   ....
j) Our company has just been bought by a multi-national.   OVER
   ....

4

Put *one* suitable
word in each
space.

a) In the army, all orders have to be *carried* out!
b) Why don't you .... up golf? It's a good pastime.
c) If I won a lot of money, I would .... some of it away.
d) Let's .... out the new food processor.
e) This room is a mess. Why don't you .... it up?
f) I've been walking all day. I feel .... out.
g) Joe is very quarrelsome, he .... out with everyone.
h) Where were you exactly when the bomb .... off?

128

i) When does your new record .... out?

j) Can you .... in for me while I go to the bank?

5

Complete each sentence with the most suitable word or phrase.

a) Brian ..*C*.. at our dinner party wearing a pink bow tie.
   A) wore out   B) showed off   C) turned up   D) tried out

b) David's wife is bound to ...... the truth sooner or later.
   A) find out   B) come out   C) make up   D) give up

c) You don't have to decide now, you can ....
   A) put it aside   B) call it off   C) tear it up   D) think it over

d) Pat was caught by the police, but Martin ....
   A) gave in   B) gave up   C) got away   D) held up

e) After the quarrel, we kissed and ....
   A) cleared up   B) looked up   C) made up   D) put up

f) Why exactly did war ....between the two countries?
   A) break out   B) set in   C) go off   D) call off

g) After a long day at work most people feel ....
   A) broken down   B) worn out   C) knocked out   D) turned down

h) I've just been offered a new job! Things are ....
   A) turning up   B) clearing up   C) making up   D) looking up

i) In the end I .... the form in disgust, and threw it away.
   A) filled in   B) worked out   C) tore up   D) put off

j) I was interested in buying the car, but a friend ....
   A) put me off   B) turned me down   C) showed me around
   D) gave me away

6

Replace the word underlined with a suitable phrasal verb listed in this unit.

a) I think that you <u>invented</u> this story. *made up*..

b) When do you think your book will <u>be published</u>? ....

c) I think that the weather is <u>improving</u>. ....

d) I can't <u>find an answer</u> to this problem. ....

e) <u>Be careful!</u> You're going to fall! ....

f) I'm afraid William tends to <u>stop trying</u>. ....

g) If you want a rest, I'll <u>carry on for you</u>. ....

h) The plane is going to <u>leave the ground</u>. ....

i) I think that Sue and Neil have <u>quarrelled</u>. ....

j) Why do you have to <u>make people admire you</u>! ....

7

Choose the best meaning for the phrase underlined in each sentence.

Other meanings for verbs listed in this unit are included (some with a change of category).

a) At half past six, the alarm clock <u>went off</u>. ..*B*..
   A) exploded   B) rang   C) disappeared

129

b) Jim is very good at <u>taking off</u> his teacher. ....
  A) flying with his teacher   B) getting rid of his teacher
  C) imitating his teacher
c) Please <u>give in</u> your papers at the end of the lesson. ....
  A) give them back   B) put them inside the desk
  C) accept whatever they say
d) Please don't <u>bring up</u> that subject again! ....
  A) start shouting about it   B) mention it   C) talk about it for hours on end
e) There is one small matter I would like to <u>clear up</u>. ....
  A) find an explanation for   B) make clean and tidy   C) get rid of once and for all
f) Shirley spends hours <u>making up</u> before she goes out. ....
  A) thinking of a good story   B) trying to get on better with her friends
  C) putting cosmetics on her face
g) Jean is really good at <u>picking up</u> languages. ....
  A) choosing languages   B) learning languages by being in a country
  C) learning languages by heart
h) All my old clothes need <u>taking up</u>. ....
  A) taking to the cleaners   B) to be replaced   C) to be made shorter
i) The whole cost of the equipment <u>works out at</u> £450. ....
  A) comes to   B) can be reduced to   C) will involve an extra
j) Jackie <u>broke down</u> and everyone felt sorry for her. ....
  A) injured herself   B) caused an accident   C) started crying

KEY POINTS

1 Check any new phrasal verb with a dictionary, to be sure what type it is.

2 Bear in mind that many phrasal verbs have more than one meaning.

3 Phrasal verbs tend to be more common in spoken language and informal written language.

SEE ALSO

Unit 30
Progress test

Unit 28 Verbs followed by infinitive or gerund and *that* clause

Explanations

1
Verbs followed by -ing or a noun

avoid, be worth, dislike, enjoy, fancy, help, keep, mind, miss, practise, risk, can't stand.
>   Try to **avoid walking** as much as possible.
>   I managed to **avoid an argument**.
>   It's not **worth waiting** for a bus at this time of day.
>   I **dislike having** to get up early.
>   Do you **enjoy meeting** people from other countries?
>   I don't **fancy going out** this evening.
>   George can't **help laughing** when he sees you!
>   I wish you wouldn't **keep interrupting**.
>   I don't **mind helping** you do the washing-up.
>   Jane **misses going** for long country walks.
>   You should **practise introducing** yourself.
>   We can't **risk starting** a fire in the forest.
>   I **can't stand going** to office parties.

2
Verbs followed by -ing, a *that* clause, or a noun.

admit, consider, deny, imagine, recollect, report, suggest
>   Jack **admitted stealing** the money.
>   Jack **admitted that** he had stolen the money.
>   When accused of stealing the money, Jack **admitted it**.
>   Have you **considered taking up** jogging?
>   You must **consider that** Jim has never driven abroad before.
>   Peter **denied stealing** the money.
>   Can you **imagine living** in California?
>   I don't **recollect meeting** you before.
>   Suddenly I **recollected that** I had another appointment.
>   Helen **reported losing** her watch to the director.
>   I **suggested going** to the beach.
>   I **suggested that** we went to the beach.

3
Verbs followed by either infinitive with *to* or -*ing* with little or no change of meaning.

attempt, begin, continue, dread, not bear, hate, intend, like, love, prefer, start
>   I **attempted to leave/leaving** but the police stopped me.
For some speakers, *like to* describes a habitual action.
>   On Sundays I **like to get up** early and go for a swim.
Would like, would love and *would prefer* are followed by *infinitive with to*.
>   I'd **like to come** to your party, but I'll be away then.

131

4
Verbs followed
by either
infinitive with *to*
or *-ing* or a *that*
clause, with
change of
meaning.

forget
> *I **forgot to buy** any coffee.*   (I didn't remember)
> *I **forgot the coffee**.*
> *I **won't forget to go** there.*   (I'll remember)
> *I **won't forget meeting** you.*   (It will stay in my memory.)
> *I **forgot that I had invited** ten people to lunch.*

go on
> *Diana **went on working** all night.*   (continue)
> *The director **went on to say** that the strike was over.*   (add)

mean
> *I **meant to phone** you but I forgot.*   (intend)
> *This **means leaving** at 6.00.*   (involve)
> *This **means that** we will have to leave at 6.00!*

regret
> *I **regret to tell** you that you have failed.*   (a formal statement)
> *Kate **regretted not buying** the house.*   (be sorry about the past)
> *Kate **regretted that** she hadn't bought the house.*
> *Kate **regretted her decision**.*

remember
> *Please **remember to lock** the door.*   (don't forget a future action)
> *I **remember locking** the door.*   (remember a past action)
> *I **remembered Sue's birthday**.*
> *I **remembered that** I had left my keys behind.*

stop
> *I **stopped going** to evening classes.*   (give up)
> *I **stopped to buy** some coffee.*   (in order to do something)
> *I **stopped the car**.*

try
> *I **tried to get up** early, but I couldn't.*   (try and fail)
> *Why don't you **try getting up** early?*   (suggesting an action)
> *I **tried a new kind of toothpaste**.*

5
Verbs followed
by infinitive
without *to*, or
-ing with change
of meaning.

feel, hear, listen to, look at, notice, see, watch
Notice can also be followed by a *that* clause.
> *I **felt** the train **moving**.*   (continuing action)
> *I **felt** the train **move**.*   (completed action)
> *I **noticed** people **waving** outside.*
> *I **noticed that there were** people waving outside.*

Some of these verbs can be used with a *that* clause with change of meaning.
> *I **feel that** you should look for another job.*   (believe)
> *I've just **heard that** the match is off.*   (receive news)
> ***See that** you lock up when you leave.*   (make sure)

6
Verbs followed
by infinitive with
to.

afford, appear, ask, choose, fail, happen, help, long, manage, offer, prepare,
refuse, tend, wait, want.
> *I can't **afford to go** on holiday abroad this year.*

*The car **appears to have broken down**.*
*David **asked me to give** this to you.*
*I **chose not to go** to university.*
*Gerry **failed to arrive** on time.*
*I **happened to be passing** so I dropped in.*

7
Verbs followed by infinitive with *to*, or a *that* clause.

agree, arrange, decide, demand, desire, expect, hope, intend, learn, plan, pretend, promise, seem, threaten, wish
  *Tom **agreed to meet** us outside the cinema.*
  *Tom **agreed that** he would meet us outside the cinema.*

Activities

1
Complete each sentence with a suitable form of the verb in brackets.

a) I really miss (play) *playing* tennis like I used to.
b) I'm sorry. I meant (write) .... to you, but I've been busy.
c) Harry says he doesn't remember (meet) .... Sally before.
d) Martin failed (pay) .... the rent on time yet again.
e) It's not worth (buy) .... a return ticket.
f) Have you ever considered (work) .... as a teacher?
g) I promise I won't forget (feed) .... the cat.
h) We've arranged (meet) .... outside the school at 4.30.
i) If you've got a headache, why don't you try (take) .... an aspirin?
j) I can't imagine (not have) .... a car!

2
Rewrite each sentence so that it contains the word in capitals, and so that the meaning stays the same.

a) Jack said that he hadn't cheated in the exam.   CHEATING
   Jack denied cheating in the exam....
b) It was difficult for me not to laugh at Wendy's letter.   HELP
   ....
c) I'm sorry but you have not been appointed to the post.   REGRET
   ....
d) I needed a drink of water and so I stopped running.   TO
   ....
e) Luckily Peter didn't pay a fine.   PAYING
   ....
f) I think it would be a good idea to take the train.   SUGGEST
   ....
g) Don't forget the lights when you leave.   OFF
   ....
h) I can hear voices upstairs.   SOMEONE
   ....
i) I think Derek has forgotten the meeting.   APPEARS
   ....
j) My neighbour said he would call the police!   THREATENED
   ....

3

Complete each sentence with a suitable form of the verb in brackets.

a) Pauline couldn't manage (eat) *to eat* all the ice cream.
b) A witness reported (see) .... Terry at the scene of the crime.
c) William pretended (not notice) .... the 'No Parking' sign.
d) One of the boys finally admitted (start) .... the fire.
e) I suppose I tend (buy) .... more books than I used to.
f) Sometimes I regret (move) .... to this part of the country.
g) Did you notice anyone (wait) .... outside when you left?
h) Mark expects (finish) .... work round about 6.00.

4

Complete each sentence with a suitable form of one of the verbs in brackets.

a) Mary was so angry that she *demanded* to see the manager.
   (demand, hope, risk, stop)
b) The weather is so awful that I don't .... going out this evening.
   (fancy, like, try, want)
c) The children could hardly .... to leave their pets behind.
   (bear, forget, regret, seem)
d) You don't .... looking after the baby, do you?
   (agree, stand, mind, notice)
e) Do you .... to know when this castle was built?
   (ask, happen, imagine, like)
f) John .... to let his children go to the concert.
   (afford, avoid, refuse, stop)
g) If I give you the information, I .... losing my job!
   (expect, mean, prepare, risk)
h) What do you .... to be doing in ten years time?
   (begin, expect, remember, suggest)
i) Do you .... to tell the police about the missing money?
   (admit, confess, deny, intend)
j) Why does Basil .... looking at his watch?
   (appear, attempt, keep, mean)

KEY POINTS

1 Check new verbs in a dictionary to be sure how they are used.

2 Note that some verbs can be used in different ways with changes of meaning.

> **SEE ALSO**
>
> **Unit 30**
> Progress test

134

Unit 29 Prepositions following verbs and adjectives

Explanations

Prepositions following verbs

1 About
agree about, argue about, boast about, dream about, know about, laugh about, read about, talk about.

2 At
guess at, laugh at, look at.

3 For
apply for, arrange for, ask for something, blame someone for, care for, forgive someone for, look for, pay for something, search for, vote for, wait for.

4 In
believe in, confide in someone, involve someone in something, specialise in, succeed in, take part in.

5 Of
accuse someone of something, (dis)approve of, die of something, dream of, remind someone of something, rob someone of something, smell of, taste of, warn someone of something.

6 On
blame something on someone, concentrate on, congratulate someone on something, depend on, insist on, rely on.

7 To
add something to, admit to, apologise to someone for something, be accustomed to, to be used to, belong to, confess to, explain something to someone, lend something to someone, listen to, object to, reply to, talk to someone about something.

8 With
agree with, argue with, begin with, charge someone with a crime, deal with, discuss something with someone, provide someone with something, share something with someone, trust someone with something.

Prepositions following adjectives

1 About
annoyed about, anxious about, certain about, excited about, happy about, pleased about, right about, sorry about, upset about.

135

2 At
angry at, annoyed at, bad/good at, surprised at.

3 By
bored by, shocked by, surprised by.

4 For
famous for, late for, ready for, sorry for.

5 From
absent from, different from, safe from.

6 In
interested in.

7 Of
afraid of, ashamed of, aware of, capable of, fond of, full of, it is good of you to do something, jealous of.

8 On
keen on.

9 To
grateful to, kind to, married to.

10 With
angry with, annoyed with, bored with, happy with, pleased with.

Activities

1

Put *one* suitable word in each space.

a) A lot of people I know really believe *in* ghosts.
b) Martin grew to be very fond .... his pet snake.
c) This bread tastes .... fish!
d) Everyone was shocked .... Susan's strange appearance.
e) The company blamed the drop in sales .... the economic situation.
f) Brenda decided to discuss her problems .... a psychiatrist.
g) When Harry made his speech everyone laughed .... him.
h) Robert has been married .... Deborah for over a year.
i) You were right after all .... the result of the election.
j) The woman who lived next door admitted .....the robbery.

2

Rewrite each sentence beginning as shown, so that the meaning stays the same.

a) Two men stole the old lady's handbag.
The old lady was *robbed of her handbag*.

b) John finds photography interesting.

John is ....

c) Helen has a good knowledge of car engines.

Helen knows a lot ....

d) The food in France is famous.

France is ....

e) I'd like to think your brother for his help.

I am very grateful ....

f) Can you and Stephen share this book, please.

Can you share this book ....

g) I find studying all night rather difficult.

I'm not used ....

h) Harry feels frightened when he sees a snake.

Harry is afraid ....

i) I'm sorry about breaking your camera.

Please forgive me ....

j) Peter knows how to draw well.

Peter is good ....

3

Put *one* suitable word in each space.

a) David was *ashamed* of what he had done, and he blushed.

b) I'm not very .... on the idea of going climbing.

c) Mary is always .... about all the famous people she has met.

d) Jim was often .... for work, and lost his job as a result.

e) There were no empty seats on the train, which was .... of soldiers.

g) Bill decided not to .... Bob with his secrets.

g) The two boys were .... of stealing a sports car.

h) We .... in persuading Carol to lend us her boat.

i) You have worked very hard! I am very .... with you!

j) I can't remember her name, but it .... with 'J'.

4

Rewrite each sentence so that it contains the word in capitals and so that the meaning stays the same.

a) William could do better work.   CAPABLE

William is capable of (doing) better work............

b) I own this car.   BELONGS

....

c) The job received over a hundred applications.   APPLIED

....

d) Mrs Jones' death was caused by old age.   DIED

....

e) 'Well done, Tony, you have passed the exam,' said Joe.   CONGRATULATED

....

f) Jean borrowed Shirley's camera.   LENT

....

g) I'm not sure exactly when the train leaves.   CERTAIN

....

h) Graham found the film very boring.   BORED

....

i) We all pitied Stephen.   SORRY

....

j) People should treat animals well.   KIND

....

5

Put *one* suitable word in each space.

a) My boss shouted at me, he was really *angry* with me!
b) I can see your point, but I just don't .... with you
c) Terry doesn't .... of his children going to rock concerts.
d) George and I .... about politics all night!
e) Can I have a .... at the evening paper?
f) This story .... me of a novel by Dickens.
g) Peter feels .... of anyone who talks to his girlfriend.
h) I didn't expect you to behave like that! I'm .... at you!
i) Oh dear, I forgot to .... any baking powder to the cake.
j) I think you should .... your boss for a rise.

6

Complete each sentence with the most suitable word or phrase.

a) Thank you very much. It's very ..*B*.. you to help me.
   A) good with   B) good of   C) good for   D) good about
b) The bad weather was ..... the series of power cuts.
   A) blamed for   B) blamed on   C) blamed with   D) blamed by
c) I'm sorry, but I ..... seeing the manager at once!
   A) arrange for   B) look for   C) agree with   D) insist on
d) Why do you spend all your time ..... your sister!
   A) arguing about   B) arguing for   C) arguing with   D) arguing at
e) Helen is very ..... going to work in Germany.
   A) excited about   B) excited for   C) excited with   D) excited to
f) The tourists were not ..... the danger of bandits in the hills.
   A) known about   B) aware of   C) provided with   D) guessed at
g) I understood the problem after it had been ..... me.
   A) explained to   B) admitted to   C) confessed to   D) replied to
h) I wish you wouldn't show off and ..... your success as much!
   A) full of   B) bored by   C) boast about   D) congratulate on
i) If you listen to music you can't ..... your homework.
   A) read about   B) arrange for   C) specialise in   D) concentrate on
j) We thought we would be ..... the storm if we sheltered under a tree.
   A) happy about   B) safe from   C) depended on   D) cared for

KEY POINTS

1   Check verbs and adjectives in a dictionary to be certain which prepositions follow them.

2   In some cases differeent prepositions give different meanings.

3   Note the difference between *used to* (see Unit 1) and *be used to*:
    I used to have a bike, but I sold it.
    This is a contrast between past and present. *To have* is an infinitive in this sentence.
    I am not used to getting up so early in the morning.
    This describes a situation which you find strange or difficult, because you are not familiar with it. In this sentence, *used* is an adjective, *to* is a preposition, and *getting up* is the noun following the verb (gerund).

SEE ALSO

Unit 30
Progress test

Unit 30 Progress test

(Units 26, 27, 28, 29)

1

Put *one* suitable word in each space.

I was reading an article last week in which the writer described how her children had changed as they (1) ..... up. When they were small she had to (2) ..... up with noisy games in the house, or (3) ..... in interminable games of football in the garden which (4) ..... her out. If the house went quiet, she wondered what the monsters were (5) ..... up to, or what crisis she would have to (6) ..... with next. She dreaded the fact that they might (7) ..... after her husband, who admitted having (8) ..... an uncontrollable child who (9) ..... most of the time (10) .... off to his friends by breaking things or (11) ..... into fights. What was worse was that (12) .... else thought he was a sweet child, and he (13) ..... away with (14) ..... most terrible things! However, she had experienced an even greater shock with her children. They had (15) ..... out of all their naughty behaviour, and (16) ..... up serious hobbies (17) ..... as chess and playing the piano. They never did anything without (18) ..... it over first, and coming to a serious decision. She had to (19) ..... up to the fact that they made her feel rather childish as they got (20) ..... , and that in some ways she preferred them when they were young and noisy!

2

Complete each sentence with an expression formed from *get.*

a) When are you going to .... to writing to the bank?
b) I'm afraid I don't .... very well with my teacher.
c) I don't understand what you are .... What do you mean?
d) How are you feeling? Have you .... your cold yet?
e) Jim chased the burglar, but unfortunately the burglar........ .

3

Complete each sentence with an expression formed from *come.*

a) Has the new book of tests .... yet?
b) It's a difficult situation and we haven't .... a solution yet.
c) I .... these old photographs in my desk yesterday.
d) Julie became rich when she .... a fortune.
e) I'm afraid we've .... a lot of problems in this project.

4

Rewrite each sentence, beginning as shown, so that the meaning stays the same.

a) I wish I could work in the evenings as I used to.
   I miss ....
b) If I take the job I'll have to move to London.
   Taking the job will ....
c) Neil wishes he hadn't sold his car.
   Neil regrets ....
d) Please see that you post all the letters.
   Please don't ....
e) Sheila has decided to take driving lessons.
   Sheila has decided to learn ....

f) Jim said he had seen the jewels but hadn't stolen them.
   Jim said he had seen the jewels but denied ....

g) How about going to the theatre tonight?
   Would ....

h) Peter will look after the children, he has no objection.
   Peter doesn't mind ....

i) 'I'll definitely be here by eight,' Ann promised.
   Ann promised she ....

j) We met in 1978. Do you remember?
   Do you remember ....

5

Put *one* suitable
word in each
space.

a) Don't go so fast! I can hardly .... up with you.

b) Don't be such a coward! .... up for yourself!

c) Please don't let me down. I'm .... on you.

d) We don't know who started the fire, but we're ..... into it.

e) I must go to the dentist's and have my teeth .... to.

f) It's raining now, but I think it'll .... up later.

g) Ronnie hit his head on the shelf and .... himself out.

h) Tony's application for the job was .... down.

i) Steve woke up when the effect of the sleeping pill .... off.

j) The efforts of the United Nations could not stop war .... out.

6

Put *one* suitable
word in each
space.

Last year I stayed for a few days in an old house in Scotland which was
famous (1) ..... its ghost. I don't really believe (2) ..... ghosts, so I'm not
afraid (3) ..... them of course. So when my hosts suggested (4) ...... up all
night to see their ghost, I simply laughed (5) ..... them. Then they told me
(6) ...... the woman who haunted their house. She had been accused (7) .....
murdering her husband in the eighteenth century because she had been
jealous (8) ..... him, but she had avoided (9) ..... tried, and had disappeared.
She appeared quite regularly, walking through the house as if she was
searching (10) ..... something. I agreed to watch that night, though it
would (11) ..... sitting for hours in the cold. The house was full (12) ..... old
furniture, and I (13) ..... getting up from my chair and walking around. I
(14) ..... one of my friends to appear, dressed as the 'ghost', and (15) ..... to
scare me, as I knew they were fond (16) ..... practical jokes. So when the
figure of a woman finally came (17) ..... me, I (18) ..... to be terrified. You
can imagine my surprise when the figure appeared to (19) ..... a knife from
her dress, and then vanished. I decided to disappear myself, and drove
home to London as (20) ..... as I could.

7

Complete each
sentence with an
expression
containing *of*.

a) Jim's boss didn't think he was .... working on his own.

b) Mrs White is very .... animals, and has six cats.

c) I know I shouldn't have stolen the money. I'm .... myself.

d) It was very .... you to help me carry my shopping.

e) Georgina is very .... anyone who dances with her husband.

8
Complete each
sentence with an
expression
containing *about*.

a) I knew I'd really seen a ghost. I was .... it!
b) Bill was very .... missing my birthday party.
c) You were .... the film. It was awful, just as you said.
d) I always get worried at airports. I feel .... missing the plane.
e) Poor Lucy has lost her job. She's very .... it.

9
Complete each
sentence with a
word ending in
-ing.

a) That's all right, I don't mind .... the washing-up.
b) Most people try to avoid .... up words in the dictionary.
c) Can you imagine .... up six small children?
d) I was considering .... up golf, actually.
e) We're rather hard up. It means .... without a holiday this year.

10
Put *one* suitable
word in each
space.

a) Have you ever thought of .... up cycling?
b) Harry had a serious illness, but he has .... over it now.
c) We have decided to .... off our holiday until next month.
d) I think that you .... up the whole story!
e) What are the children .... up to in the garden?
f) Everyone says that Chris .... after his father.
g) You'll never guess who .... up at the Christmas party!
h) Please .... over our offer before you make a decision.
i) After the party, John had to .... up all the mess.
j) Nigel found it difficult to .... up with the rest of the class.

11
Complete each
sentence with a
phrase formed
from the word
given in capitals.
This phrase may
include *it*.

a) The minister responsible has promised to .... the problem. LOOK
b) Sorry, we must end there. We've .... time. RUN
c) All passengers are asked to .... this immigration form. FILL
d) Everyone was worried in case war .... BREAK
e) I don't understand your comments. What are you .... ? GET
f) Your behaviour is intolerable! I won't .... it! STAND
g) The recipe says include garlic but I .... LEAVE
h) Have you ever .... a writer called Jack Common? COME
i) When you feel like a rest from driving, I'll .... TAKE
j) I'll do the garden soon. I just haven't .... yet. GET

Unit 31 Inversion and question tags

Explanations

Inversion after negative adverbs

Inversion in this case means that the verb is in a question form and is necessary if a negative adverb (or one with negative meaning) begins the sentence. This only occurs in formal speech, and writing.

1   Not only
    Harry not only missed the train, but also lost his case.
    ***Not only did Harry miss** the train, but (he) also lost his case.*

2   No Sooner
    The main verb is always in the Past Perfect.
    *Tim **had** no sooner **left**, than the phone rang.*
    *No sooner **had** Tim **left**, than the phone rang.*

3   Under no circumstances
    You shouldn't touch these wires under any circumstances.
    ***Under no circumstances** should you touch these wires.*

4   Seldom
    I have seldom watched a better match.
    ***Seldom** have I watched a better match.*

5   Other expressions
    which are followed by inversion are:
    little, never, not once, only then, only after, rarely

Inversion for Emphasis

The verb comes before the subject if the adverb begins the sentence.

1   Come and Go
    These are mainly used with adverbs of place.
    In this way more emphasis is put on the subject in an exclamation.
    *Here **comes** Jack!*   *There **goes** my money!*
    *Up **went** the plane into the clouds!*   *Along the road **came** Jim.*

2   Other expressions
    Live and *stand* are used in formal writing. *Now* is used with *to be*.
    *In this house **lived** Charles Dickens.*
    *On a hill outside the town **stands** the castle.*
    ***Now is** the best time to visit the Channel Islands.*

Question Tags

1 Tags are a way of adding a question to a statement, so that it becomes a question. If the intonation of the tag rises, it may be a genuine question, or a request for confirmation. If the intonation falls, the speaker expects agreement.

2 A positive statement has a negative tag, and expects the answer 'Yes'.
    You agree with me, don't you?
A negative statement has a positive tag, and expects the answer 'No'.
    You don't take sugar, do you?

3 It is possible for a positive tag to follow a positive statement, to express interest, or ask for confirmation. These are less common.
    So you like working here, do you?
Tags with *will* and *won't* can be used after imperatives.
    Don't drive too fast, will you?
Let's ... has a tag formed with *shall.*
    Let's have a drink, shall we?

4 Tags generally repeat auxiliaries, or *do/did.*
    Helen lives here, doesn't she?
    You left early, didn't you?
    Jack was born in Italy, wasn't he?
    You will help me, won't you?
    Someone's got to pay, haven't they?

Activities

1

Choose the most suitable words underlined in each sentence.

a) Let's go to London next weekend, shall we/won't we?
b) You shouldn't have told me, did you/should you?
c) Jim hasn't been waiting long, was he/has he?
d) You won't tell anyone about this, do you/will you?
e) You're not doing what I told you, do you/are you?
f) Answer the phone for me, will you/do you?
g) George can't have noticed, can he/has he?
h) You've got to leave now, don't you/haven't you?
i) Pam and Tim got married last year, didn't they/haven't they?
j) I don't think John's very friendly, does he/is he?

2

Add a question tag to each sentence. (Do not use positive tags for positive statements here.)

a) Don't leave anything behind, *will you?*
b) David is bringing some wine,....................?
c) You'll be home before midnight,..................?
d) Harry was working in Bristol then,...............?
e) Nobody knows who invented the wheel,.............?
f) You don't need me any more,....................?
g) The ticket to London doesn't cost a lot,.........?
h) Let's invite the Smiths from next door,..........?
i) You aren't too busy to talk,....................?
j) Jean owns a restaurant,..........................?

3

Rewrite each
sentence,
beginning as
shown, so that
the meaning stays
the same.

a) Tony was not only late, but he had left all his books behind.
   Not only *was Tony late, but he had left all his books behind*.

b) I had no sooner gone to bed than someone rang my doorbell.
   No sooner ....

c) I have seldom stayed in a worse hotel.
   Seldom ....

d) I have never heard such nonsense!
   Never ....

e) I realised only then that I had lost my keys.
   Only then ....

f) The economic situation has rarely been worse.
   Rarely ....

g) The manager not once offered us an apology.
   Not once ....

h) You should not send money to us by post under any circumstances.
   Under no circumstances ....

i) I understood *Hamlet* only after seeing it on the stage.
   Only after seeing *Hamlet* ....

j) The embassy staff little realised that Ted was a secret agent.
   Little ....

4

Rewrite each
sentence so that it
begins with the
word or words
underlined.

a) The best time to buy a house is <u>now</u>.
   Now is the best time to buy a house..................................

b) The bus came <u>round the corner</u>.
   ....

c) The price of petrol went <u>up</u>.
   ....

d) The Parthenon stands <u>on the top</u> of the Acropolis.
   ....

e) The wheels of the engine went <u>round and round</u>.
   ....

f) Winston Churchill lived <u>in this house</u>.
   ....

g) The flag went <u>down</u>.
   ....

h) The best part of the story comes <u>now</u>.
   ....

KEY POINTS

1   Inversion after negative adverbs is more common in formal speech and writing. The adverb has to be at the beginning of the sentence or clause.

2   Intonation carries important meaning in question tags. Rising tags are questions, level tags are checking information.
Your name's Pauline, isn't it?   (question)
Your name's Pauline, isn't it?   (checking)

3   Inversion with *come* and *go* is informal.
Look out, here comes the teacher!

> **SEE ALSO**
>
> **Unit 35**
> Progress test

Unit 32 Expressing reason, text organisers

Explanations

Reason

1   As, since and for
    As and *since* have the meaning of *because* and can begin a sentence.
    For also has the meaning of *because* but cannot begin a sentence and is
    followed by a clause. It is only used in written language.
        As/since *it was late, we decided to go home.*
        Peter has given up sailing, ***for*** *he doesn't have the time.*

2   On account of, owing to and due to
    On account of has the meaning of *because of*.
        Everyone was depressed ***on account of*** *the bad weather.*
    Due to and *owing to* also have the meaning of *because of*, and can be used in
    the same way as *on account of*. However, some grammars make this
    difference between them:
        Sue's success was ***due to*** *her hard work.* (noun + to be + due to)
        Sue succeeded ***owing to*** *her hard work.* (verb + owing to)

Text organisers

This term covers words and phrases which make clear the organisation of what
we say or write. Most of the expressions listed are more commonly used in
writing, or formal speech. The activities give examples of how these words and
phrases can be used.

1   Sequencing
    In writing, we often order the points we are making by showing their order
    or sequence. Points can be introduced by:
        *First (of all)......, secondly ...., next.........., then......, finally/lastly/last of
        all........*
    In narrative, the sequence of events can be introduced by:
        First......, then......, after that......, finally/in the end......,

2   Adding
    In writing, we can introduce additional points with these words and
    phrases. These are all formal in use:
        *Furthermore......., moreover........, in addition to this......., as well as
        this........, besides this.......*

3   Giving opinions
    Personal opinions can be introduced in writing by:
        Personally......., in my own opinion/view.........

4 Giving examples
Examples are introduced by:
   For example......, for instance.......
Such as is another way of giving examples. It is not used at the beginning of
a sentence.
   *The factory produces electrical goods, **such as** food mixers and other
   kitchen appliances.*

5 Showing result
Some formal ways of showing result are:
   Consequently......., as a result......., thus........

6 Making contrasts
In writing, a contrasting point can be introduced by:
   On the other hand......., however........., nevertheless.......
Other contrasts can be made with:
   In contrast......, in comparison.......

7 Summing up
We can introduce a summing up of our points with:
   In conclusion......., to sum up.......

Activities

1
Choose the most
suitable word or
phrase
underlined in
each sentence.

a) Many people feel nervous about flying, and worry about the possibility of an accident. Furthermore/However, according to statistics, flying is actually safer than walking down the street.

b) Our local supermarket no longer opens every day, as/on account of very few people live in our village.

c) There are a number of objections to the planned motorway. As well as this/First of all, the new road will destroy valuable farming land. In contrast/In addition to this, it will bring thousands of vehicles to our quiet area, and flood the countryside with tourists. As a result/For example, our peaceful way of life will be destroyed for ever.

d) We conducted a survey of accommodation in the town, and came up with some interesting results. The hotels we saw were rather expensive, and consequently/moreover the actual facilities on offer were not always impressive. Besides this/In contrast, there were many guest houses, offering just bed and breakfast, which were not only good value but also had much better rooms than the hotels did. Finally/Personally, I would recommend 'The Oaks', a particularly impressive guest house in Long Harbour Road.

e) Owing to/Since the increased demand for parking spaces, the company has decided to enlarge the car-park behind the main building. Consequently/Nevertheless the exit road on the west side of the car park will be closed from Monday 5th November to allow building work to begin.

2
Put *one* suitable
word in each
space.

a) *In* conclusion, I would like to thank everyone for all the help
they have given me.
b) .... it's too late to finish the work today, we'll come back tomorrow.
c) The flight was delayed .... a result of the high winds.
d) This radio is expensive, but .... the other hand it has very good reception.
e) First ...... all, I would like to welcome everyone to our annual dinner.
f) John is a hard worker. As ...... as this, he is completely reliable.
g) Science has not entirely changed the way we think. ...... instance, we still
speak of the 'sunrise' although we know it is the earth that is moving.
h) Although this building project seems attractive, in my ...... it would be a
mistake to spend so much money on it.

3
Put one of the
expressions listed
into each space in
the text. Use each
expression once
only.

| as a result   besides this   consequently   first of all   however |
| moreover   on the other hand   personally   since   such as |

Owning a car has several advantages. (1) *First of all*, you can go wherever
you want, whenever you want. You don't have to depend on public transport
and (2) .... you feel more independent. (3) .... you are able to give lifts to
friends, or carry heavy loads of shopping. (4) ...., there can be problems,
especially if you live in a city. Running a car can be expensive, and you have to
spend money on items (5) .... petrol, servicing the car, and repairs. You
might also have problems with parking, as everywhere is becoming more and
more crowded with cars. (6) ...., most people feel that the advantages of
owning a car outweigh the disadvantages. (7) .... most young people of my
age start driving as soon as they can. (8) ...., I think that cars nowadays have
become essential, but I also feel that they cause a lot of problems, (9) .... they
are noisy and dirty. (10) .... , the large number of cars on the road means that
most towns and cities are organised for the convenience of cars, and the needs
of pedestrians are ignored.

KEY POINTS

1   Text organisers help readers (and listeners to formal speeches) to follow the
organisation of the text. They make argumentative writing easier to
understand.

2   These expressions should be studied in context so that the meaning is clear.
Most of the expressions listed are formal in use.

Unit 33
It and there, it and adjectives, one, someone etc, what, whatever, possessives and reflexives

Explanations

It and there

It generally refers to something already mentioned, but is also used in some phrases which do not have a grammatical subject. *There* is used with *to be* to describe the existence of something.

> There is **a good film** on tonight. **It** stars Kim Bassinger.
> *It's raining again.*   *It's half past six.*
> *It doesn't matter.*   *It's a long way.*   *It's time to go.*

It and adjectives

It is also used in patterns with an adjective followed by an infinitive or *-ing*. In colloquial speech, *it* and the verb *to be* are often left out.

> *It's good to see you.*   **Good** *to see you.*
> *It was nice meeting you.*   **Nice** *meeting you.*

One

1 *One* can be used as a pronoun, and has a plural *ones*.
> *I don't like **this one**. I only like **green ones**.*

2 *One* can also be used with *another* to refer to both subjects.
> *Martin and David can't stand **one another**.*
> This means that Martin can't stand David, and David can't stand Martin.

3 In formal speech and writing, *one* can be used instead of *you* to refer to 'anybody'. This use of *one* is considered over-formal by many speakers.
> *What does **one** wear to a dinner of this kind?*
> *It's not pleasant to hear **oneself** described by **one's** employees.*

Someone, everyone, anyone, everyone, somewhere etc

1 *-body* can be used instead of *-one* without change in meaning.

2 Words beginning *some* or *any* follow the usual patterns for these words, with '*any*' words normally used in questions and after negatives.
> *There's **something** under the desk. Can you see **anything**?*

3 '*Some*' words can be used in questions when these refer to a definite idea.
> *Are you looking for **somewhere** to stay?*
> *Could **someone** help me, please?*

150

4 Words beginning *any* can be used in positive statements when they refer to 'every possibility'.
> *Please sit **anywhere** you like. **Anyone** who's tall will do.*

What as pronoun

What can be used as a pronoun meaning 'the thing or things which'.
> ***What** we need is a spanner.*

Whatever, whoever, wherever, whenever, whatever, why ever, however

1 These are used to add emphasis to the question word.
> *What are you doing?* becomes ***Whatever** are you doing?* (with surprise)

2 Another use adds the meaning of 'any at all'.
> ***Whatever** you say is wrong! **Anything at all** you say is wrong!*

Reflexives

1 These can be used for emphasis.
> *Why don't you do it **yourself**?   I paid for the tickets **myself**.*

2 These also include actions which involve doing something to yourself.
> *Sue **cut herself**.   I have **hurt myself**.   Did you **enjoy yourself**?*

Possessives: parts of the body

Parts of the body can be described without using a possessive adjective in some expressions after prepositions:
> *Jack gave Bill a punch **on the nose**. I grabbed him **by the arm**.*
> *Jack punched Bill **on the nose**. I looked him **in the eyes**.*

Activities

1
Rewrite each sentence, beginning as shown, so that it has the same meaning.

a) I don't mind what you do, but don't tell Jane I was here.
Whatever *you do, don't tell Jane I was here.*

b) The person who stole the painting must have been tall.
Whoever ....
c) What on earth is the time!
Whatever ....
d) I'd like to know why you told me a lie.
Why ever ....
e) Every time I go on holiday, the weather gets worse.
Whenever ....

f) Tell me where you have been!
Wherever ....

g) How on earth did you know I was going to be here?
However ....

h) Any place I hang my hat, I call home!
Wherever ....

i) I won't believe you, no matter what you say.
Whatever ....

j) If you are going to do something, do it now!
Whatever ....

2

Rewrite each sentence so that it contains the words in capitals in the order they are given.

a) John patted my back.   GAVE ME
John gave me a pat on the back.

b) Don't hold a rabbit's ears and pick it up.   BY THE
....

c) I'll never be able to look at Tanya's face again.   LOOK TANYA
....

d) Sue grabbed the thief's arm.   BY THE
....

e) Helen took the baby's hand.   BY THE
....

f) The bee stung my arm.   STUNG ME
....

g) Somebody gave me a black eye.   PUNCHED
....

h) Jane patted the dog's head.   ON THE
....

i) 'It's my arm! I'm hit!' said Billy the Kid.   WOUNDED
....

j) I felt someone pat my shoulder.   ME
....

3

Rewrite each sentence so that it begins with *it* or *there*.

a) The local cinema has a good film on at the moment.
There is a good film on at the local cinema at the moment.

b) I can't drink coffee so late at night.
....

c) Don't worry if you can't answer all the questions.
....

d) A storm is coming, I think.
....

e) The fridge is empty.
....

f) This journey has been tiring.
....

g) If you don't hurry all the beer will be gone.
....

h) The station is far away.

....

i) Let's have a break now.

....

j) I enjoyed seeing you.

....

4

Rewrite each sentence, beginning as shown, so that the meaning stays the same.

a) Was it enjoyable at the beach, Joe?
Did you *enjoy yourself at the beach, Joe?*

b) We really need a new fridge.
What ....

c) There's a lot of fog today.
It's ....

d) People who believe in ghosts are a bit crazy!
Anyone ....

e) Just call me any time you need me.
Whenever ....

f) I was very interested in our conversation.
It was interesting ....

g) John is hurt.
John has ....

h) Why did you do that?
Whatever ....

i) Never mind.
It ....

j) These bookshelves are my own work.
I made ....

5

Complete each sentence with the most suitable word or phrase.

a) I like this painting but I don't think much of those ..*C*.. .
A) rest   B) other   C) ones   D) besides

b) What would .... like to do this morning?
A) someone   B) one   C) yourself   D) you

c) Did you enjoy .... ?
A) at the party   B) the party   C) yourself the party
D) with yourself at the party

d) ....nothing much to do in this town.
A) There's   B) It's not   C) There's not   D) It's

153

e) .... you do, don't tell Harry that we've lost his camera.
    A) anything   B) what   C) whatever   D) it's better

f) One prefers to shop at Harrods, ...
    A) doesn't one   B) isn't it   C) don't you   D) isn't one

g) .... didn't you tell me that you felt too ill to work?
    A) whoever   B) whatever   C) however   D) why ever

h) Then George punched the policeman .... the face!
    A) at   B) on   C) to   D) in

i) Harry shook my hand and said, 'Pleased .... you.'
    A) to meet   B) to introduce   C) to shake   D) to acquaint

j) Please invite .... you like to the reception.
    A) one   B) anyone   C) ones   D) all

KEY POINTS

1   In some cases, *it* does not refer to another noun, but stands as the subject of verbs such as *to be* and *rain*.

2   It is possible to use *some* and words made from it in interrogative sentences, where a definite idea is referred to.
    *Are you looking for **someone**?*

3   Some verbs (*cut, enjoy, hurt*) require a reflexive (*myself* etc.) if there is no other object.
    I enjoyed the party.
    *I enjoyed **myself**.*
    Martha cut her finger.
    *Martha cut **herself**.*

SEE ALSO
Unit 35
Progress test

Unit 34 Spelling and pronunciation

Explanations

Common
spelling problems

1   Words that end in *-ful*
    These have only one 'l' when *-ful* is a suffix.
       useful   helpful

2   Doubling of consonants
    Adjectives form adverbs by adding *-ly*.
       usefully   helpfully
    Words with one syllable, ending in one vowel and one consonant double
    the consonant when adding *-ing*, *-ed* or *-er*.
       swim swimming   fit fitted   thin   thinner
    Two-syllable words also double the last consonant.
       prefer preferred   travel traveller

3   Words ending in 'y'
    (Plurals, Present Simple, Past Simple, *-ful*, *-ness*).
    One-syllable words ending in one vowel and 'y' do not change.
       try tries tried   but *boy boys*
    One-syllable words do not change when adding *-ful* and *-ness*.
       joyful   shyness
    All two-syllable words change except ones with one vowel before'y'.
       reply replies replied   happiness   beautiful
    but *destroyed*
    These rules do not apply to adding *-ing*.
       try trying   study studying   annoy annoying

4   Words with *ie* and *ei*
    The general rule is 'i' before 'e' except after 'c', as long as the sound is 'ee'.
       receive   relief   feign (the sound is not 'ee')

Spelling and
pronunciation

Note the ways of spelling the underlined sounds in each list, and that the ways
of spelling these sounds may represent different sounds in other words. Note
that schwa (ə) is an unstressed sound.

1   Vowel sounds
       /ʌ/   *l<u>o</u>ve   s<u>u</u>dden   bl<u>oo</u>d*
       /əʊ/   *b<u>oa</u>t   p<u>o</u>st   alth<u>ough</u>   kn<u>ow</u>   t<u>oe</u>*
       /eə/   *<u>air</u>   th<u>ere</u>   b<u>are</u>   w<u>ear</u>*
       /ɑ/   *h<u>ea</u>rt   p<u>a</u>rt*
       /ɜ:/   *w<u>or</u>d   h<u>ear</u>d   f<u>ur</u>ther   exp<u>er</u>t   h<u>ur</u>t*
       /aʊ/   *n<u>ow</u>   sh<u>out</u>   pl<u>ough</u>   dr<u>ow</u>n*

/ʌ/ <u>cu</u>ff r<u>ou</u>gh L<u>o</u>ndon
/eɪ/ w<u>ai</u>t g<u>a</u>te w<u>ei</u>ght gr<u>ea</u>t l<u>ay</u>
/aɪ/ br<u>igh</u>t h<u>eigh</u>t s<u>i</u>te <u>eye</u>
/ɔ/ d<u>oo</u>r p<u>our</u>
schwa /ə/ p<u>o</u>tato <u>a</u>round s<u>u</u>ggest p<u>er</u>haps neckl<u>a</u>ce

2 Consonant sounds
/ʃ/ <u>sh</u>ame deli<u>ci</u>ous posi<u>ti</u>on in<u>s</u>urance
/tʃ/ <u>ch</u>urch furni<u>t</u>ure wa<u>tch</u>es
/ʒ/ lei<u>s</u>ure confu<u>si</u>on mea<u>s</u>ure

3 Words ending in -*ough*
Like 'now' /aʊ/ pl<u>ough</u> b<u>ough</u>   Like 'cuff' /ʌf/ en<u>ough</u> r<u>ough</u> t<u>ough</u>
Like 'toe' /əʊ/ th<u>ough</u> d<u>ough</u>   Like 'off' /ɒf/ c<u>ough</u>

4 Words containing -*st* where *t* is not pronounced
listen glisten hasten fasten
castle whistle bristle mistletoe

5 Words containing -*mb* and -*bt* where *b* is not pronounced
plumber thumb comb lamb dumb tomb
debt doubt subtle

Activities

1
Correct any words spelled incorrectly.

a) studing	*studying*	reciept	....
b) destroying	....	wonderfull	....
c) donkies	....	swiming	....
d) flys	....	regreted	....
e) niece	....	hopefuly	....
f) hurryed	....	applying	....
g) furnichure	....	heard	....
h) enough	....	inshurance	....
i) wellcome	....	happily	....
j) hotter	....	advertisment	....

2
Find a word from the list which rhymes with each word given.

> home go white search store
> stuff come plumber wait cow

a) church	*search*	f) dumb	....
b) hate	....	g) plough	....
c) rough	....	h) height	....
d) throw	....	i) summer	....
e) comb	....	j) pour	....

3
Write the word
ending in the
suffix given.

a) supply (ing)   *supplying*
b) destroy (ed)   ....
c) apply (ed)   ....
d) lonely (ness)   ....
e) employ (s)   ....
f) cry (s)   ....
g) silly (ness)   ....
h) annoy (s)   ....
i) beauty (ful)   ....
j) pretty (ness)   ....

4
Find one word in
each group of
words which
does not have the
same vowel
sound (sounds
are underlined in
some words).

a) bec<u>o</u>me sung c<u>o</u>mpany cold flood *cold*
b) plate treat wait weight great ....
c) lose used choose blouse few ....
d) doubt bough ought now shout ....
e) lost post toast ghost host ....
f) mist missed list iced kissed ....
g) love done gone sunk won ....
h) bird search heart word church ....
i) two show though go owe ....
j) <u>a</u>bout wond<u>er</u> s<u>u</u>ppose ref<u>er</u> col<u>our</u> ....

5
Correct any
words spelled
incorrectly.

a) sincerly   *sincerely*   dictionry   ....
b) different   ....   intresting   ....
c) loverly   ....   necessary   ....
d) writting   ....   unninteresting   ....
e) pulover   ....   definitly   ....
f) freind   ....   responsable   ....
g) holliday   ....   quantity   ....
h) likelihood   ....   lugage   ....
i) impatient   ....   student   ....
j) finaly   ....   pavement   ....

6
Correct any
words spelled
incorrectly.

a) tomorow   *tomorrow*   glases   ....
b) conversation   ....   magasine   ....
c) atmosfere   ....   pacient   ....
d) sandwits   ....   bicycle   ....
e) gaurd   ....   running   ....
f) recomend   ....   skillfull   ....
g) tobaco   ....   acquaintance   ....
h) recieve   ....   attatch   ....
i) chimney   ....   cuboard   ....
j) electrisity   ....   expencive   ....

Unit 35 Progress test

(Units 31, 32, 33, 34)

1

Put *one* suitable word in each space.

I will always remember my first day working at the Excelsior Food Company. First of (1) ..... , I was given a greasy overall. (2) ..... had worn it before had certainly never washed it! When I mentioned this (3) ..... the foreman he said,' You're not afraid of a bit of dirt, (4) ..... you?' I wanted to say that I thought (5) ..... was supposed to be a high standard of cleanliness in a food factory, but I managed to control (6) ..... . (7) ..... I was given my first job, (8) ..... involved sweeping the floor. (9) ..... only was my overall filthy, but the whole factory looked as if (10) ..... had ever cleaned it properly. (11) ..... were also (12) ..... I later discovered to be animals' ears scattered around the place. (13) ..... it was my first day, I didn't say anything about this. (14) ..... that I had to put pies into boxes for the rest of the morning. (15) ..... were two kinds of boxes. The large (16) ..... had to be loaded onto lorries for delivery, and were sent out to places (17) ..... as hotels and restaurants. (18) .... was supposed to put the others into the cold-store, but (19) .... this person was, they had obviously forgotten about it. As a (20) ...., there was soon a huge pile of boxes waiting to be moved. Then I discovered that I was supposed to be moving them!

2

Rewrite each sentence, beginning as shown, so that the meaning stays the same.

a) Under no circumstances should you press both buttons at once.
   You ....

b) It was cold, so I decided to wear two pullovers.
   As ....

c) Did you have a good time at the party?
   Did you enjoy ....

d) Outside the cinema somebody grabbed my arm.
   Outside the cinema I ....

e) The army's defeat was due to poor organisation.
   The army was defeated ....

f) Jean not once offered her boss a word of apology.
   Not once ....

g) There's no food in the house, I'm afraid.
   There's nothing ....

h) It's pointless going on any further tonight.
   There's ....

i) It's difficult to describe what Sally saw.
   What ....

j) I have seldom had a more relaxing holiday.
   Seldom ....

158

3

Complete each sentence with the most suitable word or phrase.

a) One really shouldn't drink too much,............?
    A) does one   B) should you   C) do you   D) should one

b) ...., I would like to propose a toast.
    A) For example   B) In conclusion   C) On the other hand   D) Thus

c) Do you think .... could help me choose a pair of trousers?
    A) someone   B) anyone   C) whoever   D) there

d) .... doesn't seem to be anyone at home.
    A) It   B) One   C) There   D) Whenever

e) .... did I realise that the murderer was still in the house!
    A) Seldom   B) Under no circumstances   C) Only after   D) Only then

f) ...., I don't believe that prices will rise next year.
    A) In contrast   B) Personally   C) Not only   D) Whatever

g) You're covered in mud! .... is your mother going to say!
    A) Rarely   B) Furthermore   C) Whatever   D) On account of

h) Oh bother, ... the bus I wanted to catch!
    A) wherever   B) it's left   C) there goes   D) owing to

i) Please help yourselves to .... you like.
    A) whoever   B) nothing   C) everywhere   D) anything

j) Nobody's got to stay late this evening,..............?
    A) is it?   B) have they   C) isn't it?   D) don't they

Unit 36 Final test

1

Put each verb in brackets into a suitable tense.

a) I (wait) .... for you for the past hour! What (you do) .... all this time?

b) While I (walk) .... to the bus-stop, I realised I (leave) .... the cooker on.

c) Why didn't you phone me? If I (knew) .... you were ill, I (come) .... to see you.

d) Hello, Pat. I (phone) .... to ask if you (do) ......anything this Saturday.

e) By the time Big Jim (become) .... heavyweight boxing champion he (win) .... over thirty fights.

f) I (not see) .... you for ages. What (you do).............?

g) Hurry up! I (think) .... you (be) .... ready by now.

h) If I (be) .... you, I (not spend) .... so much money.

i) Danny's train (arrive) .... tomorrow evening at 6.00 so we (meet) .... him at the station.

j) Wish me luck! If I (get) .... the job I (let) .... you know.

2

Rewrite each sentence, beginning as shown, so that the meaning stays the same.

a) I'd prefer you not to wear jeans to the office.
   I'd rather ....

b) We won't get there on time without taking a taxi.
   Unless ....

c) 'I wouldn't go swimming on a day like this, if I were you, Tom.'
   Brian advised ....

d) Although she had twisted her ankle, Sally still won the race.
   Despite her ....

e) Mike enjoys playing golf more than I do.
   I don't ....

f) I regret selling my car.
   I wish ....

g) Nobody has cut the lawn for weeks!
   The lawn ....

h) I'm sure Dick didn't mean to offend you.
   Dick can't ....

i) Have you got a smaller size than this?
   Is this ....

j) Would you like to go out for a drink?
   Do you feel ....

160

3

Use these words and phrases to make complete sentences. The sentences are all part of a letter. Make changes and add any necessary words as in the example.

Example: After/Jim/write/letter/Mary/post.
            After Jim had written the letter, Mary posted it.

Dear Uncle Charlie,

a) I/write/thank/for/cheque/you/send/me/my birthday.
    ....

b) I/decide/save/money/because/want/buy/motorbike.
    ....

c) Although I/not old/yet/have/licence/I/be able/take/test/year's time.
    ....

d) Be/difficult/live/here/country/without/kind/transport/because/be so few/ buses.
    ....

e) So/I/look forward/day/when/not have/rely/friends/lifts.
    ....

f) Hope/see/you/Christmas/when/I go/London.
    ....

Best Wishes
Denis

4

Rewrite each sentence, beginning as shown, so that the meaning stays the same.

a) I don't play tennis as well as you do.
    You ....

b) You ought to have your house painted.
    Your house ....

c) I haven't been to the dentist's for two years.
    It's ....

d) The film was so funny that I burst out laughing.
    It was ....

e) I've never flown in a helicopter before.
    This ....

f) 'You stole the money, Joe, didn't you!' said the inspector.
    The inspector accused ....

g) It is essential that this letter is posted today.
    This letter ....

h) 'Is the London train on time?' asked one of the people waiting.
    One of the people waiting wanted to know ....

i) My advice is to inform the police.
    I think you'd ....

j) They believe a single gunman carried out the attack.
    A single gunman ....

5

Complete the numbered spaces in the dialogue.

Hotel Receptionist: Hello, Grand Hotel. Can I help you?
John Jones: Yes, I would like to book two rooms at your hotel for the weekend. Do (1).........................?
Hotel Receptionist: What (2) ....?

John Jones:	I want one double room, and another room with two beds for the children.
Hotel Receptionist:	And when (3)...?
	And for (4)...?
John Jones:	I want the rooms for Friday, Saturday and Sunday night. So that's three nights, starting Friday.
Hotel Receptionist:	I see. I'm afraid we don't have exactly what you want, but I could offer you a double room and two single rooms.
John Jones:	How (5)...?
Hotel Receptionist:	The double room is £65 per night, and the singles are £32.50 each.
John Jones:	Is (6)...?
Hotel Receptionist:	Breakfast, yes, but not any other meals of course.
John Jones:	Do (7)...?
Hotel Receptionist:	Yes, our restaurant is very highly thought of, and it's open every day for lunch and dinner.
John Jones:	Thank you for your help.
	I (8) ....
Hotel Receptionist:	Yes of course, phone at any time. We will be glad to make your booking for you, if you decide to stay with us.

6

Put *one* suitable word in each space.

Our school sports were held last week, and the whole afternoon was a disaster. For a start, very (1) ..... people bothered to turn (2) .....,and there is nothing (3) ..... than trying to win a race with only three or four people cheering you on. (4) ..... people had stayed at home to watch the Cup Final (5) ..... television, or had been (6) ..... off by the weather. It rained (7) ..... afternoon, from the moment the first starting pistol (8) ..... fired, until the last medal had (9) ..... presented. I was in the high jump, (10) ..... meant running up to do my best jump and then landing (11) ..... a pool of cold muddy water. (12)..... one point it was raining (13) ..... hard that we couldn't see the runners in the 5000 metres, and it (14) ..... out that they had all stopped (15) ..... the other side of the field (16) ..... were sheltering under a tree. My other event was the javelin, but (17) ..... time I tried to throw, the javelin kept slipping from my hand. In (18) ..... case, I couldn't see where I was throwing, and when I (19) ..... finally manage to launch my javelin into the air it disappeared in the direction of the railway line, and was never seen (20) ..... . By Monday morning most of the athletes were in bed with bad colds, two runners were in hospital with broken legs, and we were still waiting for the finish of the 5000 metres.

7

Rewrite each sentence beginning as shown, so the meaning stays the same.

a) A year ago we hadn't even met!
   This ....

b) Without your help, I wouldn't have passed the exam.
   If it ....

c) Nobody knows anything about the whereabouts of the President.
   Nothing ....

d) My teachers made me work hard at school.
   I was ....

e) 'I'm awfully sorry, Carol, but I've broken your watch,' said Jim.
   Jim apologised ....

f) Please see that you lock the door when you leave.
   Please don't ....

g) Your hair needs cutting.
   It's time you ....

h) Do you own these two fields.
   Do these ....

i) Business hasn't been so bad for a long time.
   Rarely ....

j) I won't sell the painting, no matter how much you offer me.
   Whatever ....

1 Travel and Holidays

1
Complete each sentence with a word from the list.

> buffet coach-station departure-lounge harbour quay
> cabin deck destination platform runway

a) Most of the young people on the boat slept on the ...... in their sleeping bags.
b) As the train drew in to the station, Terry could see her sister waiting on the ....
c) I was so nervous about flying that I left my bag in the ....
d) By the time I got to the ...., the express bus to Scotland had left.
e) As soon as the boat left the ......, the storm began.
f) We hadn't had anything to eat, but luckily there was a .... on the train.
g) I'm afraid there is only one first-class .... free on the boat.
h) Tim reached Paris safely, but his luggage didn't reach its ......
i) There was a queue of cars on the ...., waiting for the car-ferry to the island.
j) Our plane nearly crashed into a fire-engine on the ....

2
Choose the most suitable word or words underlined.

a) David's plane was <u>cancelled/delayed</u> by thick fog.
b) The ship's owner agreed to give the <u>crew/passengers</u> a pay-rise.
c) The plane from Geneva has just <u>grounded/landed</u>.
d) We hope that you will enjoy your <u>flight/flying</u>.
e) Because of heavy snow in London, their plane was <u>diverted/deviated</u> to Manchester.
f) I won't be long. I'm just packing my last <u>luggage/suitcase</u>.
g) A sign above the seats in the plane says 'Fasten your <u>lifebelt/seat belt</u>'.
h) You have to <u>check in/check up</u> an hour before the plane leaves.
i) All duty free goods must be <u>declared/surrendered</u> at the customs.
j) On the plane a <u>stewardess/waitress</u> brought me a newspaper.
k) The plane <u>took off/took up</u> and was soon high over the city.
l) I bought a <u>simple/single</u> ticket, as I was going to return by car.

3
Use a word or words from **1** or **2** to complete each sentence. The word may be in a different form.

a) I had to .... my tickets, because I was ill and couldn't travel.
b) The train for London is now arriving at .... three.
c) The plane .... on time but arrived half an hour late.
d) We finally reached our .... after travelling all day.
e) It was hard to find a seat on the train as there were so many ......
f) While we were waiting at the station we had a bite to eat in the ...
g) I felt seasick so I went to my .... and tried to sleep.
h) Do you want a return ticket, or a .... ?
i) The customs officer asked Bill if he had anything to ....
j) There is a small .... here for fishing boats and yachts.
k) How much .... am I allowed to take with me on the plane?
l) The 8.55 from Hull will be 30 minutes late. We apologise for the ....

4

Match these words with the definitions given.

> an expedition   a flight   a tour   a voyage   a package tour
> an itinerary   a trip   travel   a cruise   a crossing

a) A journey by ship for pleasure. ....
b) A journey by plane. ....
c) The plan of a journey. ....
d) An informal word for journey. Sometimes meaning a short journey. ....
e) A journey for a scientific or special purpose. ....
f) A holiday which includes organised travel and accommodation. ....
g) Taking journeys, as a general idea. ....
h) A journey by sea. ....
i) An organised journey to see the sights of a place. ....
j) A journey from one side of the sea to the other. ....

5

Use a word from **4** in each sentence.

a) The travel agent will send you the .... for your trip.
b) My neighbours went on a guided .... of Rome.
c) The first time I went from England to France we had a very rough ....
d) The first prize in the competition is a luxury Mediterranean ....
e) When you go on a/an ...., you pay one price which covers everything.
f) The college organised a/an .... to search for the ancient ruins.
g) Olympic Airways announces the arrival of .... OA 269 from Athens.
h) The Titanic sank on its first .... in 1912.
i) .... is one of my main interests.
j) Mr Dean is away on a business .... at the moment. Can I help you?

6

Replace the words underlined in each sentence with a word from the list.

> camp-site   book   hostel   accommodation   double
> hitch-hike   a fortnight   guest-house   vacancy   porter

a) I stayed in France for <u>two weeks</u> last year. ....
b) It's difficult to find <u>anywhere to stay</u> in this town in the summer. ....
c) We were short of money so we decided to <u>get lifts in other people's cars</u>. ....
d) I'd like a room for the night please. A <u>room for two people</u>. ....
e) The place where we stayed wasn't a hotel but a <u>private house where you pay to stay and have meals</u>. ....
f) I'd like to <u>reserve</u> three single rooms for next week, please. ....
g) It was raining, and we couldn't find a <u>place to put our tent</u>. ....
h) I'd like a room for the night please. Do you have a <u>free one</u>? ....
i) The school has its own <u>place for students to stay</u>. ....
j) We gave a tip to the <u>person who carried our bags in the hotel</u>. ....

7
Use a dictionary to find compound words beginning *sea-*. Complete each sentence with one of these words.

a) Last year we decided not to spend our holidays in the country as usual, and we went to the .... instead.
b) There's a restaurant near the harbour that serves wonderful ....
c) The beach was covered in piles of smelly green ....
d) This town is very high up. It's over a thousand metres above ......
e) We drove along the .... but we couldn't find anywhere to park.
f) Tourists were throwing bread to the .... flying behind the ship.
g) Luckily I had taken some travel pills so I didn't feel ....
h) Children were building sand castles on the ....

8
Choose the most suitable word or phrase to complete each sentence.

a) They .... all day swimming and sunbathing at the beach.
   A) passed   B) used   C) spent   D) occupied
b) The hotel room .... over a beautiful garden.
   A) viewed out   B) faced up   C) opened up   D) looked out
c) We didn't .... to the station in time to catch the train.
   A) get   B) reach   C) arrive   D) make
d) I was in such a hurry that I left one of my bags ....
   A) out   B) aside   C) on   D) behind
e) Mr Hill had his money stolen and couldn't .... his hotel bill.
   A) pay up   B) pay   C) pay for   D) pay out
f) Jane lost her case because it did not have a/an .... with her name on.
   A) ticket   B) poster   C) label   D) identification
g) Take the bus, and .... at Oxford Circus.
   A) get out   B) get off   C) get down   D) get away
h) I was too tired to .... my suitcase and hang my clothes in the wardrobe.
   A) unpack   B) empty   C) put out   D) disorder
i) On the first day of our holiday we just .... by the hotel pool.
   A) enjoyed   B) calmed   C) comforted   D) relaxed
j) The wind was blowing so much that we couldn't .... our tent.
   A) raise   B) put up   C) make up   D) build

9
Rewrite each sentence, beginning as shown, so that it contains an expression with *have*.

a) I sunbathed for a while, and then went swimming.
   I sunbathed for a while, and then ....
b) I really enjoyed my holiday last year.
   I ....
c) David crashed his car while he was driving to Spain.
   David ....
d) When we left, Maria wished us a safe journey.
   'Goodbye,' said Maria, 'and ....'
e) Most of the people on the beach were wearing very little.
   Most of the people on the beach ....
f) We couldn't decide about our holiday but then Sue thought of something.
   We couldn't decide about our holiday until Sue ....
g) There was a party at Martin's house last night.
   Martin ....

h) Brenda couldn't go away for the weekend because she was busy.
Brenda couldn't go away for the weekend because she ....

i) Ian didn't know how to water-ski, but he gave it a try.
Ian didn't know how to water-ski but he ....

j) Laura suspected that the hotel food was going to be bad.
Laura ....

2 Work and Employment

1
Match each job in list A with a place in list B. More than one answer may be possible.

A
| cashier farmer mechanic photographer typist
cook hairdresser miner pilot vicar
dentist librarian musician porter waiter |

B
| bank garage studio kitchen coal-mine
cockpit hotel office surgery salon
field concert hall restaurant church library |

cashier/bank

2
Match each job from the list with the sentence which best refers to the job.

| accountant chef estate agent plumber
architect dustman firefighter postman/woman
carpenter electrician optician vet |

a) Yesterday I had to give an injection to an injured bull. *vet* .
b) I get rather tired of picking up rubbish all day. ....
c) I can help you sell your house. ....
d) I can make new doors for the wardrobe if you like. ....
e) Make sure that the fish is fresh by looking at the eyes. ....
f) I'll come round and replace all the pipes in the kitchen. ....
g) Unless you keep the receipts you'll pay more tax. ....
h) The cause was either an electrical fault or a cigarette. ....
i) Always turn the power off at the mains before you start. ....
j) You can see the balcony on the plan for the second floor. ....
k) It's a registered parcel. Can you sign here? ....
l) This pair also protects your eyes from the sun. ....

3
Which person from **1** and **2** would you need in each situation?

a) One of the radiators has burst and flooded your bedroom. ....
b) You are very short-sighted and get headaches when you read. ....
c) You have to carry a lot of heavy bags at the airport. ....
d) You think you need three fillings. ....
e) Your fringe is too long and you want a perm. ....

167

f) The floorboards in the living room need replacing. ....

g) Your pet goat has started sneezing. ....

h) You have read the menu twice and you are feeling hungry. ....

i) When you turn on your cooker, the fridge turns off. ....

j) Your car makes a funny whistling noise. ....

4

Complete each sentence with a word from the list. The words can be used more than once.

| business   job   living   work |

a) Jack makes his .... working as a journalist.

b) She has just left to go to ...., I'm afraid.

c) They worked very hard and now have their own ....

d) There are still nearly two million people without ....

e) The cost of .... has risen greatly over recent years.

f) Stop interfering! This is none of your ....

g) Lucy has a very good .... in an international company.

h) I can't come out tonight. I've got too much .... to do.

i) Some ....-men came and dug a hole in the road outside.

j) An early .... by Picasso was sold for £2,000,000.

5

Complete each sentence with a word from the list. Use each word once only.

| call   draw   fall   get   take   come   face   fill   go   turn |

a) I think we should .... over our plan again before we tell the managing director.

b) Have you .... up with any new ideas for advertising the new products?

c) Our deal with the Chinese company may......... through, but we can sell the machinery to the German firm if necessary.

d) You have to .... in this form, and return it to the personnel manager.

e) She didn't .... on with her boss, so she left the company.

f) If they don't give us a better price, we'll .... down their offer.

g) I'm afraid we have to .... up to the fact that the company is losing money.

h) Our lawyers are going to .... up a new contract tomorrow.

i) A multi-national company is trying to .... over our firm, but we want to stay independent.

j) We had to .... off the office party because of the economic situation.

6

Complete each sentence a) to j) with one of the endings 1) to 10). Use each ending once only.

a) If you work hard, the company will give you.....

b) In a different job I could get a higher....

c) The best way to find new staff is to put a/an......

d) Because he had stolen the money, we decided that ......

e) She has a pleasant personality but hasn't got the right ......

f) In the meeting we are going to discuss the....

g) As he has three young children he doesn't want ......

h) I think it would be a good idea to send in your.....

i) I'm afraid that in this job there aren't very good ......

j) We cannot give you the job without .....

1) .... qualifications for a job of this kind.
2) .... advertisement in the local press on Friday.
3) .... application for the job as soon as possible.
4) .... promotion to a more responsible position.
5) .... full-time employment at the moment.
6) .... references from your previous employer.
7) .... dismissing him was the only possible action we could take.
8) .... prospects for the future at the moment.
9) .... salary and better conditions of employment.
10) .... appointment of a new sales representative.

7
Complete each sentence with a word formed from the word in capitals.

a) She found a good job working in an .... agency. ADVERTISEMENT
b) He is enthusiastic, but not well- .... QUALIFICATIONS
c) This company treats all its .... equally. EMPLOY
d) After her ...., she wrote a novel. RETIRE
e) Include details of all your .... for last year. EARN
f) Last week he offered the boss his .... RESIGN
g) Write all the details on this .... form. APPLY
h) After losing her job she was .... for a month. EMPLOY
i) Our firm closed down because of the ...... situation. ECONOMY
j) The sale of the company buildings was very .... PROFIT

8
Choose the most suitable word or phrase underlined in each sentence.

a) The building workers were paid their income/salary/wages every Friday.
b) She's only here for three weeks. It's a/an full-time/overtime/ temporary job.
c) When he retired he received a monthly bonus/pension/reward.
d) Apparently she earns/gains/wins over £20,000 a year.
e) While the boss is away, Sue will be in charge/in control/in place of the office.
f) Could I have two days away/off/out next week to visit my mother?
g) Paul was always arriving late, and in the end he was pushed/sacked/ thrown.
h) When I left the job, I had to hand in my application/dismissal/notice three weeks beforehand.
i) How much exactly do you do/make/take in your new job?
j) If you have to travel on company business, we will pay your costs/ expenses/needs.

9

Rewrite each sentence so that it contains the word or words given, and so that the meaning stays the same. Do not change the words in any way.

a) Terry works in a different place now.   JOB

....

b) A good boss looks after everyone in the company.   EMPLOYER

....

c) I am sure you will learn a lot in this job.   EXPERIENCE

....

d) This job is a good way to earn money, but that's all. LIVING

....

e) The firm gave me a rise after I had worked there a
year.   RAISED

....

f) The company was profitable last year.   MADE

....

g) I had to be interviewed at the head office.   ATTEND

....

h) My monthly salary is £1000.   A YEAR

....

i) Jill is employed by a firm of accountants.   WORKS

....

j) We advertised the job in the paper.   PUT

....

3 Sport and Leisure

1

Complete each sentence with a word from the list. Use each word once only.

handlebars racket rope glasses net costume
whistle saddle gloves rod club ice

a) When Brenda entered the swimming competition she bought a new ......
b) I learned to ride a horse without using a ....
c) Gemma tried to hit the golf-ball with her ...., but missed it.
d) After the tennis match, one of the players jumped over the ....
e) Diana's bike crashed into a tree, and she was thrown over the ......
f) A mountain-climber's life may depend on their ....
g) Open-air skating can be dangerous if the .... is too thin.
h) Peter put his .... in front of his face to protect himself from his opponent's punches.
i) Suddenly the referee blew his ...... and pointed to the penalty spot.
j) Skiing can be dangerous if you don't wear dark ....
k) I had to play the doubles match with a borrowed ....
l) Terry went fishing with the new .... his parents gave him.

2

Match these
words with the
comments given.

> billiards   crossword   embroidery   hiking
> camping   draughts   gambling   jigsaw
> cards   do-it-yourself   gardening   model-making

a) Catherine dealt, and gave me the ace, king and queen of hearts. ....
b) You need a small needle, and threads of different colours. ....
c) I couldn't find ten down, so I looked for words in the dictionary. ....
d) Ian glued the parts together wrongly because he didn't read the instructions. ....
e) When Ellen is losing, she tries to knock the pieces off the board. ....
f) The path we want doesn't seem to be on the map. ....
g) Nigel missed the red, and put the pink in the pocket by mistake. ....
h) I want to put £50 on 'Ealing Comedy' to win in the 4.30 at York. ....
i) These pieces with flowers on all look the same, don't they. ....
j) Graham papered the hall while I was painting the doors. ....
k) When I woke up there was a chicken inside the tent. ....
l) The daffodils I put in haven't come up this year. ....

3

Choose the most
suitable word
underlined in
each sentence.

a) Sue came first in the 5000 metre competition/game/race.
b) Jack and Eddie arranged to meet outside the football ground/field/pitch.
c) Brenda goes jogging every morning to keep exercised/fit/trained.
d) Our team beat/defeated/won the match by two goals to nil.
e) The local stadium isn't large enough for so many audience/viewers/spectators.
f) I'm afraid I don't find basketball very interested/interesting.
g) Collecting matchbox labels is Rebecca's favourite leisure/occupation/pastime.
h) Norman won first medal/prize/reward in the cookery competition.
i) All competitors/rivals/supporters for the relay race should make their way to the track.
j) The final result was a/an draw/equal/score.

4

Replace the word
or words
underlined in
each sentence
with a word from
the list. Use each
word once only.

> arranged   outdoors   record   second
> captain   postponed   referee   side
> champion   professionally   score   spare

a) Mary plays tennis as a way of earning her living.
b) Tomorrow's hockey match has been put off for another time.
c) In motor racing last year William Green was the best driver of all.
d) The player with the lowest number of points wins the game.
e) A match between the Dutch and German teams has been fixed for next month.
f) I like going swimming in my free time.
g) Jane Briggs was the runner-up in the 100 metres hurdles.
h) Who is the player in charge of in your football team?
i) She won all her matches this season, which is a best ever performance.

j)   Charles was sent off for punching the <u>person who controls the match.</u>

k)   We decided to hold this year's dancing competition <u>in the open air</u>.

l)   Everyone agreed that United were the best <u>team</u>.

5
Complete each
sentence with a
word formed
from the word in
capitals.

a)   I have decided to take up .... as a hobby.   PHOTOGRAPH

b)   John turned up on the wrong day because of a ......-.   UNDERSTAND

c)   Her collection of old coins is extremely ....   VALUE

d)   We all thought what a .... player Helen was.   SKILL

e)   The result was very strange! In fact it was ....   BELIEF

f)   My attempt to lose weight by running was a ....   FAIL

g)   The young girl's fine performance was completely
      ..... .   EXPECT

h)   Luckily George's second jump was ....   SUCCEED

i)   It was a terrible game. Our team played very ....   IMAGINE

j)   Jackson had another violent .... with the linesman.   AGREE

6
Complete the
compound word
in each sentence
using a word
given in the list.

> board court jacket repairs collection field
> making site course hooligan pools track

a)   Everyone who goes sailing must wear a life-........ .

b)   Karen's hobby is doing her own car........ .

c)   I'm afraid that Ruth doesn't have the patience for model- ......

d)   People look bored when I talk about my stamp........ .

e)   Bring your racket and I'll meet you at the tennis......... .

f)   Because Bill wears a scarf everyone thinks he is a football.......

g)   The school has sold its playing......... to a property company.

h)   Violet won half a million pounds on the football ....

i)   I enjoy walking around the golf....... and watching people play.

j)   Every morning I jog round the running .... opposite my house.

k)   Steve jumped from the diving....... wearing all his clothes!

l)   We stayed on a lovely camp........ just outside Paris.

7
Choose the most
suitable word or
phrase to
complete each
sentence.

a)   Mary stopped swimming and just .... on the surface.
      A) sank   B) floated   C) dived   D) poured

b)   Jack turned the last corner and .... for the finishing line.
      A) approached   B) arrived   C) waited   D) headed

c)   David was trying to .... another cyclist when he crashed.
      A) overpass   B) overcome   C) overtake   D) overcharge

d)   You have to .... the person with the ball until you catch them.
      A) chase   B) rush   C) jump   D) drop

e)   The fans climbed over the fence to .... paying.
      A) avoid   B) prevent   C) abandon   D) refuse

f)   I fell over while skiing and my sister had to .... a doctor.
      A) bring   B) take   C) fetch   D) carry

g)   It's very easy to ...... over when the snow is hard.
      A) slide   B) skid   C) skate   D) slip

h) Don't .... the road until all the runners have gone by.
   A) pass B) cross C) across D) pass by
i) The swimmers .... forward as they waited to begin the race.
   A) fell B) crawled C) rolled D) leaned
j) When I was hiking in the mountains I .... on a snake.
   A) tripped B) stepped C) surprised D) carried

8
Complete each sentence with a word from the list. Use each word once only.

anywhere dinner ready through back lost
right together better off stuck used

a) After Paul's leg was injured, it took him a long time to get ....
b) Unfortunately Sally rode her bike into the mud and got ....
c) An hour before the race I went to the stadium and started to get ....
d) Some of the competitors got .... because of the thick fog.
e) I tried learning to do embroidery but I didn't get ....
f) Jean worked on her stamp collection while Barry was getting the ....
g) I didn't get .... from the match till late because of the crowds.
h) David practised hitting the golf ball until he got it ....
i) Kate enjoyed riding the horse but found it hard to get ....
j) I tried to phone the tennis club but I couldn't get ....
k) We have a great time whenever our rugby team gets ....
l) I can't get .... to playing football on plastic grass!

9
Rewrite the sentences in **8** so that each one contains *one* of the words in the list, and does *not* contain a form of *get*.

answer dismount perfected strange
became home prepare succeed
cooking meets recover way

a) ....
b) ....
c) ....
d) ....
e) ....
f) ....
g) ....
h) ....
i) ....
j) ....
k) ....
l) ....

4 Clothes and appearance

1
Choose words from the list to complete the labels for the illustrations. Not all words given are suitable.

belt   costume   handbag   shoes   suit
blouse   dress   jacket   skirt   suitcase
boots   earrings   sandals   socks   tie
briefcase   glasses   shirt   stockings   waistcoat

2
Choose the most suitable word or phrase underlined in each sentence.

a) At Harry's school, the children have to wear a special appearance/style/uniform.

b) If we go to the Embassy ball we'll have to wear fashion/formal/polite clothes.

c) I really like Jack's new dress/suit/trouser.

d) In the summer I always wear shirts with short collars/cuffs/sleeves.

e) Paul answered the door wearing his pyjamas and his dressing-gown/nightdress.

f) You get really dirty repairing a car unless you wear a jumper/overalls/underwear.

g) I didn't get wet in the rain because I put on my plastic mac/overcoat/tights.

h) When it snows Freda always wears a/an anorak/glove/scarf around her neck.

i) David had to stop three times to tie up his small daughter's heels/shoe-laces/soles.

j) My hands were cold so I put them in my jacket/pockets/turn-ups.

k) I don't like that dress, it isn't in fashion/made/style.

l) Julie was given a lovely fur/hair/skin coat for her birthday.

m) All the men at the wedding were wearing top caps/hats/helmets.

n) The waitresses in this restaurant all wear white aprons/dungarees.

o) When Tom goes to a party he always wears a bow/butterfly/knot tie.

3

Complete each sentence with a word formed from the word in capitals.

a) Some young people today have a very strange ..... .   APPEAR
b) Lucy ..... quickly and got into the warm bath.   DRESS
c) Neil decided to buy a ..... shirt.   STRIPE
d) These trousers are filthy. Can you take them to the .....   CLEAN
e) Barry always does his hair with a ..... in the middle.   PART
f) This blouse is lovely, and very ..... .   FASHION
g) Don't wear that dress. It isn't ..... for a funeral.   SUIT
h) It's very hot. Why don't you ..... your collar.   BUTTON
i) That jacket is very ..... . You should buy a new one.   WEAR
j) Wear casual clothes. It's a/an ..... occasion.   FORMAL

4

Correct any errors in these sentences. Some sentences contain no errors.

a) This shirt is too small. It's not my number.
b) You have so many clothes. Why did you buy this cloth as well?
c) What costume did you wear to the fancy dress party?
d) Joan was dressed completely in white.
e) I like your new trouser. How much was it?
f) Excuse me for a moment. I have to wear some different clothes.
g) As far as I can see, the man in this photograph wears a suit.
h) The blouse is a good fit, but it isn't a very good suit.
i) What are you wearing to the party this evening?
j) You're soaked! Put out your clothes immediately!

5

Choose the most suitable word or phrase to complete each sentence.

a) When you saw Jack at the dance, what did he .....?
   A) wear   B) have on   C) dress   D) put on
b) My hands were so cold that I couldn't .... my coat buttons.
   A) open   B) remove   C) put out   D) undo
c) Those trousers are far too big. Why don't you have them ..... .
   A) taken in   B) let out   C) taken up   D) let in
d) I don't think that purple shirt ..... with your yellow skirt.
   A) suits   B) fits   C) goes   D) wears
e) This jacket is the kind of thing I want. Can I .....?
   A) wear it   B) dress it   C) take it off   D) try it on
f) You look really silly! Your pullover is on ....
   A) upside down   B) inside out   C) round and round   D) side by side
g) I don't want a pattern. I prefer just a/an ..... colour.
   A) plain   B) simple   C) clear   D) only
h) You look hot in that coat. why don't you ..... .
   A) put it on   B) take it off   C) put it away   D) take it out
i) Your diet was a success! You look wonderfully .....!
   A) skinny   B) thin   C) slim   D) underweight
j) I went shopping today and bought a new winter ..... .
   A) costume   B) outfit   C) suit   D) clothing

6

Complete the word in each sentence using. Each space represents one letter.

a) It's cold today. I'm going to put on a thick s _ _ _ _ _ _ .

b) When they go to church the women wear face s _ _ _ _ _ _ over their heads.

c) Graham usually wears a leather j _ _ _ _ _ _ .

d) My trousers are falling down! I must buy a b _ _ _ .

e) It's too hot for trousers. I'm going to wear my s _ _ _ _ _ _ .

f) Let's roll up our shirt s _ _ _ _ _ _ and start work.

g) I can't wear these jeans! They are too t _ _ _ _ _ .

h) I bought this lovely s _ _ _ scarf in Japan.

i) Don't forget to put your clothes away in the w _ _ _ _ _ _ _ .

j) I'm never cold as long as I wear my woolly u _ _ _ _ _ _ _ _ .

7

Choose the most suitable word or phrase to complete each sentence.

a) If I wear a long-sleeved shirt, I usually ..... the sleeves.
   A) put up   B) take up   C) roll up   D) get up

b) You're too fat! You have definitely ..... that roll necked jumper!
   A) grown out of   B) put away   C) worn out   D) tried on

c) That skirt is very short. Why don't you have it .....
   A) left out   B) set in   C) let down   D) taken round

d) The thief wore gloves so that his fingerprints didn't .....
   A) give him in   B) give him away   C) give him out   D) give him out

e) I can't walk in these high-heeled boots. I keep .....
   A) falling out   B) falling back   C) falling out   D) falling over

f) What do you mean, my swimming costume is too small? What are you ..... ?
   A) seeing to   B) getting at   C) making up   D) putting out

g) I'm ..... money every week to buy a new sports jacket.
   A) making for   B) getting over   C) putting aside   D) turning in

h) Some of the young people in my town ..... very strange hair-cuts!
   A) go out with   B) go in for   C) go through with   D) go back on

i) Before we choose a dress for you, let's ..... all the shops.
   A) look into   B) look through   C) look up   D) look around

j) If you work in a bank, you can't ..... wearing an open-necked shirt.
   A) get round to   B) get into   C) get away with   D) get out of

8

Complete the text by putting *one* word in each space.

Are you one of the thousands of people who eagerly follow every new (1) ..... that appears? Or are you one of those who go to the shops and just buy whatever they can find in their (2) ..... that (3) ..... them? Or perhaps you order from a mail-order catalogue, and then have to send everything back because nothing (4) ..... ? Whatever (5) ..... of shopper you are, one thing is certain. Everyone finds (6) ..... important. According to a recent survey, people spend more time either buying clothes, or thinking about buying them, or looking at them in shop (7) ....., than they do on most other products, (8) ..... from food. And the reason is obvious. Clothes are an important part of our (9) ..... . At work, you may need to impress a customer, or persuade the boss that you know what you are doing, and clothes certainly help. (10) ..... dressed people, so they say, get on in the world. And as far as attracting the opposite sex is concerned, clothes also play a vital role. If a friend who has been (11) ..... the same old jacket or the same old dress suddenly appears in the (12) ..... fashion, you can be sure that romance is in the air. And apart from work and romance, there are the influences of sport, music and leisure on the way we (13) ..... . So excuse me while I (14) ..... on my tracksuit and training (15) .... I'm just dashing off for some fast window-shopping.

5 Towns and Buildings

1

Choose the most suitable word underlined in each sentence.

a) As you can see, the garden has two ornamental iron <u>doors/gates</u> and there is a stone <u>path/pavement</u> leading to the house.

b) This is the front <u>entry/entrance</u>, but there is another door at the <u>edge/side</u> of the house.

c) All the rooms have <u>covered/fitted</u> carpets.

d) All the <u>cupboards/wardrobes</u> in the kitchen and the <u>bookshelves/ library</u> in the living room are included in the price.

e) There is a beautiful stone <u>chimney/fireplace</u> in the living room, and there are <u>sinks/washbasins</u> in all the bedrooms.

f) At the top of the <u>stairs/steps</u> there is a 19th century <u>coloured/stained</u> glass window.

g) The bathroom has a <u>shower/washer</u> and modern mixer <u>pipes/taps</u>.

h) At the top of the house there is a/an <u>attic/cellar</u> and the garden contains a <u>glasshouse/greenhouse</u> and a garden <u>hut/shed</u>.

i) There is a wooden <u>fence/wall</u> on one side of the garden, and a <u>bush/ hedge</u> on the other.

j) All in all, this is a fine <u>single/detached</u> house in a quiet residential <u>neighbourhood/suburb</u>.

2

Match these words with an explanation. Not all words given are possible.

aerial	curtains	drive	parking	shelf
central heating	dishwasher	furniture	radiator	stool
cook	doormat	landing	rug	stove
cooker	door knocker	letter box	settee/sofa	washing machine

a) Rectangular hole in the front door. ....

b) Kitchen appliance running on gas or electricity. ....

c) Long narrow rectangular piece of wood or metal fixed to the wall. ....

d) Short road between the street and a house or its garage. ....

e) Use this if you want someone to open the front door. ....

f) Put the dirty dishes in this. ....

g) This system makes the house warm. ....

h) A small carpet. ....

i) More than one person can sit on this. ....

177

j) This helps a radio or television to receive a broadcast. ....
k) An area at the top of some stairs. ....
l) Wipe your feet on this before you enter the house. ....
m) Pull these to cover the windows. ....
n) Small seat without back or arms. ....
o) Put your dirty washing in this. ....

3

Complete each sentence a) to j) with one of the endings 1) to 10) so that the meaning of the word underlined is clear. Use each ending once only.

a) I would prefer to live in a <u>cottage</u>...
b) The shopping centre has a <u>multi-storey car-park</u>...
c) My grandmother bought a <u>bungalow</u> ...
d) Jenny lives in a small <u>flat</u> ...
e) This street is only for <u>pedestrians</u> ...
f) Helen and John live in a <u>square</u> ...
g) Peter has moved to a London <u>suburb</u> ...
h) This village is surrounded by lovely <u>countryside</u> ...
i) Sue's new house is <u>unfurnished</u> ...
j) My house is <u>semi-detached</u> ...

1) ... on the third floor of a modern block.
2) ... and he commutes to work in the centre.
3) ... with room for over 2000 vehicles.
4) ... but the rent is so high that she cannot afford much furniture.
5) ... which has a beautiful garden in the middle.
6) ... in a small village in the country.
7) ... and the neighbours often bang on the wall.
8) ... because she had difficulty climbing stairs.
9) ... with views of the distant mountains.
10) ... and cars and lorries are not allowed.

4

Complete each sentence with the words *home*, *house*, or a word formed from one of these words.

a) The old couple decided to live in an old people's ....
b) Jane can't stand washing and ironing and other ....
c) Graham bought a terraced .... in a quiet city street.
d) Many .... people sleep in the streets in London.
e) Jack was unable to look after his children so he employed a ....
f) I come from Newcastle. It's my .... town, you could say.
g) Paul used to live on the river on a ....-boat.
h) When I went to boarding school I felt very ....-sick at first.
i) Our first home was on the ....-estate on Oakwood Hill.
j) Pour yourself a drink and make yourself at ....

5

Choose the most suitable word or phrase to complete each sentence.

a) The view from the skyscraper ...... over New York harbour.
   A) shows up   B) sees about   C) stands up   D) looks out
b) The old houses opposite are going to be ....
   A) broken down   B) knocked down   C) put down   D) taken down
c) ......! You're about to push the wheelbarrow over my foot!
   A) Hang up   B) Stop off   C) Get away   D) Look out

178

d) Please ...... the rubbish because the dustman is coming tomorrow.
   A) take in   B) make up   C) put out   D) tie down
e) Please come and unblock our drains! I'm .... you!
   A) doing without   B) counting on   C) seeing to   D) waiting for
f) I can't put these plants in pots. I've .... earth.
   A) run out of   B) put up with   C) given up   D) come up with
g) We .... through the window by climbing up a ladder.
   A) fell out   B) got in   C) ended up   D) set off
h) I've been planting trees all day and I'm ....
   A) worn out   B) taken in   C) run down   D) grown up
i) A lot of tiles .... our roof after the high wind.
   A) came off   B) took off   C) put off   D) got off
j) The car went out of control and .... hitting a lamp-post.
   A) speeded up   B) ran up   C) turned up   D) ended up

6
Complete each
sentence with a
word formed
from the word in
capitals.

a) I prefer living in a quiet ....   NEIGHBOUR
b) It will take a lot of money to .... this large
   house.   FURNITURE
c) Water is coming through the ceiling!
   What's happening ....?   STAIRS
d) Some people think that men are better .... than
   women.   COOK
e) There is a great .... of housing in this city.   SHORT
f) Water came through our roof but luckily my books
   were ....   DAMAGE
g) What is the exact .... of your garden?   LONG
h) Richard made a large profit from the ....
   of his house.   SELL
i) I couldn't afford to buy a flat so I
   took out a ....   LEND
j) The church was damaged in the war but it
   has now been ....   BUILD

7
Choose the most
suitable word or
phrase
underlined in
each sentence.

a) Laura was sitting beside in fire in a comfortable <u>armchair/sofa.</u>
b) We drove out of the village along a winding <u>lane/path</u>.
c) Steve redecorated his room with flowery <u>posters/wallpaper</u>.
d) Put the meat in the <u>cooker/oven</u> for two hours.
e) These plums are ripe. They need <u>picking/picking up</u>.
f) Peter was in the garden mowing the <u>flowers/lawn</u>.
g) We used to keep the coal downstairs in the <u>cave/cellar</u>.
h) Why don't you put the car in the <u>car-park/parking</u>?
i) Kate lives in a flat on the first <u>floor/storey</u>.
j) Put your wet socks on the <u>central heating/radiator</u> to dry.
k) Let's take the <u>runway/motorway</u>, we'll get there faster.
l) Go and get the lawnmower. The grass <u>is/are</u> very long.
m) I like the painting but I don't like the <u>frame/surrounding</u>.

n) Mary has a lot of small ornaments on her window shelf/sill.

o) There's someone at/on the door. Can you see who it is?

8
Match these words with the explanations given.

| shutters ceiling chimney pillow kennel |
| blind cushion roof rubbish urban |
| bunk eiderdown kerb litter rural |

a) Put this over you if you are cold in bed. .....

b) Put this behind your back if you are sitting uncomfortably. .....

c) This describes city places. .....

d) These protect your windows outside and can be closed in bad weather. .....

e) This is paper dropped in the street. .....

f) This is the top of the room. .....

g) This is a bed with others above it. .....

h) This describes country places. .....

i) This is the top of the house. .....

j) Put this under your head when you go to sleep. .....

k) Close this to keep the sunlight out of your room. .....

l) This is anything you throw away in the dustbin. .....

m) This is home for your pet dog. .....

n) This is the stone edge of the pavement at the side of the road. .....

o) The smoke goes up this from the fireplace. .....

6 Vehicles and Transport

1
Choose the most suitable word or phrase underlined in each sentence.

a) I enjoy taking the baby out in its cart/pram/trailer.

b) The train fare is expensive, it's cheaper to go by carriage/coach/waggon.

c) Terry and Bill rode around the island on their bicycle/trolley/tandem.

d) A farmer gave me a lift across the muddy field on his dustcart/lorry/tractor.

e) Cars made between 1916 and 1930 can be called racing/sports/vintage cars.

f) The first person who arrived at the scene of the accident phoned for a/an ambulance/stretcher/trolley.

g) Lorries, motorbikes and sports cars are all kinds of cars/motors/vehicles.

h) Jack was nearly run over by a fire engine/hosepipe/tanker on its way to a put out a serious blaze.

i) You need a powerful car to tow a camping/caravan/sleeper in the mountains.

j) Most buses in London are double decks/decked/deckers and you can see the sights from upstairs.

2

Complete each sentence with a word from the list. Use each word once only.

captain	crew	guard	pedestrian
chauffeur	cyclist	mechanic	steward
conductor	driver	motorist	traffic warden

a) The company chairman has a Rolls-Royce driven by a ....

b) When my car broke down a passing .... towed it to a garage.

c) The police wanted me to describe the .... of the car.

d) The four passengers on the ship had dinner with the ....

e) The train couldn't leave until the .... waved his green flag.

f) Hilary was given a parking ticket by a ....

g) Before take-off, the .... told me to fasten my seat belt.

h) When I got on the ship, one of the .... helped me find my cabin.

i) There isn't a .... on this bus, you pay the driver.

j) Eddie is a keen .... and rides his bike to work every day.

k) The bus mounted the pavement and injured a ....

l) Jim works as a .... in a local garage.

3

Choose words from the list to complete the labels for the illustration.

roof rack   bonnet   bumper   tyre   exhaust
windscreen   wheel   engine   headlight   mirror
steering wheel   aerial   boot   wipers   wing

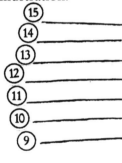

4

Choose the most suitable word or phrase to complete each sentence.

a) The ship stopped because two passengers had fallen ....
   A) upside down   B) overboard   C) underground   D) inside out

b) The .... was crowded with passengers waiting for the train.
   A) platform   B) quay   C) runway   D) pavement

c) We had to stop for petrol at a filling ....
   A) garage   B) service   C) pump   D) station

d) Mary looked up the fastest train to Glasgow in the ....
   A) catalogue   B) timetable   C) dictionary   D) programme

e) The train was very crowded because there were only four ....
   A) coaches   B) waggons   C) trucks   D) cars

f) Peter's car .... off the icy road and fell into a ditch.
   A) crashed   B) collided   C) hit   D) skidded

g) I dropped my wallet from the boat but luckily it ....
   A) drifted   B) floated   C) sank   D) rescued

181

h) Everything went dark when the train entered a/an ....
   A) underground   B) tunnel   C) tube   D) metro

i) David missed his train because of the queue in the ticket ....
   A) office   B) agency   C) room   D) lounge

j) To get to our hotel we had to cross the railway ....
   A) road   B) route   C) rails   D) line

5
Complete each sentence with a word formed from the word in capitals.

a) The police car was in .... with a fire engine.   COLLIDE
b) I couldn't help it, the accident was ....   AVOID
c) The passengers suffered only light .... in the crash.   INJURE
d) There is always a traffic jam here. The road needs .... WIDE
e) This small car is .... for long journeys.   SUIT
f) My new car has .... back seats.   REMOVE
g) The driver who gave us a lift refused to accept ....   PAY
h) All the bikes we manufacture have .... saddles.   ADJUST
i) The car in front braked .... and I ran into it.   EXPECT
j) The thick fog caused the .... of many trains.   CANCEL

6
Complete each sentence with the word *sail* or *ship*, or a word formed from one of these words.

a) Jack has been working as a .... for ten years.
b) We're all flying home but our furniture is being ....
c) What time does the ferry set .... ?
d) We are expecting a .... of coffee from Brazil this week.
e) We have decided to go for a .... tomorrow afternoon.
f) When Paul was young he .... round the world.
g) It's time you were aboard .... We're leaving soon.
h) Do you like ....? Or do you prefer water-skiing?
i) Graham works in the harbour as a .... clerk.
j) The boats on the lake had brightly coloured ....

7
Match these words with the descriptions given.

accelerator   chain   gear   parachute   bonnet   cockpit
handlebars   reverse   brakes   deck   oar   wings

a) An aeroplane has two of these. ....
b) Change this in a car to change speed. ....
c) Hold these when you ride a bicycle. ....
d) This will save your life if you fall from a plane. ....
e) You need this to row a boat. ....
f) This might be on a bicycle or around your neck. ....
g) Put these on if you want to stop. ....
h) Your car engine is usually under this. ....
i) Walk on this when you are on a ship. ....
j) The pilot of a plane sits in this. ....
k) Put your foot on this to make the car go faster. ....
l) Go into this if you want to go backwards. ....

8

Complete each sentence with *one* suitable word.

a) I'm really .... forward to sailing in Jean's new yacht.
b) In cities, cars and other vehicles .... up most of the space..
c) We'll come with the van and .... up the rest of the furniture.
d) When the storm began, the small boat .... for the nearest harbour.
e) How can you .... up with all those exhaust fumes!
f) We can't .... up with that speedboat in this rowing boat!
g) Jane likes .... off by driving her sports car at 100 miles an hour.
h) A fire engine arrived and soon .... out the fire.
i) Little Johnny is in the garden .... out his new tricycle.
j) One way of .... with the pollution problem is to use unleaded petrol.

7 Food, Restaurants and Cooking

1

Choose the most suitable word or phrase underlined in each sentence.

a) Waiter, could you bring me my account/bill/addition please?
b) It's a very popular restaurant, we should apply for/book/keep a table.
c) If you're hungry, why not ask for a large dish/plate/portion.
d) Please help/serve/wait yourself to salads from the salad bar.
e) Waiter, can I see the catalogue/directory/menu, please?
f) This fish is not what I called/commanded/ordered.
g) This dish/plate/serving is a speciality of our restaurant.
h) Have you tried the crude/raw/undercooked fish at the new Japanese restaurant? It's great!
i) Paul never eats meat, he's a vegetable/vegetarian/vegetation.
j) Have you decided what to have for your main course/food/helping?

2

Complete each sentence a) to j) with one of the endings 1) to 10). Use each ending once only.

a) Dinner's nearly ready. Can you lay...
b) There's some meat in the fridge. Just warm...
c) Keep an eye on the milk or it might boil...
d) Jack likes his steak rare but I prefer mine well...
e) When we finish lunch, I'll do the washing...
f) I always cut roast beef with an electric carving...
g) Mary bought a lovely set of cups and...
h) They serve a very cheap three course...
i) I really enjoyed that freshly ground...
j) If you have finished eating I'll clear...

1) .... up if you dry and put the dishes away.
2) .... it up in the microwave oven for a few minutes.
3) .... coffee you made for me this morning.
4) .... meal at the pub opposite the supermarket.

5) .... knife as it makes really thin slices.
6) .... the small table in the dining room.
7) .... saucers in the sales last week.
8) .... done, but not burnt if you see what I mean.
9) .... away the plates and bring the next course.
10) .... over and make a mess on the cooker.

3
Complete each phrase with the most suitable word from the list. Use each word once only.

bacon   butter   forks   pepper
beer   chips   grapes   saucers   bread
chocolate   instant coffee   wine

a) cups and ....   e) eggs and ....   i) a can of ......
b) fish and ....   f) salt and ....   j) a bar of ......
c) knives and .....   g) a loaf of ......   k) a jar of ......
d) bread and ......   h) a bottle of ....   l) a bunch of ......

4
Choose words from the list to complete the labels for the illustrations.

frying pan   saucepan   casserole   jar   kettle
jug   bowl   tin opener   mug   food mixer

5
Complete each sentence with *one* suitable word.

a) I'm trying to cut down .... fatty food.
b) Don't worry! The smell of garlic wears .... after a while.
c) Let's look .... the market before we buy any vegetables.
d) I can't understand this recipe. Can you work .... what it means?
e) I'm afraid I don't feel up .... eating another cream cake.
f) I visited a farm once, and it put me .... eating meat for a week.
g) I haven't got .... to cleaning the fish yet.
h) Why don't we warm .... last night's leftovers for lunch?
i) Keith usually makes .... his recipes as he goes along.
j) The waiter seemed a bit put .... when we didn't leave a tip.

6

Choose the most suitable word or phrase to complete each sentence.

a) Would you prefer .... potatoes or chips?
   A) poached   B) ground   C) mashed   D) powdered

b) I bought this bread four days ago and now it's ....
   A) stale   B) off   C) bad   D) rotten

c) Don't forget to buy a packet of .... peas.
   A) chilled   B) frozen   C) frosted   D) chilly

d) Can you give me the .... for this pie? It's delicious.
   A) prescription   B) instructions   C) ingredients   D) recipe

e) There was a wonderful smell of .... bread in the kitchen.
   A) cooking   B) roasting   C) baking   D) grilling

f) Don't buy those fish, they aren't very ....
   A) fresh   B) new   C) recent   D) young

g) I'd like to eat more of this cake, but it's very ....
   A) fat   B) fatty   C) fattened   D) fattening

h) Waiter, I can't eat this meat. It's under- ....
   A) done   B) developed   C) nourished   D) weight

i) Is the hamburger for you to eat here, or to .... ?
   A) go out   B) take away   C) carry on   D) sit down

j) That was fantastic. Could I have a second .... please?
   A) plate   B) course   C) helping   D) service

7

Complete each sentence with a word formed from *cook*. Use each word once only.

a) The hospital has over twenty .... working in the kitchen.

b) We bought David a .... book when he left home.

c) Do you like my new electric .... ?

d) The meals were large but not very well ....

e) I don't mind shopping, but I can't stand ....

f) You can boil these shellfish, or you can eat them ....

8

Complete each sentence with a word from the list. Use each word once only.

| add | beat | cool | grate | heat |
| melt | peel | pour | slice | sprinkle |

a) ...... the potatoes and .... them thinly.

b) ...... the eggs in a bowl, and then .... them to the mixture.

c) ...... the butter in a saucepan and .... gently for two minutes.

d) ...... the mixture into a bowl and leave to ....

e) ...... some cheese, and .... over the potatoes.

9

Make a word or compound word to match the description.

a) A spoon used for putting sugar in tea. *a teaspoon*

b) A cloth put on the table at meal times. ....

c) A metal device for opening bottles. ....

d) A pot in which tea is made. ....

e) An electrical appliance for making toast. ....

f) A cup specially made for coffee. ....

g) An omelette containing mushrooms. ....

h) An electrical appliance for mixing food. ....

i) A napkin made of paper. ....
j) The amount contained in a tablespoon. ....
k) An electrical appliance for washing dishes. ....

8 Shops and Shopping

1
Choose the most suitable word or phrase underlined in each sentence.

a) That new clothes shop has a lot of very good <u>bargains/sales</u>.
b) On Saturday morning the High Street is full of <u>customers/shoppers</u>.
c) It costs £2.50, so give her £3, and she'll give you 50p <u>change/rest</u>.
d) I don't go to that supermarket, it's a bit <u>priced/pricey</u>.
e) You cannot return goods without the original <u>recipe/receipt</u>.
f) Supasoft Soaps are <u>for sale/on sale</u> here.
g) A carrier bag is free with each <u>buyer/purchase</u> over £5.
h) If you pay cash we can give you a 10% <u>cutting/discount</u>.
i) How much did you <u>pay/spend</u> for your new shoes?
j) This is a good shoe shop, but the <u>costs/prices</u> are very high.

2
Rewrite each sentence so that it includes the word given in capitals.

a) I can't manage to see what the price is. Let's ask inside. MAKE
....
b) Is this coat the right size? Can I check? TRY
....
c) Two masked men robbed the supermarket yesterday. HELD
....
d) You need a new coat. Your old one is too small. GROWN
....
e) I've been shopping all morning. I feel exhausted. WORN
....
f) I'll come and collect the goods on Thursday. PICK
....
g) Sorry, we don't have any bread left. RUN
....
h) Are you going to the chemist's? CALLING
....
i) I don't like supermarkets. I can't bear the queues. PUT
....
j) I don't know whether to buy this car. I'll consider it. OVER
....

3

Complete each sentence with a word from the list. Use each word once only.

| change | deliver | find | fit | go | help |
| order | pay | queue | serve | try | wrap |

a) You have to .... for ages to pay in this supermarket.

b) In the London area, we .... furniture free of charge in our van.

c) The trousers I bought are the wrong size, I'd like to .... them.

d) Could somebody .... me please? I've been waiting for ten minutes.

e) Is this a present? Would you like me to .... it for you?

f) I like the colour of this skirt, but it doesn't .... me.

g) Good morning, madam. Can I .... you?

h) We don't have your size at the moment, but we can .... it for you.

i) Can you .... at the other cash desk please.

j) Would you like to .... on this green pair?

k) I went shopping but couldn't .... exactly what I wanted.

l) Food is so expensive now. The prices seem to .... up all the time.

4

Complete each sentence a) to j) with one of the endings 1) to 10). Use each ending once only.

a) I bought my new television from a department...

b) Don't forget to write a shopping...

c) Can you pay over there? This cash...

d) Most of the tourists went bargain...

e) Why don't we go to the new shopping...

f) Quite late at night the little corner...

g) It would be much better to buy an economy...

h) Don't forget that we have to stop at the filling...

i) There's a very nice suit on display in the shop...

j) Mary has just started work as a shop...

1) ...... centre near the public library?

2) ...... register doesn't work.

3) ...... window of that new shop next to the post office.

4) ...... size box of paper tissues.

5) ...... store in the town centre.

6) ...... shop down the road is still open.

7) ...... assistant in a shoe shop.

8) ...... list before we go to the market tomorrow.

9) ...... station to get some petrol.

10) ...... hunting in the old part of the city.

5

Choose the most suitable word or phrase to complete each sentence.

a) I bought these jeans very cheaply in the ....
   A) bargains   B) reductions   C) sales   D) discounts

b) The washing instructions for this shirt are given on the ....
   A) label   B) badge   C) notice   D) mark

c) All the small .... closed their shops in protest at the price rises.
   A) shop assistants   B) shoppers   C) shopkeepers   D) shop stewards

d) We don't have the cassette, I'm afraid. It's out of ....
   A) order   B) stock   C) shelf   D) sale

187

e) The street market was full of .... selling fruit and vegetables.
A) counters B) boutiques C) tables D) stalls
f) The shop opposite my house sells a variety of ....
A) objects B) purchases C) goods D) productions
g) I'm sorry, but the dress you want is not .... in red.
A) possible B) economical C) suitable D) available
h) Every Friday you can buy cheap vegetables in the market ....
A) street B) place C) store D) sales
i) I like street markets, because you shop in the open ....
A) prices B) sunshine C) bargains D) air
j) I like your new car. What .... is it?
A) brand B) make C) name D) label

6

Complete each sentence with a word from the list. Use each word once only.

| baked beans   chocolates   jam   orange   juice   soap |
| breakfast cereal   flowers   margarine   paper tissues   toothpaste |

a) a tube of ....
b) a bunch of ....
c) a pot of ....
d) a tin of ....
e) a box of ....
f) a box of ....
g) a packet of ....
h) a bar of ....
i) a carton of ....
j) a tub of ....

7

Match these words with the descriptions given.

| advertisement   bargain   catalogue   deposit   list |
| manager   purse   receipt   trolley   wallet |

a) You push this in the supermarket and fill it with food. ....
b) You are given this as proof of buying something. ....
c) This tries to persuade you to buy something. ....
d) You put money, especially banknotes, in this. ....
e) This person is in charge of a shop. ....
f) You might make this before you go shopping. ....
g) Leave this if you can't pay now but want to buy later. ....
h) Do this if you want to get a better price. ....
i) Coins are usually carried in this, especially by women. ....
j) Read this to find descriptions of goods. ....

8

Complete each sentence with a word formed from the word in capitals.

a) I prefer fresh food to .... food.   FREEZE
b) Those shoes are not waterproof. They are ....
   for winter.   SUIT
c) I'd like to make a .... about this radio I bought here.   COMPLAIN
d) We don't have any onions. There's a .... at the moment.   SHORT
e) There is not much .... of our being able to afford it.   LIKELY
f) Pushing into a queue is considered extremely ....   POLITE
g) Whoever designed this lovely shopping centre
   was very ....   IMAGINE

h) There are some good .... in the sales.   REDUCE
i) This is a good quality carpet, but actually very ....   EXPENSE
j) I thought this was an antique, but in fact it's ....   WORTH

9 Crime and the Law

1

Choose the most suitable word or phrase underlined in each sentence.

a) Sally didn't realise that she had broken/countered/denied the law.
b) The police have banned/cancelled/refused parking in this street.
c) I must remember to get a/an agreement/licence/permission for my television.
d) The president admitted that there had been a breakdown of law and crime/government/order.
e) Jim's parents wouldn't agree/allow/let him go to the demonstration.
f) Carlos was arrested because he had entered the country falsely/illegally/wrongly.
g) Talking to other students is against the law/orders/rules of the examination.
h) The two men were arrested before they could commit/make/perform any more crimes.
i) I had to take the company to court/justice/law to get the money they owed me.
j) Smoking is compulsory/prohibited/refused near the petrol tanks.

2

Match each person in the list with the description given.

| blackmailer forger hooligan murderer shoplifter vandal |
| burglar hijacker kidnapper pickpocket smuggler witness |

a) This person takes control of a plane or boat by force. ....
b) This person sees what happens during a crime or accident. ....
c) This person brings goods into the country illegally. ....
d) This person might steal food from a supermarket. ....
e) This person kills someone on purpose. ....
f) This person takes people and demands money for their return. ....
g) This person makes illegal copies of paintings, documents etc. ....
h) This person damages other people's property. ....
i) This person might steal your wallet in a crowd. ....
j) This person steals from houses. ....
k) This person gets money from others by threatening to tell secrets. ....
l) This person causes trouble at football matches. ....

3

Complete each part sentence a) to j) with one of the endings 1) to 10). Use each ending once only.

a) I decided to buy a burglar alarm after someone broke...
b) When Alan was arrested he ended...
c) As it was Sheila's first offence she was let...
d) After climbing over the prison wall, Peter managed to get...
e) The old couple who live opposite were taken...
f) At the end of the trial Hilary was found...
g) My neighbours admitted denting my car but got away...
h) The bank at the end of the street was held...
i) Nobody saw Jack cheating and he got away with...
j) The hijackers took fifteen people...

1) .... in by a salesman who cheated them out of their money.
2) .... away by stealing a car parked nearby.
3) .... station and charged with shoplifting.
4) .... it, although everyone suspected what had happened.
5) .... into my house and stole my stereo.
6) .... off with only a warning.
7) .... with paying only £50 damages.
8) .... hostage and demanded £1,000,000 from the authorities.
9) .... guilty and sentenced to six months in prison.
10) .... up by two masked men last week.

4

Complete each sentence with a word from the list. Use each word once only.

| accused evidence guilty lawyer statement |
| charged fine jury sentence suspect |

a) The customs officers arrested Bob and .... him with smuggling.
b) The police spent all morning searching the house for ....
c) Jean left her car in a no-parking area and had to pay a/an ....
d) Unfortunately at the end of the trial my brother was found ....
e) The trial took a long time as the .... couldn't reach a verdict.
f) George won his case because he had a very good defence ....
g) The police visited Dawn and asked her to make a/an ....
h) Because of his past criminal record, Brian was the main ....
i) Pauline decided to sue the police because she had been wrongly ....
j) The murderer of the children received a life ....

5

Choose the most suitable word or phrase to complete each sentence.

a) Most schools in my country no longer have .... punishment.
   A) physical B) capital C) bodily D) corporal
b) The policemen following the robbers were in .... clothes.
   A) plain B) ordinary C) normal D) simple
c) The two old ladies were .... of their purses.
   A) stolen B) attacked C) robbed D) snatched
d) At the end of the story, the hero manages to arrest the ....
   A) offenders B) villains C) wrongs D) evils
e) I had to answer question A because it was ....
   A) compulsory B) necessary C) a must D) an obligation

f) Charles could not .... having been at the scene of the crime.
   A) refuse   B) object   C) deny   D) alter
g) As there was no evidence, the judge dismissed the ....
   A) trial   B) witness   C) court   D) case
h) If your dog damages your neighbour's property, you could be ....
   A) guilty   B) liable   C) payable   D) illegal
i) After ten years in prison, Stephen was .... and set free.
   A) pardoned   B) released   C) innocent   D) forgiven
j) The police sergeant told the young .... to make some tea.
   A) officer   B) official   C) guardian   D) constable

6

Rewrite each sentence, beginning as shown, so that the meaning stays the same.

a) They said that John had stolen the money.
   They accused..
b) Ian said that he hadn't punched anybody.
   Ian denied..
c) 'OK, Andy, you can go now,' said the detective.
   The detective gave Andy..
d) 'James Frogget, you will go to prison for ten years,' said the judge.
   The judge sentenced ....
e) 'I forged the signature,' said Mary.
   Mary admitted ....
f) Harry stole £30,000 and was arrested.
   Harry was arrested ....
g) 'We saw the accused break into the car,' said the witnesses.
   The witnesses stated ....
h) Graham said that he wouldn't go to the police station.
   Graham refused ....
i) 'It's true,' said Norman, 'I murdered Alan.'
   Norman confessed to ....
j) 'Can you come with me, please,' the detective said to Helen.
   The detective asked ....

7

Complete each sentence with a word formed from the word in capitals.

a) The bank robbers were sentenced to ten years ....   PRISON
b) We believe that severe .... is not the answer.   PUNISH
c) Nobody reported the .... of the Chinese vase.   THIEF
d) Stuart was charged with three motoring ....   OFFEND
e) The value of the .... goods was over £10,000.   STEAL
f) The judge told Arthur he was a hardened ....   CRIME
g) Susan could say nothing in her own ....   DEFEND
h) Everyone at the trial believed in Bill's ....   INNOCENT
i) Joan said she had .... destroyed her passport.   ACCIDENT
j) The painting I stole turned out to be ....   WORTH

8

Choose the most suitable word or phrase underlined in each sentence.

a) Harry was told that fishing in the lake was <u>against/by/over</u> the law.
b) Catherine led a secret life <u>for/in/of</u> crime before she was caught.
c) Having trouble with your phone? Send <u>at/for/to</u> Fix-a-phone!
d) I regret to tell you that you are <u>for/in/under</u> arrest.
e) I only attacked the young man <u>from/in/with</u> self-defence.
f) David was often <u>at/in/with</u> trouble with the police when he was young.
g) The robbers' car was hidden <u>below/by/from</u> sight behind the bank.
h) The kidnappers have been caught, and the child is no longer <u>at/in/on</u> danger.
i) Tony was caught by a policeman who was <u>off/out/away from</u> duty and cycling to work.
j) The thieves took the wrong painting <u>by/in/under</u> mistake.
k) The suspicious manager left the safe unlocked <u>from/on/with</u> purpose.
l) The robbers met to plan the bank raid <u>from/in/with</u> secret.

10 Entertainment and the Arts

1

Choose the most suitable word or phrase underlined in each sentence.

a) I like this book, and I've read six <u>capitals/chapters/prefaces</u> already.
b) It's not a proper drawing, only a <u>rough/plan/sketch</u>.
c) The play is very long but there are three <u>breaks/intervals/rests</u>.
d) At the cinema I don't like sitting too near the <u>film/screen/stage</u>.
e) We heard a piece by Mozart performed by a German <u>band/group/orchestra</u>.
f) Her second book was very popular and became a best <u>buy/seller/volume</u>.
g) I like the painting but I can't stand its ugly <u>border/frame/square</u>.
h) Robert's new book will be <u>broadcast/published/typed</u> in August.
i) I liked the acting, and the <u>costumes/dressing/outfits</u> were good too.
j) The best <u>act/place/scene</u> in the film is when Jack meets Kate.

2

Complete each sentence with a word from the list. Use each word once only.

announcer	composer	critic	editor	playwright
author	conductor	director	novelist	sculptor

a) The orchestra would not be so successful with a different ....
b) I want a book on sailing, but I can't remember the name of the ....
c) We must see the new film by that Italian ....
d) The .... said that the sports programme is on after the news.
e) Harry writes for the theatre, but he is not only a ....
f) We saw some interesting metal objects made by a French ....
g) That's a nice piece of music. Who is the .... ?
h) Peter Smith was the only .... who wrote in praise of the film.
i) Charles Dickens is probably the best known British ....
j) The .... of the newspaper usually decides what it contains.

3

Complete each sentence by putting *in, on, at* or *out of* in each space.

a) Harry Potter is hard .... work writing his new screenplay.
b) The music was terrible and the singer was .... tune.
c) I can't tell what that is ...... the background of the picture.
d) Jane's new book is coming out .... paperback next year.
e) Is there anything any good .... Channel 4 this evening?
f) The school put on *Hamlet* .... modern dress.
g) The critics found Joe's kind of writing rather .... date.
h) In the last scene, all the actors are .... stage together.
i) When David took his place ...... the piano the audience went wild.
j) The film stars Doris Fleck .... the part of Queen Elizabeth.
k) I had to read her latest book .... professional interest.
l) Margaret's new sculptures are .... display in the park.

4

Complete each sentence with a word from the list. Use each word once only.

current electric humorous modern public special dull gripping live popular readable still

a) No recording can be as good as a .... concert in my opinion.
b) It was a very .... story and made me laugh a lot.
c) I couldn't put that book down, it had such a .... plot.
d) Most people find it difficult to understand .... art.
e) My favourite television programmes are about .... affairs.
f) Of course it's possible to like both classical and .... music.
g) Everyone enjoyed the .... effects in the 'Star Wars' films.
h) I don't buy books because there's a good .... library nearby.
i) We both found it a very .... film I'm afraid.
j) George doesn't paint people, but mainly does .... life paintings.
k) It was an interesting book, and very ....
l) Unfortunately the boy upstairs is learning the .... guitar.

5

Choose the most suitable word or phrase to complete each sentence.

a) Susan's first painting was a/an .... portrait.
   A) self B) own C) selfish D) auto
b) The audience enjoyed the play so much that they .... for ten minutes.
   A) booed B) screamed C) applauded D) handed
c) Peter sings every Sunday in the local church ....
   A) concert B) chorus C) opera D) choir
d) I bought this book mainly because it has a very attractive ....
   A) folder B) cover C) coat D) wrapping
e) The play was a success and had very good ...... in the papers.
   A) reviews B) critics C) advertisements D) notes
f) If you can't find what you are looking for in the book, use the ....
   A) preface B) directory C) list D) index
g) The average .... watches television for about 15 hours a week.
   A) viewer B) audience C) spectator D) observer
h) First we see their faces from far away, and then we see a ....
   A) side by side B) foreground C) replay D) close up

i) Please note that the next programme is .... for children.
   A) unusual   B) unsuitable   C) unmistakable   D) unreasonable

j) All the members of the ..... had a party after the play was over.
   A) scene   B) cast   C) circle   D) drama

6

Complete each sentence with a word formed from the word in capitals.

a) Ann gave a brilliant .... as Juliet in the school play.   PERFORM
b) To be a novelist you really have to be very ....   IMAGINE
c) The book contains some delightful ....   ILLUSTRATE
d) The audience gave Mary a long round of ....   APPLAUD
e) Watching videos is becoming a popular form of ....   ENTERTAIN
f) The film was well made but not very ....   AMUSE
g) Alex usually .... Diana at the piano when she sings.   COMPANY
h) I think there is too much .... on television.   ADVERTISE
i) The editor said Joe's articles were so bad they
   were ....   PRINT
j) Julia is really a very .... kind of person.   ART
k) Most people enjoyed the new .... of *Macbeth*.   PRODUCE
l) The actors all helped with the painting of the ....   SCENE

7

Complete the compound word in each sentence, using a word given in the list. Use each word once only.

back   book   fair   operas   rehearsal
biography   circle   ground   piece   scripts

a) Edward's third book is usually considered his master.......... .
b) A lot of people enjoy watching soap .... on television.
c) I found the Prime Minister's auto .... very interesting.
d) Some of the actors still did not know their lines at the dress ....
e) I won't buy the book until it comes out in paper.......... .
f) We had very good seats in the dress ....
g) There is a black cat painted in the fore......... of the picture.
h) Writing film .... is rather like writing for the theatre.
i) I was fined because I forgot to return my library ....
j) The scene showed them on a roundabout in a children's fun.......... .

8

Replace the verb underlined in each sentence with a verb from the list, so that the meaning stays the same. Change the tense and word order where necessary.

call off   go over   pick up   take over   turn up
come out   look up   put on   take up   work out

a) My radio doesn't <u>receive</u> the BBC World Service very easily.
   ....

b) Our school is going to <u>do</u> *The Tempest* next month.
   ....

c) The management <u>cancelled</u> the performance an hour before the opening.
   ....

d) I <u>searched for</u> the reference in the index.
   ....

e) I can't hear the radio. Can you <u>make it louder</u>?
   ....

f) Colin's new book <u>is published</u> next week.

....

g) The conductor <u>studied</u> the music carefully before the concert.

....

h) The publishing company was <u>bought</u> by a Japanese firm.

....

i) I like detective stories where I can't <u>think</u> who did the murder!

....

j) Jim has <u>started</u> painting as a hobby.

....

11 The Natural World

1
Choose the most suitable word or phrase underlined in each sentence.

a) The fields were flooded after the river burst its <u>banks/edges/sides</u>.
b) After the rain the street was full of <u>floods/lakes/puddles</u>.
c) During the storm, the climbers sheltered in a <u>cave/cliff/valley</u>.
d) A small <u>river/stream/torrent</u> runs across the bottom of our garden.
e) It was difficult to swim because the <u>waters/waves/tides</u> were so high.
f) From the <u>peak/summit/top</u> of the hill you can see the sea.
g) You must carry a lot of water when you cross the <u>desert/plain/sand</u>.
h) In the middle of the square there is an old <u>fountain/source/tap</u>.
i) I think it's going to rain. It's very <u>clouded/clouding/cloudy</u>.
j) The church caught fire when it was struck by <u>hurricane/lightning/thunder</u>.

2
Complete each sentence with a word from the list. Use each word once only.

forest	leaves	plant	seeds	trunk
lawn	peel	roots	stone	twig

a) We cut down the tree but then we had to dig up its ....
b) The road goes through a beautiful pine ....
c) When Tom was eating a cherry, he accidentally swallowed the ....
d) In autumn, these paths are covered in fallen ....
e) Who is going to cut the .... while I am away?
f) We bought Diana a beautiful indoor .... for her birthday.
g) A tree fell, and its massive .... blocked the road.
h) Harry buys .... and grows all his own vegetables.
i) The bird was carrying a .... to build its nest.
j) Some people like eating orange ....

3

Complete each
sentence a) to j)
with one of the
endings 1) to 10).
Use each ending
once only.

a) A large green snake...
b) A small brown duck...
c) A large black and yellow wasp...
d) A shiny green crab...
e) An enormous black spider...
f) A bright green frog...
g) A black and white puppy...
h) A herd of cattle...
i) A dirty black lamb...
j) A small ginger kitten...

1) .... was spinning its web across the window.
2) .... was plodding across the field, mooing loudly.
3) .... was buzzing around the jar of honey on the table.
4) .... was sitting on a branch and miaowing.
5) .... was slithering across the floor towards me.
6) .... was sitting on a leaf and croaking.
7) .... was following the flock, baaing quietly.
8) .... was swimming on the pond and quacking loudly.
9) .... was barking furiously outside the gate.
10) .... was pinching Fiona's toe as she stood on the sea shore.

4

Match these
words with the
descriptions
given.

| bee dolphin giraffe moth rabbit whale |
| camel fly leopard pig shark worm |

a) It lives in a hole in the ground and has long ears. ....
b) It flies at night and is attracted to light. ....
c) It lives in a hive and makes honey. ....
d) It has yellow fur and a long neck. ....
e) It is a large dangerous fish. ....
f) It lives in the earth and we can use it when we go fishing. ....
g) It is a large member of the cat family with spotted fur. ....
h) It is the largest kind of animal in the world. ....
i) It is used for transport in desert countries. ....
j) It is a fat pink animal which lives in a sty. ....
k) It is a large intelligent sea animal. ....
l) It is an insect which spreads diseases. ....

5

Choose the most
suitable word or
phrase to
complete each
sentence.

a) The dog .... its tail furiously when it saw the children.
   A) shook   B) wagged   C) moved   D) rubbed
b) A large .... of the tree broke off in the storm.
   A) trunk   B) bark   C) twig   D) branch
c) There was field after field of golden .... waving in the wind.
   A) corn   B) bushes   C) grass   D) herbs
d) Before railways were built, many goods were carried on ....
   A) channels   B) water   C) canals   D) river.

e) The children enjoyed rolling down the grassy ....
   A) mountain   B) cliff   C) stone   D) slope
f) What kind of .... is your dog?
   A) breed   B) race   C) mark   D) family
g) Some wild animals will become .... if they get used to people.
   A) peaceful   B) tame   C) organised   D) petty
h) There's a .... of blackbirds at the bottom of the garden.
   A) house   B) home   C) cage   D) nest
i) Many people are interested in watching ....
   A) wildlife   B) wilds   C) wilderness   D) wildly
j) You have to sleep under a net to avoid being bitten by ....
   A) lobsters   B) geese   C) cockroaches   D) mosquitoes

6

Complete each sentence with a word formed from the word in capitals.

a) Jane's parents decided that her rat was an ....pet.   SUIT
b) My dog never does what it is told, it's very ....   OBEY
c) If wild animals had more .... they wouldn't be in danger.   PROTECT
d) Of course it's a daffodil! It's shape and colour are .... MISTAKE
e) Many wild animals are shot by :......... simply for sport.   HUNT
f) An elephant has tremendous ....   STRONG
g) Some animals can escape from a .... cage.   WOOD
h) People who suffer from .... should buy a pet.   LONELY
i) Everyone is worried about the .... of the rainforests.   DESTROY
j) Some people are afraid of dogs from early ....   CHILD

7

Complete the compound word in each sentence, using a word given in the list. Use each word once only.

| forecast hive house side top |
| fountain hole mower skin trap |

a) There were so many mice we had to buy a mouse.......... .
b) Paula was cutting the grass with an electric lawn.......... .
c) There's a drinking .... on the other side of the park.
d) What's the weather .... for tomorrow?
e) The hill.......... was covered in beautiful wild flowers.
f) You can see the mountain.......... among the clouds in the distance.
g) At the end of the field was a large stone farm.......... .
h) We collect honey from our own bee.......... .
i) There's a rabbit.......... in the corner of this field.
j) Martin was wearing imitation snake.......... boots.

8

Complete each sentence with *one* suitable word.

a) I think this fruit juice has gone .... It smells funny.
b) Mind ....! Our cat has very sharp claws!
c) I keep my dog on a lead, but I let it .... in the park.
d) Would you like me to show you .... in the park.
e) I like the idea of camping, but I am put .... by the insects.
f) Our dog never got used .... sleeping in its kennel.
g) I don't think I want to find .... whether that bull has sharp horns!

h) After they made ...., George gave Silvia a bunch of roses.

i) My puppy managed to tear .... three of my school books.

j) I've taken .... going for long walks in the countryside.

12 People and Behaviour

1

Choose the most suitable word or phrase underlined in each sentence.

a) Please don't push. It's very <u>bad-tempered/rude/unsympathetic</u>.

b) Jack hates spending money. He's rather <u>frank/greedy/mean</u>.

c) Our teacher is very <u>proud/strict/tolerant</u> and won't let us talk in class.

d) Helen never does her homework. She is rather <u>gentle/lazy/reliable</u>.

e) I didn't talk to anyone at the party because I felt <u>ambitious/lonely/shy</u>.

f) When Harry saw his girlfriend dancing with Paul he felt <u>jealous/selfish/sentimental</u>.

g) I don't like people who are noisy and <u>aggressive/courageous/sociable</u>.

h) Thank you for bringing us a present. It was very <u>adorable/grateful/thoughtful</u> of you.

i) Teresa never gets angry with the children. She is very <u>brave/patient/pleasant</u>.

j) Tom always pays for everyone when we go out. He's so <u>cheerful/generous/honest</u>.

2

Match these words with the descriptions given. Use each word once only.

> bad-tempered   determined   lazy   reliable
> cheerful   frank   mean   selfish
> considerate   honest   punctual   sympathetic

a) You always arrive on time. ....

b) You are always happy. ....

c) You do what you say you will do. ....

d) You say exactly what you think. ....

e) You don't think about the needs of others. ....

f) You have a strong wish to get what you want. ....

g) You are unkind, or not willing to spend money. ....

h) You easily become angry with others. ....

i) You think about the needs of others. ....

j) You tell the truth and obey the law. ....

k) You understand the feelings of others. ....

l) You try to avoid work if you can. ....

3

Complete each sentence with a word from the list. Use each word once only.

| ambitious greedy polite sociable brave imaginative proud stubborn grateful kind snobbish tolerant |

a) I think I'll stay here on my own, I'm not feeling very .... today.
b) Diana wants to get to the top in her company. She is very ....
c) It's not .... to stare at people and say nothing!
d) I think you have to be very .... to write a novel.
e) Thank you for helping me. It was very .... of you.
f) Peter refuses to change his mind, although he is wrong. He's so ....
g) It was very .... of Sheila to put out the fire on her own.
h) Our neighbours look down on us. They are a bit ....
i) Don't eat all the cakes! You really are becoming .... !
j) If you lend me the money I'll be very ....
k) I am very .... of my new motorbike.
l) My parents don't mind my crazy hair style. They are very ....

4

Complete each sentence with a word formed from the word in capitals.

a) The two men were accused of robbery with .... VIOLENT
b) Please don't tell lies. It is very .... HONEST
c) I can't stand our little brother. He's really .... ANNOY
d) Paul is a good employee, and is very .... CONSCIENCE
e) Mary never stops chatting! She is a very .... person. TALK
f) I was very touched by her .... in helping me. KIND
g) We asked for directions but people were rather .... HELP
h) Jane gets into trouble at school. She's not very .... OBEY
i) David was given a medal for .... BRAVE
j) I didn't like the local people. They were very .... FRIEND
k) Please don't shout! It's rather .... POLITE
l) Maria takes great .... in her work. PROUD

5

Choose the most suitable word or phrase to complete each sentence.

a) You can't tell what someone is like just from their ....
   A) character B) appearance C) personality D) looking
b) I was born in Scotland but I .... in Northern Ireland.
   A) grew up B) raised C) brought up D) rose
c) Edward was named after one of his father's distant ....
   A) family B) brothers C) members D) relations
d) Jane and Brian got married a year after they were ....
   A) divorced B) proposed C) engaged D) separated
e) Graham works well in class, but his .... could be better.
   A) rudeness B) behaviour C) politeness D) acting
f) Julie had a terrible .... with her parents last night.
   A) row B) discussion C) argue D) dispute
g) I got to .... Steve well last year when we worked together.
   A) introduce B) know C) meet D) sympathise
h) Is Brenda married or ....? I don't like to ask her.
   A) spinster B) alone C) bachelor D) single

199

i) Parents and teachers have to try hard to understand the younger ....
    A) generation B) people C) adolescents D) teenagers

j) My father likes to be called a 'senior citizen', not an old age ....
    A) person B) relative C) gentleman D) pensioner

6
Match each person from the list with a suitable description. Use each name once only.

| adult | colleague | nephew | toddler | best man | fiancé |
| niece | twin | bride | neighbour | sister-in-law | widow |

a) The son of your brother or sister. ....
b) A woman on the day of her marriage. ....
c) A young child who is learning to walk. ....
d) What a woman calls the man she is engaged to. ....
e) One of two children born at the same time. ....
f) A person who lives near you. ....
g) The daughter of your brother or sister. ....
h) A person who is fully grown. ....
i) A woman whose husband has died. ....
j) At a wedding, the friend of the bridegroom. ....
k) The sister of the person you marry. ....
l) A person you work with. ....

7
Complete each sentence with *one* suitable word.

a) After a few days they realised they were .... love.
b) I went .... with a very interesting girl last week.
c) Andrew acts as .... he was the most important person in the room.
d) After two years, their marriage broke ....
e) John discovered that he was related .... his next door neighbour.
f) My parents keep treating me .... a child, but I'm not one!
g) I was brought .... by my aunt after my parents died.
h) It was very kind .... you to give me a lift.
i) Teachers should be patient .... small children.
j) James was very disappointed .... his new job.
k) It's very .... of character for Bill to behave like that.
l) Most famous people behave quite normally .... private.

8
Complete each sentence by replacing the words underlined with one of the verbs in the list. Use each verb once only.

| call in | fall out | give away | put up with | turn down |
| count on | get on well with | look up to | take after | turn up |

a) The wedding was cancelled when the bride failed to <u>arrive</u>. ....
b) Susan feels that her boss is someone to <u>respect</u>. ....
c) I'm sorry, but I just can't <u>stand</u> your behaviour any longer. ....
d) My brother and I really <u>have a good relationship with</u> our parents. ....
e) Why don't you <u>visit my house</u> on your way home from the shops? ....
f) Tony felt that he could <u>rely on</u> his friend Mary. ....
g) The millionaire decided to <u>make a present of</u> his money to the poor. ....
h) Paula and Shirley are good friends but sometimes they <u>quarrel</u>. ....
i) Jean decided to <u>refuse</u> Chris's offer of marriage. ....
j) All three children <u>behave</u> like their father and are very sociable. ....

13 Technology and Machines

1

Choose the most suitable word or phrase underlined in each sentence.

a) This is a small car, but it has a powerful <u>engine/machine</u>.
b) Do you use an <u>electric/electrical</u> toothbrush?
c) I can't see anything. Where's the light <u>plug/switch</u>?
d) I've decided to buy a new <u>typewriter/typist</u>.
e) You can't use the lift. It's out of <u>order/work</u>.
f) If you don't press this button the washing machine won't <u>go/move</u>.
g) Use this torch. The other one doesn't <u>act/work</u>.
h) The lights have gone out. It must be a power <u>break/cut</u>.
i) A car <u>factory/industry</u> has just been built in our town.
j) Who exactly <u>discovered/invented</u> the computer?

2

Choose words from the list to complete the labels for the illustrations. Not all the words in the list are possible.

| axe file needle razor scissors spade |
| corkscrew hammer pin saw screwdriver spanner |

3

Complete each sentence with a suitable word from **2**. Use each word once only.

a) You can cut that plank in half with this ....
b) You need a .... to open this bottle of wine.
c) I've split my trousers. Do you have a .... and thread?
d) I can't open the back of the television without a special ....
e) You can make the edges smooth with a ....
f) I've cut myself shaving again. I think I'll buy an electric ....
g) We could chop this tree down if we had a sharp ....
h) Until I can sew this, I'll fix the edges together with a ....
i) I was going to dig the garden but I can't find the ....
j) Oh bother! I've hit my thumb with the .... instead of the nail!
k) You can cut this cardboard if you have some sharp ....
l) This nut is impossible to undo. I need a larger ....

4

Complete each sentence a) to j) with one of the endings 1) to 10). Use each ending once only.

a) It's very hot in here. Why don't you...
b) I can't make out what it is. I think I'll...
c) We haven't got much time but I can...
d) I need to put up these shelves, so I'm going to...
e) It's a long way up. I think we should use...
f) The lamp does work. You'll have to...
g) The radio isn't very loud. I must...
h) This would make a nice picture. Hang on while I...
i) A seat on the morning flight? Let me just...
j) The tyre's a bit flat. I'll have to...

1) .... get the pump out of the boot.
2) .... fetch my camera from the living room.
3) .... heat up the food very quickly in the microwave.
4) .... the lift, but we can walk down if you like.
5) .... put on the air conditioning.
6) .... find out from the computer.
7) .... put in a new light bulb.
8) .... borrow William's electric drill.
9) .... go and get my binoculars.
10) .... buy some new batteries.

5

Choose the most suitable word or phrase to complete each sentence.

a) James is going to be late. His car has ....
   A) broken out   B) broken up   C) broken in   D) broken down
b) If your camera is faulty, you should return it to the ....
   A) creator   B) manufacturer   C) inventor   D) builder
c) It is hard to get ...... parts for this car if something goes wrong.
   A) extra   B) spare   C) additional   D) emergency
d) I bought this electric drill from a ....-it-yourself shop.
   A) do   B) repair   C) make   D) fix
e) This clock .... on two small batteries.
   A) goes   B) works   C) runs   D) moves
f) Lift the .... and listen for the dialling tone.
   A) microphone   B) dial   C) receiver   D) number
g) Don't touch that wire! You'll get an electric ....
   A) surprise   B) current   C) charge   D) shock
h) It's difficult to repair a car unless you have the right ....
   A) gadgets   B) instruments   C) appliances   D) tools
i) This knife is really .... I'll have to sharpen it.
   A) blunt   B) dull   C) flat   D) frank
j) Don't forget to .... your alarm clock for 6.30.
   A) put   B) set   C) ring   D) go off

6

Complete each sentence with a word formed from the word in capitals.

a) This bag contains all my photographic ....
b) This company's .... include radios and televisions.
c) This drill is .... It doesn't work at all!
d) Two bulldozers were .... the road.
e) You can't open the top unless you .... it first.
f) These scissors won't cut. They need.......... .
g) Peter studied civil .... at university.
h) I've always wanted to ride a .... motorbike.
i) .... is probably the cleanest form of energy.
j) Brenda always wanted to be a ....

EQUIP
PRODUCE
USE
WIDE
SCREW
SHARP
ENGINE
POWER
ELECTRIC
SCIENCE

7

Complete each sentence by putting *one* word in each space.

a) There's nothing good on the television. Why don't you turn it .... ?
b) Can you plug the electric fire .... for me?
c) Hurry up sir. We're just going to lock .... for the night.
d) The machine is quite automatic, it does everything .... itself.
e) We'd better stop for some petrol. We've nearly run ....
f) The parts come from Japan, but we put them .... here in Italy.
g) The word processor consists .... a keyboard, a screen and a printer.
h) This looks like wood but actually it's made .... plastic.
i) What exactly is a file used .... ?
j) These two metal sections are then bolted .... to make one.

8

Replace the words underlined in each sentence with one of the verbs from the list.

| break down go off keep up with pick up run out |
| do without hang up look out put off stand for |

a) My car isn't as fast as yours. I won't be able to <u>stay near</u> you. ....
b) The torch doesn't work. The batteries must have <u>been used up</u>. ....
c) This radio doesn't <u>receive</u> the BBC World Service very well. ....
d) The car is making a funny noise. I think it's going to <u>stop working</u>. ....
e) I was going to buy a motorbike, but I was <u>discouraged</u> by my parents. ....
f) People call me on the phone, but then <u>put down the receiver</u>. ....
g) <u>Be careful</u>! You're going to give yourself an electric shock! ....
h) It's difficult to <u>manage if you don't have</u> a washing machine. ....
i) The letters CD <u>mean</u> compact disc, actually. ....
j) Without a fridge, fresh food will <u>become bad</u> very quickly. ....

14 Problems

1

Choose the most suitable word or phrase underlined in each sentence.

a) Many people were injured when the building <u>demolished/collapsed</u>.
b) The ship radioed to say that it was in <u>difficulties/dangers</u>.
c) The government has announced plans to help the <u>poor/poverty</u>.
d) The driver of the bus admitted that he had <u>done/made</u> an error.
e) Everyone agrees that the <u>environment/nature</u> must be protected.

f) There has been another <u>increase/rising</u> in the amount of crime.

g) There are few jobs here and many people are <u>away from work/unemployed</u>.

h) The train was in <u>accident/collision</u> with a bus on a level crossing.

i) No ships are sailing today because of the <u>high/storm</u> winds.

j) There was a large <u>demonstration/manifestation</u> against nuclear power in Manchester yesterday.

2
Complete each sentence with a word from the list. Use each word once only.

disaster   emergency   hooliganism   living
disease   famine   injuries   rubbish
earthquake   floods   invasion   slums

a) Food has been sent to areas in Africa suffering from ....

b) Many people live in overcrowded .... on the edge of the city.

c) The cost of .... has risen steadily this year.

d) Thousand of buildings fell down during a severe ....

e) .... at football matches has been reduced this year.

f) The .... of Ruritania has been condemned by the United Nations.

g) The eruption of the volcano was a terrible ....

h) Hundreds of people were drowned during the .... in China.

i) Two of those involved in the crash had serious ....

j) Large cities face the problem of what to do with household ....

k) Doctors announced that there was now a cure for the ....

l) During the storm there were hundreds of .... calls.

3
Complete each sentence with the best word or phrase.

a) Most young people want to .... more about environmental problems.
   A) look up   B) find out   C) deal with   D) make out

b) Everyone knows about pollution problems, but not many people have .... any solutions.
   A) thought over   B) got round to   C) looked into   D) come up with

c) Many factories break the anti-pollution laws and ....
   A) put up with it   B) take it over   C) get away with it   D) come round to it

d) Disposing of waste and rubbish is a hard problem to ....
   A) carry out   B) put up   C) get away   D) deal with

e) More people in cities should .... cycling instead of using cars.
   A) rely on   B) take up   C) set up   D) get around to

f) Most governments seem to just .... dealing with environmental problems.
   A) put off   B) make up for   C) do without   D) take after

g) In some countries environmental organisations have been .... to inform people and gain their support.

h) Unless we .... the problem, many animals could become extinct.
   A) face up to   B) look up to   C) turn up to   D) get up to

i) Quite soon, the world is going to .... energy resources.
   A) run out of   B) get into   C) keep up with   D) come up against

j) The important thing is to believe that problems can be solved, and not to ....
   A) make up   B) look up   C) give up   D) put up

4

Replace the words underlined in each sentence with a word or phrase from the list.

banned ignored increased polluted solved flooded improved overpopulated protected unemployed

a) Smoking has been <u>made illegal</u> in public places in some countries. ....
b) Famine is a serious problem, and it hasn't been <u>dealt with</u> yet. ....
c) Many kinds of wild animals need to be <u>guarded by the law</u>. ....
d) Living conditions have been <u>made better</u> in some parts of the world. ....
e) Our local lake has been <u>made dirty</u> by nearby factories. ....
f) A problem which is <u>not thought about</u> does not simply go away. ....
g) A lot of people in industrial areas are <u>without work</u> at the moment. ....
h) After the recent storms, the town was <u>filled with water</u>. ....
i) Some countries are <u>inhabited by too many people</u>. ....
j) Recently the number of people riding bicycles has <u>grown larger</u>. ....

5

Choose the most suitable word or phrase to complete each sentence.

a) I'm glad I .... my plane! I've just heard that it's been hijacked.
   A) lost   B) refused   C) missed   D) altered
b) The cruise ship hit a rock and ....
   A) sank   B) drowned   C) flooded   D) crashed
c) I lost the keys to my house and had to climb in ...... the window.
   A) by   B) to   C) through   D) with
d) The village was completely .... in an earthquake.
   A) collapsed   B) destroyed   C) ruined   D) broken
e) The bus driver couldn't .... the accident.
   A) protect   B) control   C) provide   D) prevent
f) After police found drugs there, the disco was ....
   A) closed down   B) banned   C) ignored   D) abolished
g) During the match, someone .... fire to the stadium.
   A) set   B) put   C) opened   D) caught
h) We decided not to go camping because of the .... rain.
   A) great   B) amount   C) heavy   D) extra
i) I had to shut the window because the noise outside was ....
   A) shouting   B) unbearable   C) in danger   D) enormous
j) When the fire broke out, an electronic alarm ....
   A) came in   B) opened up   C) went off   D) put out

6

Complete each sentence with a word formed from the word in capitals.

a) People living in cities often suffer from ....   LONE
b) There was a head-on .... between two trains yesterday.   COLLIDE
c) The government is searching for a .... to the problem.   SOLVE
d) When the crew of the ship were rescued they were ....   EXHAUST
e) Living conditions in the slums were very ....   HEALTH
f) The old hospital was filthy and ....   ORGANISE
g) Floods caused the .... of the old church.   DESTROY
h) The traffic problem has shown .... lately.   IMPROVE
i) During the cold weather, the river was .... over.   FREEZE
j) The unemployment situation has improved ....   EXPECT

7

Match these words with the descriptions given.

> aid   conservation   drought   famine   riot
> charity   demonstration   emergency   pile-up   strike

a) An organisation which collects money to help those in need. ....
b) When an area is desperately short of water. ....
c) The act of protecting animals, or parts of the environment. ....
d) When people march through the streets to show their opinions. ....
e) A collision involving several vehicles. ....
f) When an area is desperately short of food. ....
g) Something unexpected which must be dealt with quickly. ....
h) When people stop working through disagreement with their employers. ....
i) Help (money, food etc) given by governments or other organisations. ....
j) When a crowd of people is violent and out of control. ....

8

Put *one* word in each space in these sentences.

a) The fireman put his life .... risk to rescue the child.
b) Teachers have decided to go .... strike next month.
c) Sue has a lot of work to do and is .... stress at the moment.
d) The coach driver went through a red light .... mistake.
e) Many people are dying .... hunger in the desert area.
f) The boat which sank was crowded .... people.
g) The two countries are now .... war with each other.
h) .... an emergency, break the glass.
i) When the fire brigade arrived, the church was no longer .... fire.
j) When the volcano erupted, a party of tourists was .... danger.

15 Health and the Body

1

Choose the most suitable word or phrase underlined in each sentence.

a) There were ten people waiting in the doctor's office/surgery/ward.
b) After I ate the shellfish I experienced/fell/happened ill.
c) George's cut arm took over a week to cure/heal/look after.
d) David fell down the steps and twisted his ankle/heel/toe.
e) Everyone admired Lucy because she was tall and skinny/slim/thin.
f) I've been digging the garden and now my back aches/pains/injures.
g) Whenever I travel by boat I start feeling hurt/sick/sore.
h) The doctor can't say what is wrong with you until she cures/examines/recovers you.
i) Use this thermometer and take his fever/heat/temperature.
j) I seem to have caught/infected/taken a cold.

2

Replace the words underlined in each sentence with one of the words from the list. Use each word once only.

agony	body	breath	look	stomachache
beard	brains	heart	spine	tongue

a) Janet fell from her horse and injured her <u>backbone</u>. ....

b) I had a very bad toothache, and was in <u>great pain</u> all night. ....

c) The police discovered the <u>dead person</u> buried in the garden. ....

d) One thing you can say about Ann, she has certainly got <u>intelligence</u>. ....

e) They have a new house right in the <u>centre</u> of the countryside. ....

f) Italian is actually Mary's native <u>language</u>. ....

g) Before I dived in the water, I took a deep <u>mouthful of air</u>. ....

h) After dinner, Jack had a <u>pain from eating too much</u>. ....

i) Shirley had a strange <u>expression</u> on her face. ....

j) David managed to grow a <u>lot of hair on his face</u>. ....

3

Complete each sentence with a word from the list. Use each word once only.

cheek	knees	neck	throat	waist
chin	lips	nose	thumb	wrist

a) After speaking for two hours, the lecturer had a sore ....

b) Terry was on his hands and ...., looking for the fallen coin.

c) Paul gave his aunt an affectionate kiss on the ....

d) There was such a terrible smell that I had to hold my ....

e) Stan is deaf, but he can understand people by reading their ....

f) I never wear a watch because I don't like the weight on my ....

g) One of the boxers punched the other on the .... and knocked him out.

h) When Diane was a baby, she used to suck her ....

i) I've lost a lot of weight, especially around the ....

j) Norma wears a heart on a gold chain around her ....

4

Complete each sentence a) to j) with one of the endings 1) to 10). Use each ending once only.

a) I think we should send for an ambulance...

b) Some people go jogging every morning...

c) It would be a good idea for you to go to the dentist's...

d) The doctor gave Andy an injection...

e) I'm going into hospital tomorrow...

f) We took the cat to the vet...

g) Susan took two aspirins...

h) Nobody could find a stretcher...

i) The doctor gave Helen a prescription...

j) I bought some special cream...

1) ... to have that bad tooth of yours taken out.

2) ... to check whether it had recovered from its accident.

3) ... to take old Mrs Jones to hospital.

4) ... to put on my sunburnt arms and legs.

5) ... to get rid of her headache.

6) ... to reduce the pain and help him sleep.

7) ... to take to the chemist's.

8) ... to keep fit, or to lose some weight.

9) ... to carry the injured man out of the building.

10) ... to have an operation on my foot.

5

Choose the most suitable word or phrase to complete each sentence.

a) Martin hasn't quite .... his illness yet.
   A) recovered   B) got over   C) looked after   D) suffered

b) Pauline .... birth to a baby girl yesterday afternoon.
   A) was   B) put   C) had   D) gave

c) Your leg isn't broken but it is badly ....
   A) fractured   B) bruised   C) bandaged   D) bent

d) Several angry drivers shook their .... at me as I drove away.
   A) fists   B) arms   C) hands   D) elbows

e) That was a bad fall! Have you .... yourself?
   A) harmed   B) damaged   C) wounded   D) hurt

f) Each time I sneezed, everyone said, '....... you!'
   A) cough   B) bless   C) cold   D) thank

g) Stop making that noise! You're getting on my ....!
   A) muscles   B) brains   C) nerves   D) blood

h) As the little boy cried, large .... rolled down his cheeks.
   A) drips   B) tears   C) puddles   D) streams

i) I had severe toothache and half my face was badly ....
   A) swollen   B) rounded   C) exploded   D) injured

j) I've got a headache, and I don't feel very ....
   A) healthy   B) fit   C) sane   D) well

6

Complete each sentence with a word formed from the word in capitals.

a) You should try to lose some more ....

b) Eddie had a funny .... on his face.

c) Everyone was very .... by the good news.

d) Arnold is very tall and ....

e) The doctor recommended a new course of ....

f) Everyone is praying for the Prime Minister's ....

g) Unfortunately, your illness is ....

h) Stephen was bitten by a .... snake.

i) Can you tell me whether this disease is .... ?

j) Don't touch my knee, it's very ....

WEIGH
EXPRESS
HEART
MUSCLE
TREAT
RECOVER
CURE
POISON
INFECT
PAIN

7

Match each sentence a) to j) with a sentence from 1) to 10) which has the same meaning.

a) Henry's heart was in the right place. ...

b) Paul held his tongue. ...

c) Richard jawed away for at least an hour. ...

d) Dave had a lot of cheek to talk like that. ...

e) Keith couldn't stomach his new boss. ...

f) Harry backed his boss. ...

g) William kept poking his nose in. ...

h) Graham thumbed a lift to work. ...

i) Charles put his foot in it. ...

j) Jack's heart ached to be where he belonged. ...

1) He talked.
2) He supported him.
3) He said the wrong thing.
4) He was kind.
5) He was rather rude.
6) He didn't say anything.
7) He interfered in other people's business.
8) He hitch hiked.
9) He missed home.
10) He didn't like him.

8
Complete each sentence with *one* suitable word.

a) I am afraid she is suffering .... an incurable disease.
b) I was .... agony all night with earache.
c) I think you've put .... a lot of weight lately.
d) The effect of this drug will slowly wear ....
e) You really get .... my nerves sometimes!
f) After Jack fainted it was several minutes before he .... round.
g) Is Coral being operated .... tomorrow?
h) Harry went .... with flu during his holiday.
i) Peter was treated .... minor injuries and shock.
j) Don't worry. I'll take care .... you myself.

16 Money

1
Choose the most suitable word or phrase underlined in each sentence.

a) I haven't got enough money I'm afraid. Could you <u>borrow/lend</u> me some?
b) It's a good school, but the <u>fares/fees</u> are rather high.
c) This car is too expensive. We can't <u>afford/pay</u> it.
d) It was a very good meal. Can we have the <u>account/bill</u> please?
e) There's a small flat to <u>hire/let</u> in Bridge Street.
f) How much do you <u>earn/gain</u> in your new job?
g) She's a good dentist, but she doesn't <u>charge/spend</u> too much.
h) I bought this coat in the sales. It was <u>decreased/reduced</u> a lot.
i) Jack made his <u>fortune/treasure</u> buying and selling property.
j) How much do you <u>reckon/value</u> that house would cost?

2
Replace each word or phrase underlined with a word or phrase from the list which has the *opposite* meaning.

| cash generous profit save well off |
| expensive poverty purchase take out worthless |

a) I was surprised by how <u>mean</u> Charles was. ....
b) Janet says that she is very <u>hard up</u> at the moment. ....
c) Last year their business made a huge <u>loss</u>. ....
d) I'd like to <u>pay in</u> £100 please. ....
e) That part of Spain always seems very <u>cheap</u> to me. ....

f) Most people in the city live in great <u>prosperity</u>. ....
g) The manager insisted that I paid <u>by cheque</u>. ....
h) Some people manage to <u>spend</u> most of their money. ....
i) Jean was able to make only one <u>sale</u> during the morning. ....
j) The old painting I found in the loft turned out to be <u>valuable</u>. ....

3

Complete each sentence with a word from the list. Use each word once only.

| coin | guarantee | pension | rent | tip |
| credit | card | loan | receipt | safe | wealth |

a) The old couple had only a small .... to live on.
b) My uncle Sam acquired his considerable .... selling cars.
c) David never carries cash with him and pays for everything by ....
d) I wouldn't have been able to buy my boat without a bank ....
e) The shop won't change any goods without the original ....
f) Keith didn't like the waiter so he didn't leave a ....
g) The house is not in very good condition so the .... is low.
h) The food mixer has a twelve month ....
i) We keep all our money and valuables in this .... in the floor.
j) The five pence .... is so small that everyone dislikes it.

4

Choose the most suitable response to each sentence a) to j) from the sentences 1) to 10). Use each response once only.

a) Who do I make the cheque out to? ...
b) We seem to be spending a lot of money lately. ...
c) The house has burnt down! What are we going to do? ...
d) How much do you want for this drawing? ...
e) Did you inherit this house? ...
f) Your dog must have cost a lot of money. ...
g) Do we still owe the bank any money? ...
h) How much do you make a year? ...
i) Can we change money at the hotel to pay the bill? ...
j) Why are you putting so much money in the bank? ...

1) Sorry, but it's not for sale.
2) I'm saving up to buy a new motorbike.
3) Perhaps we should try to economise a bit.
4) Yes, my Aunt Clara left it to me.
5) Well, we've nearly paid it all back.
6) To JB Woolbury PLC.
7) Actually I got it for nothing.
8) I think they accept travellers cheques anyway.
9) I've got quite a good salary actually.
10) Don't worry, we're insured.

5

Choose the most suitable word or phrase to complete each sentence.

a) I bought these shoes in the sales. They were a real ....
   A) cheap   B) economy   C) bargain   D) purchase
b) If you put your money in the bank, it will earn ten per cent ....
   A) interest   B) profit   C) deposit   D) investment
c) John asked his parents if they would pay off his ....
   A) rents   B) debts   C) accounts   D) credits
d) Adults have to pay £2.50 to get in, but children under 14 are ....
   A) free   B) nothing   C) penniless   D) open
e) I'm interested in this old car. Is it .... ?
   A) selling   B) a sale   C) to sell   D) for sale
f) I'm trying to save for my holidays so I'm .... some money each week.
   A) putting in   B) putting aside   C) putting behind   D) putting up
g) Just a minute! You've forgotten to .... your cheque!
   A) mark   B) make   C) place   D) sign
h) I like your typewriter. How much did it .... exactly?
   A) pay   B) cost   C) afford   D) spend
i) The blackmailer asked for the money in used ....
   A) notes   B) cheques   C) paper   D) cash
j) I gave the assistant £10 and she gave me four pounds ....
   A) rest   B) money   C) coins   D) change

6

Complete each sentence with a word formed from the word in capitals.

a) Harry spends a lot each month on his .... policy.   INSURE
b) The bank .... asked to see my passport.   CASH
c) This is not my .... on the cheque.   SIGN
d) I've just spent all my .... on a holiday in Mexico.   SAVE
e) We had to take out a .... from the bank to buy the car.   LEND
f) In the end, the old vase proved to be ....   WORTH
g) The millionaire lived in a .... mansion.   LUXURY
h) I'm afraid that my business is not very ....   PROFIT
i) £1000! Thank you for your ....   GENEROUS
j) Steve inherited £1,000,000 from a .... relative.   WEALTH

7

Complete each sentence with a word or phrase formed from *pay*. Each space represents one word.

a) You can pay the full price now, or make six monthly ....
b) If you lend me the money, I'll .... next week.
c) I haven't got enough money to .... the suit now.
d) We .... a lot of money on the decorating for this house.
e) Whenever Alan loses a bet he refuses to ....
f) Thank goodness it's Friday today. It's ....
g) I must do something about all these .... bills.
h) Please make the cheque .... to R.D. Smith.
i) Take this money and .... the bank.
j) I like my job, and it's very ....

8

Match each person from the list with a suitable description. Use each name once only.

| accountant cashier heir manager pensioner |
| agent customer investor miser swindler |

a) Someone who likes to keep money and not spend it. ....
b) Someone who inherits money or property. ....
c) Someone who runs a bank. ....
d) Someone who has retired. ....
e) Someone who keeps or checks financial records. ....
f) Someone who buys things in a shop. ....
g) Someone who pays out money in a bank. ....
h) Someone who represents others in business. ....
i) Someone who puts money into a business. ....
j) Someone who cheats people out of money. ....

17 Feelings and Opinions

1

Choose the most suitable word or phrase underlined in each sentence.

a) When Dick saw his neighbour kick his dog he became angry/nervous.
b) Sue wasn't really interested/interesting in the film.
c) We were both afraid/anxious that we would miss the plane.
d) Please accept our faithful/sincere congratulations.
e) I wish you wouldn't snap your fingers. It's very annoying/worrying.
f) Your friend Judith is extremely attractive/striking.
g) You're not scared/thrilled of spiders, are you?
h) If we forget to do our homework, our teacher gets cross/terrifying.
i) Tim completely lost his temper! He was absolutely furious/upset.
j) Your written work is full of careless/naughty mistakes.

2

Replace the word or words underlined with one of the words from the list. Use each word once only.

| confused delightful fascinating irritating scared |
| depressed dull glad naughty upset |

a) I'm afraid the children have been very badly-behaved today. ....
b) I felt a bit frightened when I went into the dark room. ....
c) Jean was very unhappy when her kitten was run over. ....
d) The film we saw last night was rather boring. ....
e) This is a really interesting book. You must read it. ....
f) I'm so happy that Helen got the job she wanted. ....
g) Sometimes when I hear the news I feel very miserable. ....
h) He always interrupts everyone! It's very annoying. ....
i) We had a wonderful evening with some Scottish friends. ....
j) Sorry I gave you the wrong tickets. I got a bit mixed up. ....

3

Complete each sentence with a suitable word or phrase from the list. Use each word or phrase once only.

> blush   grin   shake your head   scream   whisper
> cry   nod your head   shrug your shoulders   wave   yawn

a) When you feel embarrassed you might ....
b) When you feel tired or bored you might ....
c) When you want to talk without being heard you might ....
d) When you want to show agreement you might ....
e) When you want to show great amusement you might ....
f) When you want to show that you don't know or care you might ....
g) When you feel upset you might ....
h) When you want to show disagreement you might ....
i) When you are scared or in pain you might ....
j) When you want to attract someone's attention you might ....

4

Choose a suitable comment or reply from 1) to 10) for each sentence a) to j). Use each comment once only.

a) How do you feel about folk music? ...
b) Do you think I should order the tickets in advance? ...
c) Do you have any comment on the Prime Minister's decision? ...
d) I feel really miserable today. ...
e) Is it all right if I invite some friends round? ...
f) Shall I do the washing up? ...
g) I like this vase. Is it an antique? ...
h) Don't you think you should treat your mother better? ...
i) Is my homework all right? ...
j) Did you enjoy the concert? ...

1) You can do whatever you like, as far as I'm concerned.
2) In my opinion, the most important matter has been forgotten.
3) I didn't think much of it, actually.
4) No, it's not worth it.
5) Mind out, you might drop it!
6) I'm sorry. but it just won't do.
7) I'm not very keen on that kind of thing, to be honest.
8) No, don't bother, I'll do it.
9) Why don't you mind your own business!
10) Never mind, cheer up!

5

Match each word or phrase from the list with each description.

> co-operative   determined   helpful   obedient   realistic
> dependable   embarrassed   imaginative   quarrelsome   tolerant

a) If you are this, you can't put up with people looking at you ....
b) If you are this, you get on well working with others. ....
c) If you this, you face up to facts. ....
d) If you are this, you might make up stories. ....
e) If you are this, you carry out instructions. ....
f) If you are this, you don't give up easily. ....
g) If you are this, you put up with other people's differences. ....

h) If you are this, people can count on you. ....
i) If you are this, you keep falling out with other people. ....
j) If you are this, you might put yourself out for someone else. ....

6

Choose the most suitable word or phrase to complete each sentence.

a) The thief returned the old lady's money, because he had a guilty ...
   A) heart   B) feeling   C) conscience   D) mind
b) I wanted to complain about my boss, but I didn't ....
   A) dare   B) risk   C) courage   D) attempt
c) I'm hungry. Do you .... going out for a pizza?
   A) like   B) want   C) desire   D) fancy
d) Let's go to a different cinema. I'm not very ...... on horror films.
   A) keen   B) interested   C) enthusiastic   D) impressed
e) All my friends have big new cars. I'm becoming ...... of my old Mini.
   A) embarrassed   B) ashamed   C) guilty   D) upset
f) I'm sorry I screamed. Something .... me.
   A) afraid   B) terrifying   C) scared   D) depressed
g) How do you ...... about the pollution problem in this country?
   A) feel   B) think   C) believe   D) view
h) I'm sorry to ...... you, but could I make a phone call?
   A) trouble   B) upset   C) worry   D) mind
i) I don't think this programme is .... for young children.
   A) wonderful   B) suitable   C) worth   D) keen
j) The African workers accused the European company of racial ....
   A) judgement   B) beliefs   C) argument   D) prejudice

7

Complete each sentence with a word formed from the word in capitals.

a) You have made a lot of mistakes. You are too ....   CARE
b) You are safe after all! What a ....   RELIEVE
c) A dog will always be .... if you treat it well.   FAITH
d) Please accept this present as a token of our ....   GRATEFUL
e) What was your first .... of Ron?   IMPRESS
f) The soldier was accused of .... because he ran away.   COWARD
g) Harry was filled with .... for Susan's work.   ADMIRE
h) The children thought the little kittens were ....   ADORE
i) To be honest, I found the film rather ....   OFFEND
j) Colin always feels bad-tempered and .... in the morning.   IRRITATED
k) The main .... of the job is the opportunity for travel.   ATTRACT
l) You need more confidence, and .... in yourself.   BELIEVE

8

Complete each sentence by putting *one* suitable word in each space.

a) In reply to Jack's question, Sue shook .... head.
b) You should be ashamed .... your behaviour!
c) Cheer ....! Try laughing for a change!
d) Do you like chocolate cake? I am very fond .... it.
e) Young David has got .... trouble as usual.
f) Are you laughing .... me? Do I look funny?
g) That was a terrible thing to do! I'm extremely cross .... you!
h) I don't believe .... spending a lot of money on clothes.

i) You look a bit fed .... Is anything the matter?
j) I'm very keen .... classical music, actually.

18 Education and Learning

1

Choose the most suitable word or phrase underlined in each sentence.

a) Jack decided to take a <u>course/lesson</u> in hotel management.
b) Sheila always got good <u>marks/points</u> in algebra.
c) After leaving school, Ann <u>studied/trained</u> as a teacher.
d) Peter decided not to <u>go in/enter</u> for the examination.
e) My sister <u>learned/taught</u> me how to draw.
f) I can't come to the cinema. I have to <u>read/study</u> for a test.
g) In history we had to learn a lot of dates by <u>hand/heart</u>.
h) I hope your work will improve by the end of <u>course/term</u>.
i) Martin <u>failed/missed</u> his maths exam and had to sit it again.
j) If you have any questions, <u>raise/rise</u> your hand.

2

Complete each sentence with a word from the list. Use each word once only.

| cheat copy memorise pay revise |
| concentrate divide pass punish underline |

a) Our teachers used to .... us by making us stay behind after school.
b) The teacher saw Jerry trying to .... in the test.
c) Try to .... the most important rules.
d) It is difficult to .... attention in a noisy classroom.
e) Pauline tried her best to .... the end of year examinations.
f) Your work is the same as Harry's. Did you .... his work?
g) Your mind is wandering! You must .... more!
h) Helen decided to .... all her work at the end of every week.
i) It's a good idea to .... important parts of the book in red.
j) If you .... twenty seven by nine, the answer is three.

3

Match each person from the list with a description. Use each name once only.

| classmate examiner learner principal pupil |
| coach graduate lecturer professor tutor |

a) Someone who teaches at a university. ....
b) Someone who has a college degree. ....
c) The head of a school. ....
d) Someone who studies at primary or secondary school. ....
e) The most important teacher in a university department. ....
f) Someone who teaches one student or a very small class. ....
g) Someone in the same class as yourself. ....
h) Someone who trains a sports team. ....
i) Someone who writes the question papers of an examination. ....
j) Someone who drives but has not yet passed a driving test. ....

4

Complete each
sentence a) to j)
with one of the
endings 1) to 10).
Use each ending
once only.

a) Joe was absent most of the time...
b) Sue wanted to do the experiment for herself...
c) James was a very gifted pupil...
d) Lucy couldn't find a duster to clean the board...
e) Dave could pick up languages very easily...
f) Brenda wanted to leave space for corrections...
g) Tony didn't pay attention in class...
h) Helen was educated at home by her parents...
i) Brian attended evening classes in photography...
j) Cathy wanted to get into university...

1) ... so he didn't have any problems passing his exams.
2) ... so he started talking in French after only a few days.
3) ... so she had to study for the entrance examinations.
4) ... so his name was removed from the register.
5) ... so he didn't go out with his friends much during the week.
6) ... so she wrote her answers in the corner.
7) ... so she didn't have many friends of her own age.
8) ... so she wrote everything on alternate lines.
9) ... so she went to the science laboratory.
10) ... so he could never remember what the teacher said.

5

Choose the most
suitable word or
phrase to
complete each
sentence.

a) Helen's parents were very pleased when they read her school ....
   A) report   B) papers   C) diploma   D) account
b) Martin has quite a good .... of physics.
   A) result   B) pass   C) understanding   D) head
c) In Britain, children start .... school at the age of five.
   A) kindergarten   B) secondary   C) nursery   D) primary
d) Edward has a .... in French from Leeds University.
   A) certificate   B) degree   C) mark   D) paper
e) My favourite .... at school was history.
   A) topic   B) class   C) theme   D) subject
f) It's time for break. The bell has ....
   A) gone off   B) struck   C) rung   D) sounded
g) Our English teacher .... us some difficult exercises for homework.
   A) set   B) put   C) obliged   D) made
h) Before you begin the exam paper, always read the .... carefully.
   A) orders   B) instructions   C) rules   D) answers
i) If you want to pass the examination, you must study ....
   A) hardly   B) enough   C) thoroughly   D) rather
j) Most students have quite a good sense of their own ....
   A) grasp   B) ability   C) idea   D) information

6

Complete each sentence with a word formed from the word in capitals.

a) John should pay more .... in class.
b) This book is terrible. It's completely ....
c) Can you explain why you have so many ....?
d) Brian went on to be a very .... student at university.
e) No, I didn't say it. You must be ....
f) We're going to do some .... before the exams.
g) Jim was a very .... pupil, and learned easily.
h) This book has a very interesting ....
i) Most schools have now abolished corporal ....
j) Ann's teacher persuaded her she was not a ....

ATTEND
READ
ABSENT
SUCCEED
MISTAKE
REVISE
GIFT
INTRODUCE
PUNISH
FAIL

7

Complete each sentence with a form of *do, make* or *take*.

a) Have you .... Exercise Three yet?
b) I can't come this afternoon. I'm .... an English exam.
c) Jack has .... very well this term.
d) I'm afraid that you haven't .... any progress.
e) Sue didn't know the answer, so she .... a guess.
f) You all look tired. Let's .... a break.
g) This is a good composition, but you have .... a lot of errors.
h) I think you should .... yourself more seriously.
i) The teacher gave a lecture, and the class .... notes.
j) Paul finds maths difficult, but he .... his best.

8

Complete each sentence with a word beginning as shown. Each space represents one letter.

a) Charles has a good k _ _ _ _ _ _ _ _ of the subject.
b) These children are badly behaved! They need more d _ _ _ _ _ _ _ _ _ .
c) Everyone agrees that a good e _ _ _ _ _ _ _ _ is important.
d) If you don't know a word, look it up in your d _ _ _ _ _ _ _ _ _ .
e) Maths is easy if you are allowed to use a c _ _ _ _ _ _ _ _ _ .
f) Keith spent four years studying at u _ _ _ _ _ _ _ _ _ .
g) Some apes seem to have as much i _ _ _ _ _ _ _ _ _ _ _ as humans!
h) I find listening c _ _ _ _ _ _ _ _ _ _ _ _ tests rather difficult.
i) At the age of eleven I went to s _ _ _ _ _ _ _ _ school.
j) I enjoyed doing e _ _ _ _ _ _ _ _ _ _ in the laboratory.

9

Complete each sentence with *one* word.

a) If you have a problem, put .... your hand.
b) Please pay attention .... what your teacher says.
c) Mary has a degree .... civil engineering.
d) David was punished .... throwing chalk at the teacher.
e) I was very good .... maths when I was at school.
f) What's the answer if you multiply 18 .... 16 ?
g) We had to write a composition .... 'Our Ideal School'.
h) Please write this .... your exercise books.
i) You might not understand things even if you learn them .... heart.
j) When Sue visited Italy, she soon picked .... the language.

Word Formation 1

1

Use your
dictionary to
complete the
word in each
sentence.

a) The children never do what I tell them to! They are very dis.......... .
b) It won't rain in August, surely! That seems extremely un.......... .
c) No, I told you <u>not</u> to sell the shares! You must have mis.......... .
d) Jack gets very good marks, and is an out.......... student.
e) If you co.......... with the police you will receive a light sentence.
f) Dave was in the first sub.......... that sailed under the North Pole.
g) Just heat up the rice, it's been pre.......... .
h) Mr Jones is incredibly rich. In fact he's a multi-.......... .
i) The ship hit a rock, but the lives of the passengers were not en.......... .
j) I just can't answer this question! It's im.......... .

2

Complete each
sentence with a
word formed
from the word
underlined,
beginning as
shown. Begin the
word with a
prefix from the
list.

dis- in- non- over- re- trans- un- vice-

a) I'm not <u>satisfied</u> with your work. I am .... with it.
b) She doesn't have the <u>usual</u> kind of haircut. It's very ....
c) We haven't <u>decided</u> where to go yet. We are ....
d) Mary is sailing across the <u>Atlantic</u>. She is on a .... voyage.
e) Dan is the <u>president</u>'s assistant. He is the ....
f) Terry is no longer a <u>smoker</u>. Now he is a ....
g) Don't wear a <u>formal</u> suit. The dinner is quite ....
h) I don't think this rule is fair. It's .... to older students.
i) You haven't <u>written</u> this clearly. It'll have to be ....
j) This steak is <u>cooked</u> too much. It's ....

3

Complete each
sentence with a
word formed
from a word
given in the list,
ending as shown.

astonish fool great music thought
back free lead short trumpet

a) I don't want to be a slave! I demand my ....dom.
b) How kind of you to bring flowers! That was very ....ful.
c) Martin plays the guitar, but he isn't a very good..........ian.
d) Our school has closed because there is a ....age of teachers.
e) Brian is one of the world's ....ing architects.
f) Imagine my ....ment when the cat started to speak!
g) Don't be ....ish ! There is no such thing as a ghost!
h) I prefer to begin at the end and go ....wards.
i) I always wanted to be a ....er in a jazz band.
j) A small country can still achieve ....ness.

4

Complete each sentence with a word formed from a word given in the list using one of the prefixes or suffixes given.

| care employ home postpone satisfied |
| charged friend night pronounce skirts |

| dis- mis- out- over- -less -ment -ship -ee |

a) I travelled to Scotland on the .... train and slept all the way.
b) You're always breaking things! Why are you so .... ?
c) Jane knows a lot of French words, but she tends to .... them.
d) We all believe in .... between the people of different nations.
e) Bad weather caused the .... of nearly all the football programme.
f) George was very .... with the service at the hotel.
g) We live in a flat on the .... of London.
h) Patsy thought the shop assistant had .... her.
i) David was tired of being a/an .... so he started his own company.
j) The government is providing more money to help .... people.

5

Complete each sentence with a word formed from the word in capitals.

a) The storms caused widespread .... in the countryside.   DESTROY
b) The soldier was given a medal for ....   BRAVE
c) Bill has taken up .... as a hobby.   CARPENTER
d) Mary decided to go on a .... course.   SECRETARY
e) I try not to buy .... food, as it is unhealthy.   FREEZE
f) Please give details of your present ....   OCCUPY
g) I don't think that there is a .... to this problem.   SOLVE
h) Unfortunately Tom's bid for the 100 metre record was ....   SUCCEED
i) I think that you owe me an ...., don't you?   EXPLAIN
j) Joe's first attempt to swim the Channel ended in ....   FAIL

6

Complete the compound word in each sentence, using a word given in the list.

| bow cut helmet powder storm |
| case fire place steps writing |

a) I could hear the sound of gun.......... coming from the main square.
b) We had to take shelter during a severe thunder.......... .
c) Nobody can read the doctor's hand.......... .
d) You look awful. Why don't you have a hair..........?
e) I wanted to do some washing but I've run out of soap ....
f) If you ride a motorbike you have to wear a crash ....
g) There isn't room in here for another book.......... .
h) After the shower, the sun came out and there was a rain.......... .
i) I could hear the sound of foot.......... . Someone was coming!
j) At one end of the room is a lovely old stone fire.......... .

7

Choose the most suitable word or phrase underlined in each sentence.

a) Helen doesn't look well. She is extremely <u>slim/thin</u>.
b) It's really hot today, but it's nice and <u>chilly/cool</u> in here.
c) Peter <u>nodded/shook</u> his head in agreement.
d) I can't pay you anything for this old coin. It's <u>priceless/worthless</u>.
e) The house was surrounded by a <u>high/tall</u> fence.
f) The sun is shining, and it's a/an <u>attractive/lovely</u> day.
g) This chicken is good. It's very <u>tasteful/tasty</u>.
h) Be careful of the next corner. It's rather <u>dangerous/harmful</u>.
i) Graham left the film before the end because he was <u>bored/lazy</u>.
j) When I saw the child scratch my car I became very <u>angry/nervous</u>.

8

Complete each sentence with a word formed from a word in the list.

do fall get make set
draw feel give put take

a) Those children next door are .... a lot of noise.
b) I don't really .... like going out this evening.
c) You don't have to hurry. You can .... your time.
d) Armstrong was the first person to .... foot on the moon.
e) The director .... us permission to park our motorbikes here.
f) Can you .... me a favour? I need some help with the garden.
g) I can't talk now. I'm just .... lunch.
h) When something goes wrong, people always .... the blame on me!
i) Tom has just .... in love yet again!
j) I would like to .... your attention to these instructions.

9

Rewrite each sentence so that it has the same meaning, and contains the word given in capitals. Do not change the word in any way.

a) The forest outside the town started burning last night. CAUGHT
....

b) Suddenly Janet started crying. TEARS
....

c) What's your occupation? DO
....

d) We'll have to decide soon. DECISION
....

e) Can you look after my plants while I'm away? TAKE
....

f) You will write or phone, won't you? TOUCH
....

g) Diane had a baby boy last week. GAVE
....

h) Peter always remains calm in an emergency. HEAD
....

i) Stop holding the steering wheel! LET
....

j) He can't possibly win the race. STANDS
....

10
Complete each
sentence with *one*
suitable word.

a) I've been searching high and .... for this book!
b) That man's been walking up and .... the street all day.
c) I think we've been going round and .... in circles!
d) He promised to stick by her through thick and ....
e) When we finish this, we'll be home and ....
f) Make sure you are here bright and .... in the morning.
g) It's very important! It's a matter of life and ....
h) I've been going backwards and .... to the shops all morning.
i) We cleaned the kitchen until it looked spick and ....
j) The police kept a watch on the house day and ....

Word Formation 2

1
Add one of the
prefixes in the list
to each
incomplete word
so that it makes
sense. Use each
prefix once only.

| auto- dis- ex- in- mis- |
| non- over- semi- sub- un- |

a) Dick was very tired and suffering from ....work.
b) We couldn't see the magician! He had become ....visible.
c) I could only cross the road by going down a ....way.
d) Nobody believed what Mary wrote in her ....biography
e) Let me introduce you to Janet, my ....-wife.
f) What he said was not clear. In fact it was rather ....leading.
g) Unfortunately our football team lost in the ....-final.
h) Mr Smith regrets that he is ....able to accept your invitation.
i) This is a good train, it goes to Manchester ....-stop.
j) Oh bother, my pencil sharpener has ....appeared again.

2
Complete each
sentence with a
word formed
from a word
given in the list,
ending as shown.

| drink equal hand hope partner |
| employ green harm neighbour wide |

a) Carol and Andy have just moved into a new ....hood.
b) My new ....er is paying me a much higher salary.
c) The local council have decided to ....en the main road.
d) Jerry picked up a ....ful of the money and smiled.
e) I'm a terrible card player. I'm really ....less.
f) It's a kind of blue colour, but a bit ....ish too.
g) Bill now works in ....ship with two other architects.
h) Don't drink from the stream. You don't know if the water is ....able.
i) Most people say that they believe in the ....ity of men and women.
j) Doctors have proved that smoking is ....ful.

3

Complete each sentence with a word formed from a word given in the list using one of the prefixes or suffixes given.

| art | cycle | friend | hope | national |
| circle | edible | ground | mountain | young |

| fore- | in- | inter- | semi- | tri- | -eer | -ful | -ist | -ly | -ster |

a) I can't eat this! It's completely ....
b) John has been interested in sailing ever since he was a/an.......... .
c) The teacher arranged the desks in a/an ....
d) I like it here. The people are really ....
e) There are two figures in the .... of the picture.
f) You have to have a good head for heights if you are a ....
g) It's much safer for a young child to ride a/an ....
h) Scientists are .... that a cure for the disease will be found.
i) Most countries have signed a/n .... agreement banning whaling.
j) Paintings by this .... have been sold for millions of pounds.

4

Complete each sentence with a word formed from the word in capitals.

a) You have some good ideas but your work is very .... ORGANISE
b) It was a bad accident, but luckily we were .... INJURE
c) The .... of the diamonds came as a shock to us all. THIEF
d) How terrible for you! I really .... SYMPATHY
e) Margaret had a successful career as a .... POLITICS
f) Tom's .... makes his social life difficult. SHY
g) Don't worry. We'll try to .... out the problem. STRAIGHT
h) I find computers rather cold and .... PERSON
i) As the plane approached the airport, it began its .... DESCEND
j) Tony has left his job, so we need a .... PLACE

5

Choose the most suitable compound word underlined.

a) The bus from Glasgow arrives at the Central bus station/bus stop.
b) Bob only works half-time/part-time at the moment.
c) Joan has lovely clothes and is always well-dressed/well-worn.
d) Some of Bill's ideas are rather old-aged/old-fashioned.
e) We left our car in the multi-storey car-park/car-parking.
f) Martin is now a well-known/well-written novelist.
g) Thank you. You gave me a good haircut/haircutting.
h) Excellent. That was a first-class/first course lunch!
i) I prefer self-made/home-made jam to the jam you buy in shops.
j) I sent back the chicken because it was half-baked/half-cooked.

6

Complete the compound word in each sentence, using a word given in the list.

| clothed | handed | hearted | looking | mouthed |
| eared | headed | legged | minded | tempered |

a) Thank you for helping me, and being so kind-.......... .
b) We searched all day, but had to return home empty-.......... .
c) Paul didn't have time to think, but jumped into the river fully-..........
d) It seems that long-.......... people can run faster.
e) Try to concentrate and remember! You are so absent- ....

f) Mary is very attractive, and her husband is good-.......... too.
g) Stop shouting! I'm tired of your loud-.......... comments!
h) Mike gets angry easily. He's a bit short-.......... .
i) Steve's book was dirty and dog-.......... .
j) Red-.......... people usually dislike being called 'Ginger'!

7
Complete each sentence with *one* suitable word which is the *opposite* of the word underlined.

a) The team expected an easy <u>victory</u>, but suffered a crushing ....
b) The bridge is <u>dangerous</u>! It's not .... to cross it.
c) I'm sorry, I can't <u>accept</u> your invitation. I have to .... it.
d) David thought he would <u>fail</u> the exam, but he managed to ....
e) We had a good <u>take-off</u>, but the .... was a bit bumpy.
f) This loaf isn't <u>fresh</u>! Do you always sell .... bread?
g) The pirates <u>dug up</u> the treasure, and then .... it somewhere else.
h) These books are supposed to be <u>different</u>, but they are very ....
i) I enjoyed the <u>opening</u> of the film, but not the ....
j) The water <u>freezes</u> at night, but the ice .... during the day.

8
Complete each sentence using one of the words given in the list. Use each word once only.

| bear | catch | gain | make | think |
| break | drop | lose | take | waste |

a) Don't .... such a fuss! I'll only be gone for a week!
b) I try not to .... touch with my old friends.
c) What this paper says doesn't .... much relation to the truth.
d) Please .... me a line and tell me all your news.
e) Come on, hurry up, don't .... time.
f) I managed to .... sight of the prince through the crowd.
g) He says he's going to walk, but he'll probably .... better of it.
h) Ann was able to .... a lot of experience in her first job.
i) Please .... a seat. I'll be with you in just a moment.
j) I will .... the news to Dave of his sister's accident.

9
Rewrite each sentence so that it has the same meaning, and contains the word given in capitals. Do not change the word in any way.

a) Nothing you do will alter anything.   DIFFERENCE
....

b) I hope I'm not inconveniencing you.   TROUBLE
....

c) Let's measure the room.   TAKE
....

d) Mark looked disappointed when I told him my name.   FELL
....

e) The old car suddenly started burning.   FLAMES
....

f) Susan didn't know where she was.   WAY
....

g) I can't bear to look at that boy!   SIGHT
....

h) Helen became responsible for the business.   CHARGE

....

i) What did you do while you were waiting for
the train?   TIME

....

j) I now think differently about this matter.   MIND

....

10
Complete each
sentence with *one*
suitable word.

a) The little boy who had lost his parents was .... tears.
b) I met Jack at the airport completely .... chance.
c) This wasn't an accident! You did it .... purpose.
d) We have similar tastes, and a lot of other things .... common.
e) Don't worry! Everything is .... control.
f) I'm going to study much harder .... now on.
g) Our birthday presents took him completely .... surprise.
h) This painting is now .... loan to the National Gallery.
i) Let's go to Brighton this year .... a change.
j) Go away. I want to be .... myself.

Formation Rules

1 Tenses

Present Simple

I/you/we/they like.
Do you like?
You don't like.

She/he/it likes.
Does she like?
He doesn't like.

Present Continuous

I am going.
She/he/it is going.
Are you going?
I am not going.
She isn't going.

You/we/they are going.
Am I going?
Is she going?
You aren't going.

Present Perfect

I/you/we/they have left.
Have they left?
They haven't left.

She/he/it has left.
Has she left?
He hasn't left.

Present Perfect Continuous

I/you/we/they have been
waiting.
Have you been waiting?
Has she been waiting?
He hasn't been waiting.

She/he/it has been waiting.

We haven't been waiting.

Past Simple

1. I/you/she/he/it/we/they started. (Regular)
   Did you start?
   You didn't start.
2. I/you/she/he/it/we/they went. (Irregular)
   Did you go?
   You didn't go.

Past Continuous

I/she/he/it was going.
Was he going?
She wasn't going.

You/we/they were going.
Were you going?
You weren't going.

Past Perfect

I/you/she/he/it/we/they had left.
Had he left?
They hadn't left.

Past Perfect Continuous

I/you/she/he/it/we/they had been waiting.
Had they been waiting?
He hadn't been waiting.

Future Perfect
I/you/she/he/it/we/they will have finished.
Will they have finished?
They won't have finished.

Future Perfect Continuous
I/you/she/he/it/we/they will have been waiting.
Will they have been waiting?
They won't have been waiting.

Will
See Units 3 and 19.

2 Indirect Speech

'I always drink milk.'	He said that he always drank milk.
'I'm leaving.'	She said she was leaving.
'I'll be back soon.'	He said he would be back soon.
'I've forgotten it.'	She said she had forgotten it.
'I took it.'	He said he had taken it.
'I was reading.'	She said she had been reading.
'I had left by then.'	She said she had left by then.
'I must go.'	She said she had to go/must go.
'I can help.'	He said he could help.
'I would like to help.'	She said she would like to help.
'If I had a car, I'd go.'	He said that if he had a car he would go.

3 Passive Tenses

He helps.	He is helped.
He is helping.	He is being helped.
He has helped.	He has been helped.
He helped.	He was helped.
He was helping.	He was being helped.
He will help.	He will be helped.
He will have helped.	He will have been helped.

4 Infinitives

Present:	to like
Passive:	to be liked
Past:	to have liked
Past passive:	to have been liked

5 Participles
(-ing Forms)

Present:	liking
Present passive:	being liked
Past:	having liked
Past passive:	having been liked

Word List

broadcast (v) 10
bruised 15
buffet 1
bulb 13
bungalow 5
bumper 6
bunk 5
burglar 9
bush 5, 11
button 4
buzz 11

cabin 1
call in 12
call off 10
camel 11
camp-site 1
canal 11
cancel 6,9
cancelled 1
cap 4
capital punishment 9
caravan 6
carpenter 2
carpet 5
carriage 6
cart 6
case 9
cash 16
cashier 16
cast (n) 10
catalogue 8
catch a cold 15
catch fire 14
cave 11
carving knife 7
cashier 2
casserole 7
casual 4
cause trouble 9
ceiling 5
cellar 5
central heating 5
certificate 18
chain 6
champion 3

change (n) 8, 16
channel 11
chapter 10
character 12
(in) charge 2
charge (v) 9, 16
charity 14
chat 12
chauffeur 6
cheap 16
cheat (v) 9, 18
check in 1
cheek 15
cheer up 17
cheerful 12
chef 2
chemist 8
cheque 16
chimney 5
chin 15
choir 10
chop (v) 13
chorus 10
cliff 11
close down 14
close up 10
clothing 4
cloudy 11
club (golf) 3
coach (n) 6
coach (v) 18
cockpit 2, 6
cockroach 11
coin 16
collapse (v) 14
collar 4
colleague 12
collect 14
collection 3
collide 6, 14
collision 14
come out 10
come up 3
commit 9
commute 5
competition 3

competitor 3
complain 8
composer 10
compulsory 9
computer 13
concentrate 18
concert 10
condemn 14
condition 14
conductor (bus) 6
conductor (music) 10
confess 9
confidence 17
confused 17
conscience 17
conservation 14
considerable 16
considerate 12
constable 9
control 14
cooker 5
cool 7
corn 11
corporal punishment 9
costume 3, 4, 10
cottage 5
cough (v) 15
count on 12
countryside 5
courage 17
courageous 12
course 3, 7, 18
court 3, 9
covered 5
coward 17
crab 11
credit card 16
crew 1, 6
crime 9
criminal 9
critic 10
croak 11
cross (adj) 17
crossing 1
crossword 3
cruise 1

cry (v) 17
cuff 4
cupboard 5
cure (v) 14, 15
current (adj) 10
curtains 5
cushion 5
customs officer 1

damage (v) 5, 15
damages (n) 9
dare 17
deaf 15
deal 3
deal with 3, 14
debt 16
deck 1, 6
declare 1
decrease 16
defeat 3
defence 9
defend 9
degree 18
delayed 1
delightful 17
deliver 8
demand 9
demolish 5,14
demonstration 14
dentist 2,15
deny 9
department store 8
departure lounge 1
deposit 8, 16
depressed 17
desert 11
desperately 14
destination 1
destroy 11
detached 5
determined 12
dial (v) 13
disappointed 12
disaster 14
discount 8
discover 13

disease 11, 14
dish 7
dishwasher 5
dismiss 2
dismissal 2
dismount 3
on display 8
dive 3, 15
diverted 1
divide 18
divorced 12
do-it-yourself 3, 13
do without 13
dolphin 11
doormat 5
double (room) 1
double decker 6
drain 5
drama 10
draughts 3
draw (n) 3
dressing-gown 4
drift 6
drill (n) 13
drip 15
drive (n) 5
drought 14
drown 14
duck (n) 11
dull 10, 17
dungarees 4
dustcart 6
dustman 2, 5

earring 4
earth 5
earthquake 14
economise 16
economy 2, 16
edge 5, 11
editor 10
educate 18
eiderdown 5
elbow 15
electric 13
electrical 13

electrician 2
embarrassed 17
embroidery 3
emergency 14
employ 2
employer 2
employment 2
engaged 12
engine 6, 13
entertain 10
enthusiastic 17
entrance (n) 5
entry 5
environment 14
equal 3
equip 13
error 14
eruption 14
estate 5
estate agent 2
evidence 9
examine 15
examiner 18
exhaust 6
expect 3
expedition 1
expenses 2
experience 2
experiment 18
expression 15
extinct 14

factory 13
fail 18
faithful 17
fall ill 15
fall out 12
falsely 9
famine 14
fancy dress party 4
fare 16
fascinating 17
fashion 4
fattening 7
faulty 13
fee 16

hurt (v) 15
hut 5

ignore 14
illegally 9
illustrate 10
imagine 3
imaginative 12
impress 17
improve 14
income 2
increase 14
incurable 15
index 10
industrial 14
infect 15
ingredients 7
inhabited 14
inherit 16
injection 2, 15
injure 6
injury 14, 15
innocent 9
inside out 4
instrument 13
insure 16
intelligence 15
interest (n) 16
interested 17
interesting 17
interfere 15
introduce 18
invasion 14
investment 16
investor 16
involve 14
interval 10
interview (n) 2
invent 13
irritate 17
itinerary 1

jacket 4
jar 7
jealous 12
jigsaw 3

judge 9
jug 7
jumper 4
jury 9
justice 9

keen 17
keep fit 3
keep up with 13
kennel 5
kerb 5
kettle 7
kidnapper 9
kindergarten 18
kitten 11
knee 15
knock out 15

laboratory 18
label 1, 8
ladder 5
lake 11
lamb 11
lamp-post 5
landed 1
landing 5
lane 5
law 9
lawn 5, 11
lawyer 9
lay the table 7
lazy 12
learner 18
lecturer 18
lend 16
leopard 11
let 9, 16
let down 4
let out 4
letter box 5
level crossing 14
liable 9
librarian 2
licence 9
lifebelt 1
(give a) lift 6

lightning 11
likely 8
lip 15
list 8
litter 5
living (n) 2
loaf 7
loan 16
lobster 11
lonely 12
look after 15
look out 13
look out (over) 1
look up 10
look up to 12
lorry 6
lose 14
lose your temper 17
loss 16
luggage 1
luxury 16

mac 4
machinery 2
mains 2
make (n) 8
make out 13, 16
mansion 16
manufacturer 13
mark (n) 18
market place 8
mashed 7
mean (adj) 12, 16
mechanic 2, 6
medal 3
melt 7
memorise 18
menu 7
microwave 13
mind (v) 17
mine (coal) 2
miner 2
miser 16
miserable 17
miss (v) 14, 18
model-making 3

mosquito 11
mouthful 15
moth 11
motorist 6
motorway 5
mug 7
multiply 18
murderer 9
muscle 15

naughty 17
neck 4, 15
needle 3, 13
neighbourhood 5
nephew 12
nerve 15
nervous 17
nest 11
net 3
niece 12
nightdress 4
nil 3
nod 17
note (n) 16
notice (n) 2
novelist 10
nursery 18
nut 13

oar 6
obey 11
object (v) 9
off (adj) 7
offence 9
offend 17
offender 9
operation 15
opponent 3
optician 2
order (v) 7, 8
order (n) 9
out of order 13
outdoors 3
outfit 4
open-air 8
opera 10

orchestra 10
oven 5
overall 4
overboard 6
overcoat 4
overcrowded 14
overpopulated 14
overtake 3
overtime 2

pack (v) 1
package (tour) 1
pain 15
parachute 6
pardon 9
parking ticket 6
pass 18
pastime 3
path 5
patient (adj) 12
pavement 5, 6
pay attention 18
pay back 16
pay into 16
peak 11
pedestrian 5, 6
peel (v) 7
peel (n) 11
pension 2,16
pensioner 12, 16
perform 10
performance 3, 10
permission 9
personality 2, 12
personnel manager 2
petrol 13
photographer 2
pick 5
pick up (receive) 10, 13
pick up (learn) 18
pickpocket 9
pig 11
pile-up 14
pillow 5
pin 13
pinch 11

pitch 3
plain 4, 11
plant (n) 11
plate 7
platform 1, 6
playwright 10
pleasant 12
plod 11
plug (v) 13
plumber 2
poached 7
point (n) 18
poison (n) 15
police station 9
polite 4, 8, 12
polluted 14
(football) pools 3
porter 1, 2
portion 7
position (job) 2
poster 5
pour 7
poverty 14, 16
powdered 7
power cut 13
pram 6
preface 10
prejudice 17
prescription 15
prevent 14
priced 8
pricey 8
primary 18
principal 18
print (v) 10
prize 3
produce (v) 10
professionally 3
professor 18
profit 2, 16
progress (n) 18
prohibited 9
promotion 2
propose 12
prospects 2
prosperity 16

protect 14
proud 12
provide 14
publish 10
puddle 11
pump 13
punch (n) 3
punch (v) 15
punctual 12
punish 18
punishment 9
puppy 11
purchase (n) 16
(on) purpose 17
purse 8
put (money) aside 16
put away 4
put off 13
put on 4, 10
put up with 12
quack 11
qualifications 2
quarrel 12
quay 1, 6
queue (v) 8

rabbit 11
race 3
racket 3
radiator 5
railway 6
raise (v) 2, 12, 18
raw 7
razor 13
receipt 2, 8, 16
receiver 13
recipe 7
reckon 16
recommend 15
recording 10
recover 15
reduce 8, 14, 16
reduction 8
referee 3
references 2
refuse 9

register 18
registered 2
rehearsal 10
related 12
relation 12
relationship 12
relax (v) 1
release 9
reliable 12
relieve 17
rely 12
remove 6
rent (n) 5, 16
report (n) 18
rescue 6
respect (v) 12
resign 2
result 3
retire 2
return (ticket) 1
reverse 6
review 10
revise 18
reward 3
riot 14
rise 12, 18
rival 3
roast 7
robe 4
rod 3
roof rack 6
root 11
rope 3
rotten 7
round and round 4
row (n) 12
row (v) 6
rub 11
rubbish 2, 5
rude 12
rug 5
run out 13
runway 1, 6
rural 5

sack (v) 2

saddle 3
safe (n) 16
salary 2, 16
for sale 8, 16
on sale 8
sales representative 2
sandal 4
sane 15
saucepan 7
save 16
save up 16
saw 13
scared 17
scarf 4
scene 10
science 13
scissors 13
score (n) 3
scream 17
screen 10
screw 13
screwdriver 13
script 10
sculptor 10
sculpture 10
seasick 1
seat belt 1, 6
secondary 18
seed 11
self-defence 9
selfish 12
semi-detached 5
sentence 9
sentimental 12
separated 12
serve 7, 8
service 7
service station 6
set 13, 18
set fire 14
settee 5
shake 17
shark 11
sharp 13
shed 5
shock 13

token 17
tolerant 12
tongue 15
tool 13
toothache 15
toothpaste 8
top 11
tour 1
track 3
tracksuit 4
tractor 6
traffic jam 6
traffic warden 6
train (v) 18
transport 14
trap 11
treasure 16
treat (v) 12, 15
trial 9
trolley 6, 8
trunk 11
try on 4
tube 6
tune 10
tunnel 6
turn down 12
turn up 3, 10, 12
turn-up 4
tutor 18
twig 11
twin 12
twist 15
type 10
typewriter 13
typist 2, 13
tyre 6

unbearable 14
undercooked 7
underline 18
underwear 4
undo 4, 13
unemployed 14
unexpected 14
unfurnished 5
uniform 4
unpack 1
unsympathetic 12
upset 17
upside down 4
urban 5

vacancy 1
valley 11
value 9, 16
valuable 16
valuables 16
vandal 9
vegetarian 7
vehicle 6
verdict 9
vet 2, 15
vicar 2
viewer 3, 10
villain 9
vintage 6
violent 14
volcano 14
volume 10
voyage 1

wag 11
wages 2

waggon 6
waist 15
waistcoat 4
wallet 8
ward 15
wardrobe 5
warm up 7
washbasin 5
wasp 11
waterproof 8
wave (n) 11
wave (v) 17
wealth 16
weight 15
well off 16
whale 11
wheelbarrow 5
whisper 17
whistle 3
widow 12
wildlife 11
windscreen 6
wing 6
wipers 6
wire 13
witness 9
work 2
work out 10
worm 11
worrying 17
worthless 16
wound 15
wrap 8
wrist 15

yawn 17

Grammar Index